IN
SLAVERY'S
WAKE

IN SLAVERY'S WAKE

MAKING BLACK FREEDOM IN THE WORLD

In Association with
the National Museum of African
American History and Culture

Smithsonian Books
Washington, DC

Edited by
Paul Gardullo
Johanna Obenda
Anthony Bogues

Preface by
Christina H. Paxson

Foreword by
Lonnie G. Bunch III

Contributions by
Martha Abreu
Geri Augusto
Fatoumata Camara
Bambi Ceuppens
Michelle D. Commander
Alexandra Creighton
Yhuri Cruz
Sherri V. Cummings
Lisa Edison
Candra Flanagan
Diana Ferrus
Shanaaz Galant
Miles Greenwood
Keila Grinberg
Mônica Lima e Souza
Minkah Makalani
Kate McMahon
Gabrielle Chantal Miller
Aline Montenegro Magalhães
Jennifer L. Morgan
Vinícius Natal
Ivie Orobaton
Marcus Rediker
Alexander Scott
Mongane Wally Serote
Amadou Thiam
Ibrahima Thiaw
Paul Tichmann
Shana Weinberg
Kevin Young

TABLE OF CONTENTS

PREFACE

Christina H. Paxson

Roots, Romare Bearden, 1977. Bearden created this work to commemorate the TV broadcast of a miniseries based on Alex Haley's best-selling novel *Roots: The Saga of an American Family.* Collaging together the African continent, an American flag, and a slave ship, Bearden draws connections between Africa and the Americas.

Over the years, Brown University has played a leadership role in confronting the difficult legacies of transatlantic slavery. As the president of Brown, I commend the commissioning of the international, multilingual exhibition *In Slavery's Wake*, which has been catalyzed by Brown University's Ruth J. Simmons Center for the Study of Slavery and Justice, and the Center for the Study of Global Slavery at the Smithsonian's National Museum of African American History and Culture. This companion volume includes many essays, a selection of poems, and even a playlist that shed light on the history of racial slavery and the agency with which the enslaved and formerly enslaved fought for their freedom and humanity.

This significant project explores the trajectory and long-term consequences of slavery and features distinct contributions from multiple museums across four continents. It has been made possible through the extraordinary collaboration of institutions, an international curatorial team, collections, and scholarship that ordinarily would be isolated by region, nationality, language, or any other number of factors. What's more, this innovative traveling exhibition will transform to include regional content as it moves across South America, Africa, and Europe, while also presenting an international perspective on the business of slavery and colonialism and the concepts of race and identity.

Based upon the current state of our country's, and the world's, confrontation of systemic racism, we know that the commitment to equity is a perpetual and uneven march. As we consider the impact of this exhibition, it is prudent to reflect on the ways in which we address society's most complex issues as we seek to stimulate meaningful change.

Through scholarship, institutions of higher education address pressing challenges such as health inequities, mass incarceration, economic inequality, educational access, climate change, and housing discrimination. A critical first step of any consequential examination through scholarship begins with truth telling. This is exactly what *In Slavery's Wake* challenges us to consider.

From careful collection and stewardship of oral histories from communities that discuss the lived experiences and historical memories of enslaved Africans and their descendants, to recognizing how slavery and colonialism have shaped our modern world economically, socially, and beyond, *In Slavery's Wake* urges us to confront uncomfortable truths. Just as important, the exhibition and publication tell the stories of how enslaved and colonized people have resisted global forces and fought for self-determination. Recalling the failures of our past and recognizing the humanity and persistence of colonized and enslaved people are essential to informing our future.

As Brown has engaged in the work of documenting the university's own complex and painful history with the Transatlantic Slave Trade and its terrible legacies of inequity and injustice, one frequent assertion we have heard is that studying an issue does not effect change. This would be true if the work did not extend beyond identifying a challenge and discovering its history. As we have learned, society's reckoning with slavery, or any other complex issue, does not end with the completion of a report or the launch of an exhibition. Rather, these projects can and should mark new beginnings in our collective commitment to create a more equitable and inclusive society—one in which we embrace a new standard for examining our past with a foundation in accountability. A route through scholarship, when stewarded thoughtfully, does lead to transformation. It is through this continuous arc of reflection and action that we will transform our nation and our world for the better.

"Roots"   Romare Bearden

FOREWORD

Lonnie G. Bunch III

Though the slavery question is settled, its impact is not. It is in our homes, on our streets, on our highways, in our schools, in our courts and in our politics, all the day, everyday.
—Cornelius Holmes, *Federal Writers' Project: Slave Narrative Project, South Carolina*, 1936

As the founding director of the Smithsonian's National Museum of African American History and Culture, I, along with my colleagues, wrestled with the challenge of how to interpret and present to a public audience the foundational role that slavery played in the shaping of the United States, an impact that continues to this very day. We soon realized that the nation and many other parts of the globe were grappling, or should be grappling, with the legacy, impact, and contemporary resonance of an institution that shaped the modern world. And by exploring the history of enslavement, the museum would also reveal the powerful urgency for freedom, forever coupling slavery and freedom.

Yet encouraging public engagement with slavery is not for the faint of heart. In many ways, slavery—its impact and meaning—is the last great unmentionable in American discourse. I always imagined that if I needed to exit a dinner party early, all I had to do was mention slavery and the gathering would abruptly end. Prior to the opening of the museum, I was walking in downtown Washington, DC, when an elderly African American woman stopped me. She thanked me for helping to create the museum, but as she hugged me, she whispered, "Whatever you do, please don't talk about slavery in the museum." Her comment echoed the concerns of many. Some African Americans expressed embarrassment about their enslaved ancestors. Others believed that while slavery was important in antebellum America, it has little meaning for the present day.

Fear of this public discourse has become a national issue. The ability to explore, teach, and understand the centrality of slavery in American life is threatened. Nearly 50 percent of the states have introduced or passed legislation that would limit teaching the fullness and diversity of the American past. A strong current of political leaders wants to prevent the public from engaging with Black history, which they deem "too divisive," and create a culture of silence, especially around the issue of slavery. This desire to limit the full understanding of America's past also prevents Americans from celebrating the resiliency, power, and lasting impact of freedom.

In Slavery's Wake shatters that silence by exploring the central role that slavery and the pursuit of freedom played in remaking not just the United States but the modern world. A major factor in both the planning and the success of the Smithsonian's National Museum of African American History and Culture was the notion that the impact and importance of African Americans transcend their own lives and communities. In essence, African Americans shaped and reshaped the American experience in ways, often unacknowledged, that, by centralizing freedom and fairness, have challenged America to live up to the ideals stated in its founding documents. This country was improved by the unrelenting pursuit of equality and justice for all that flowed from the moment when the first enslaved person was brought to America with freedom on his or her mind.

no world, Kara Walker, 2010. Walker's title and work play on the colonial concept of the "New World." Rather than an idealized place of new beginnings—as imagined by European colonizers—the "New World" signified pain, heartache, and bondage for the kidnapped Africans who arrived shackled on slave ships.

An equally important foundational tenet of the museum was the recognition that, throughout the world, many other nations and their citizens were also wrestling with the legacies of slavery and the struggle for freedom. There was much to learn from those experiences that would contribute mightily to countering notions of American exceptionalism. Implicit in this idea was the hope that by acknowledging and recognizing how comparable, though individually unique, each nation's experience of slavery was,

the museum could create a sense of international collaboration that, at the very least, could lead to a shared history and, at best, could contribute to profound racial change on a global scale. The Smithsonian's National Museum of African American History and Culture had the massive responsibility and the freedom of crafting those stories and building its collections directly with members of the American public. The Museum taught us important lessons about the responsibilities that institutions

Detail of *The Universe of Freedom Making*, Daniel Minter, 2024. For the *In Slavery's Wake* exhibition, Minter created a large-scale installation materializing a universe of freedom-making practices that weaves together constellations of Black liberatory actions and symbols.

have, not just in telling the truth, but in holding cultures in one's hands, and acting in concert with communities that have long been held distant from the power and authority that these institutions wield. This sense of shared stewardship is not one that the wider Smithsonian historically practiced, nor did most of the world's museums whose collections were built in the context, ideology, and practices of colonialism during the slavery era.

As a historian, I have always felt that a full, unvarnished, honest telling of history is the only way for us to move forward as a people, as a nation, and as institutions. *In Slavery's Wake* addresses this history and its continuing effects upon our present in ways that are also visible in the Smithsonian's new ethical returns and human remains policies, which focus on returning objects, remains, and most important, authority, dignity, and rights to communities long dismissed and historically marginalized. These initiatives symbolically exist hand in hand with global curatorial projects like *In Slavery's Wake*. They are not simply about the necessities of truth-telling or repatriation or the business of illuminating the dark corners of our past through our exhibition. They are also about interrogating and dismantling the racism that helped to build key collections and institutional structures. These projects and initiatives recognize that we have the shared responsibility to collaborate with and lead museums and universities around the world in like-minded efforts bent on change both outward-facing and inward-looking.

This publication, and the connected exhibition and Global Curatorial Project, imbued with possibilities of international transformation, is at the forefront of a long-overdue reckoning about repair and reconciliation. It is informed by the work of numerous scholars and community members alike and the participation of several museums in Africa, Europe, and North and South America. This global context enriches and complicates our understanding of the national and regional frameworks through which slavery is traditionally viewed, but it also serves as a provocation that we must do better. In doing so, we build on the hopes and dreams of the enslaved whose lives changed the course of nationhood and freedom making internationally.

INTRODUCTION

Paul Gardullo and Johanna Obenda

On the shores of our present, we are met by the waves of our past. Although the practice of slavery dates to ancient cultures across the world, the form of racialized slavery that grew out of the intertwined connections between European colonialism and the birth and growth of capitalism has a unique connection to our lives in the twenty-first century. Slavery and colonialism were central to building the world we inhabit today, structuring our economic, social, and political landscapes. They form the foundation of our understandings of race and racism, our modern systems of finance and banking, and the exploitation of people and land in a quest for profit and power.

In our parks and ports, town squares and cityscapes, museums, schools, and religious institutions, the history of slavery and colonialism is an ever-present reminder that the past is not yet past. Instead of fading away, the often unacknowledged painful legacies are growing more visible and virulent. They reverberate in debates about Confederate monuments in the United States or monuments to colonizers in Europe and Africa, in the unearthing of slave wharves in Brazil, and over questions about the continued economic exploitation of African nations. These questions also concern the return of the voluminous number of cultural and sacred treasures stolen from Africa and from Indigenous peoples worldwide. Painful legacies resonate through the continued epidemic of anti-Black racism and amplification of white nationalism throughout and beyond the Diaspora, and through rising questions of citizen-

ship, human rights, and belonging for formerly colonized peoples.

We are living in slavery's "wake," a productive term borrowed for this book and the exhibition of the same name from the scholar Christina Sharpe. In her groundbreaking work *In the Wake: On Blackness and Being*, Sharpe illuminates myriad ways that Black lives are swept up in the enduring afterlives of slavery. Like the turgid waves emanating behind a ship, this history continues to churn. The wake began with the departure of the very first slave ship from the West African coast and continued as thousands more, on their hundreds of thousands of legal and illegal voyages, trafficked millions of souls in the most inhumane conditions over a period of four hundred years. The tides of these floating dungeons continue to envelop our present. This can be seen in the trajectories of contemporary forced migrations and shipping routes born from the trade routes carved out centuries earlier. Slavery's wake reshaped global cultural, environmental, and economic geographies, turning them into a conception that the writer Amitav Ghosh calls "the world-as-resource," where violence upon people and the environment have become naturalized and mutually reinforcing, from the field-based factories of the plantation to the wide set of urban landscapes crafted by European colonial expansion.

The wake has created a planet in crisis. For Sharpe, however, Black life in the wake is not only a story of catastrophe and mourning but also one of agency and power. "Here there is disaster and

Diáspora: As Histórias Que O Brasil Não Conta (Diaspora: The Stories Brazil Doesn't Tell), J. Cunha, 2022. This tapestry brings together critical elements of Afro-Brazilian history, featuring the arrival of a slave ship, scenes of rebellion, and an inscription that translates to "the Black struggle has always existed."

possibility," she observes. Along with this immense story of ongoing subjugation is a history of resistance and resilience, of freedom-making too often shorn from, deeply hidden in, or willfully misrepresented within the official institutions built by the practice of colonialism—including museums, archives, and universities. This hidden history is composed of the myriad ways that enslaved and colonized people resisted overwhelming oppression, refused dehumanization, and planted seeds of liberation across geographies and centuries. These seeds have been tended to and replanted by their descendants and kept in communities and families through story and song, through a universe of gestures and cultural expressions, in addition to political and social formations. These practices of individual and collective freedom have also shaped our world, and they are as important to illuminate as the histories and practices of "unfreedom" and dehumanization. It is in this space of possibility, amid peril, that this book and a broader curatorial project emerge to illuminate domination and freedom making by studying the past, with an eye toward the future.

A Global Curatorial Project

There is a palpable hunger and an urgent need worldwide for important and useful conversations about how the past relates to our present and the vital role that institutions can play in fostering and advancing those conversations on both local and global terrain that reach past normal boundaries of race and nation. In 2014, our coeditor and co-convener of this network, Anthony Bogues, initiated conversations at Brown University in Providence, Rhode Island, that invited key staff from several world museums to address the topic of telling the story of racial slavery and colonialism as a world system and core element of modernity. This group, which included representatives from the National Museum of African American History and Culture in Washington, DC; the Wereldmuseum Amsterdam, the Netherlands; the AfricaMuseum in Tervuren, Belgium; Les Anneaux de la Mémoire in Nantes, France; the Musée d'Histoire de Nantes in Nantes, France; and the Iziko Museums of Cape Town, South Africa, began to discuss the unique role museums play in present-

ing the history and ongoing legacies of racial slavery and colonialism. A Global Curatorial Project (GCP) was born from this discussion. Over several years, more museums joined the GCP network, including the Institut Fondamental d'Afrique Noire or IFAN in Dakar, Senegal; the International Slavery Museum in Liverpool, United Kingdom; and the Museu Histórico Nacional in Rio de Janeiro, Brazil. Increasingly, provocative discussions developed amongst the network's members in meetings and public conferences in Providence, Rhode Island; Washington, DC; Amsterdam; Liverpool; Glasgow, Scotland; Dakar, Senegal; Cape Town; and Rio de Janeiro. Key questions emerged, such as: How do we craft stories that are international in scope while paying attention to the very different historical developments in different localities? How do we work sensitively across diverse linguistic, economic, racial, and cultural contexts while practicing a politics of equity between organizations and individuals? How do we contribute to the work of transforming institutions, particularly museums, that were built as part of the colonial project by using colonial languages and archives?

As a result of these conversations from 2014 to 2018, the GCP created a ten-year road map to expand and interrogate our practices of truth telling and knowledge production in museums and public institutions. We wanted to begin this process with concrete steps to offset the following shortcomings: (1) exhibitions and museums that engage with the history of slavery and colonialism too often isolate and localize important stories or tell them purely within national narratives; (2) storytelling traditionally disconnects the past from the present, and, perhaps most important for this project, such exhibitions often focus on the processes of dehumanization and victimization without illuminating and reckoning with history from the point of view of the enslaved and colonized; and (3) these historical figures and their viewpoints are distorted by or excised from the archives built by colonialism.

The GCP decided to root its work from 2018 to 2028 in two interrelated collaborations: a traveling exhibition, *In Slavery's Wake: Making Black*

Abou Mamadou Ba interviewed as a part of Unfinished Conversations in Orkadiéré, Senegal, 2021. *Unfinished Conversations* is an oral history initiative central to the development of *In Slavery's Wake*. Participants in the United States, Brazil, South Africa, Senegal, Belgium, Democratic Republic of Congo, and the United Kingdom shared their stories in communal gatherings and individual interviews.

Freedom in the World, and an archival collection and community engagement project, Unfinished Conversations, bringing together institutions, curators, collections, and scholarship with a new model of collaboration that repositions the histories of slavery and colonialism as globally connected and tied to our present. The GCP seeks to rectify historical silences by including new voices from scholars and everyday people around the world to help provoke questions and provide new answers that often go against the existing archive. It also seeks to make the "violences" perpetrated historically more visible and understood.

To expand our collective cultural memories and historical consciousness to include more viewpoints and narratives of people who were enslaved and colonized, the collaboration realized it needed to move beyond the extant collections of many of our institutions and begin to craft a new, people-centered archive, born from conversations with community members in each of our countries. Inspired in part by the cultural theorist Stuart Hall, who believed that cultural identity and history are not fixed but rather the subject of an "ever-unfinished conversation," the GCP initiated the Unfinished Conversations

project, which recorded video narratives and oral histories on topics related to key themes of slavery, memory, history, race, and place. These interviews form a new global archive built on a model of shared stewardship that will help researchers understand the legacies of racial slavery and colonialism around the world, in the words of everyday people. Edited recordings inform the exhibition's content and will be on display in all of its locations, from Washington, DC, to Rio de Janeiro, Cape Town, Dakar, Brussels, and Liverpool.

In Slavery's Wake draws upon Unfinished Conversations. A small portion of this living and growing archive graces the exhibition and the pages of this publication, providing a vital sample of the voices of people as they reflect on the past and share their visions for the future. It has been an essential part of our practice as collaborators on this project to incorporate the voices and expertise of people across nations, disciplines, and cultural spheres to address and grapple with this history and its legacies. This book reflects that ethos with contributions from academia, museums, and the public. Curators, historians, archaeologists, art historians, anthropologists, cultural theorists, farmworkers, fisherfolk, activists, imams, pastors, griots, tour guides, *sambistas*,

Flag of the Haitian Republic, early nineteenth century. This historic flag, an emblem of the first independent Black republic in the Americas, served as a beacon of abolition and hope across the globe.

barbers, retired footballers, quilters, shopkeepers, and artists from across the project and around the globe have made important contributions. Their voices are vital to building new visions for our future.

In Slavery's Wake opens in December 2024 in Washington, DC, and travels to South America, Africa, and Europe afterwards. The exhibition will engage hundreds of thousands of visitors and foster conversations around the Atlantic world. We hope those conversations are constructed with the same practices of reckoning and freedom making that inspired the historical figures in this book and the wider project, refashioning the turgid wakes of slave ships into new arcs of justice, repair, and reconciliation. We similarly hope that this book is one more tool that helps establish a long-term vision of, and forum for, global collaboration through ongoing work with scholars and communities in Africa and worldwide.

A Universe of Freedom Making

As the collaborators from the GCP began to conceptualize the stories of the exhibition and this accompanying book, we asked ourselves how we could illuminate the disasters of slavery and colonialism alongside African and African diasporic people's agency in the wake. On the one hand, it was crucial to make plain the complex, centuries-long processes throughout which Western European colonial thought and action imagined the world and its natural resources to be conquerable and extractible. But on the other hand, focusing on these factors ran the risk of recentering or re-inflicting violence and pain that are ongoing. Importantly, this focus also ignores the histories of enslaved, colonized, and liberated people whose practices and beliefs shaped the world and continue to inspire global action. The modern world is a product not merely of colonial intervention but also of Black life, resistance, and creation. To understand this history, it is crucial to prioritize the voices of those who navigated its waters.

The curatorial and editorial team made the decision to devote significant space in the exhibition and book to elevating the stories of people engaged in what we have termed "A universe of freedom making," a cosmos of varied constellations of actions and beliefs. Moving away from

a linear, textbook retelling of this history and toward one that centers the ideas and practices of Black abolitionism and the legacy of Black freedom making is challenging at best and fraught at worst. The construction and bias of the colonial archive have marginalized, silenced, and oftentimes wholly absented Black voices and histories. To piece together stories of enslaved and colonized people is often to work with fragmented records, half-truths, lies, and uncertainty. Telling more complete stories of Black lives necessitates a framework that eschews disciplinary boundaries, welcomes risk and debate, and, importantly, demands care and creativity.

Curatorial collaborators brought to the table stories of people whose lives and voices speak to the histories of slavery and colonialism in their regions. The stories of Paánza, Marème, Jan, Tòya, William, the rebels of *La Amistad*, Anastácia, Tahro, Roosje, and more that you will encounter in these pages, and in the exhibition, chronicle the Atlantic world and centuries of history, addressing topics of marronage, kinship, art, and revolution. They are stories not of victims but of people making history and seeking freedom, often in circumstances not of their own making. Through an assemblage of historic artifacts, first-person testimonies, archival images, contemporary art, and interpretive text, fragments of these freedom navigators' lives are patched together. The silences in the archive became an invitation to imagine and listen more deeply, rather than obstacles to avoid.

Vignettes of everyday people navigating extraordinary conditions are woven together in a meditation on what it means to practice freedom, even in the most oppressive environments. This vast universe of freedom practices is heard in the abolitionist activism of William Powell, a Black sailor and "son of the ocean," in Liverpool, UK. It is found in the herbal remedies of Jan Smiesing, an enslaved healer in Cape Colony, South Africa. It is shaped in the kaolin clay of Tahro, an enslaved Kongo potter in South Carolina. Each personal story expands into broader explorations of collective freedom-making practices, moving readers from the intimate experiences of motherhood and spiritual ritual to histories of critical collective efforts for liberation, like the Haitian Revolution and the West African Banama Slave Exodus.

An enslaved woman photographed with her child, Salvador, Bahia, Brazil, 1884. Due to both the high population of enslaved people and the longevity of the institution of slavery, Brazil holds some of the largest archives of images of enslaved people in the world. These archives—while originally constructed through a colonial gaze—provide glimpses into the world of the enslaved.

In this project, freedom is conceptualized not as a single destination or moment but rather as an ongoing, unfinished set of practices. Even while Black abolitionists and freedom fighters secured legal emancipation across the Atlantic world, their rights and dignity were threatened. The story of Black freedom making does not end at emancipation or colonial independence. This exhibition and publication pay particular attention to how the official end of racial slavery and the escalation of European colonialism in Africa intersect. We present a narrative thread that connects the practices of racism, resource extraction, and wealth disparity birthed through the collision of racial slavery and colonialism beginning in the late fifteenth century to the reinscription and adaptation of these practices in the late nineteenth century.

As Black revolutionaries and abolitionists pushed forward, hastening the end of racial slavery, systems were created and extended to uphold old practices and power structures. They included new laws to maintain racial hierarchies, new waves of colonialism to expand influence, and new means of exploitation to maximize profits. Taking the form of colonial rule across Africa, racial segregation in the Americas, and apartheid in South Africa, the wake continued in new and familiar ways, from the nineteenth century to now. Amidst these enduring and evolving structures of violence and exploitation, communities on the continent of Africa and across the Diaspora continued to refuse dehumanization and fought for sovereignty and equity. Anti-colonial freedom fighters defined independence on their own terms, activists worked to dismantle segregation, and scholars, storytellers, and artists reclaimed stolen histories and crafted new narratives.

In Slavery's Wake moves us to our present moment, introducing a new generation of Black freedom makers who are confronting ongoing indignities and imagining freer futures. From Lagos and Luanda to Lisbon and Los Angeles, Africans and people of the Diaspora have redefined politics, identity, and Blackness on their own terms. They have built upon visions of the Black abolitionists and revolutionaries of generations past, to not only dismantle violent systems but also to create new systems, ideas, and actions. Today, descendant communities across the globe are honoring ancestors, demanding reparative justice, and composing soundtracks for liberation and healing through projects like Black Lives Matter, Rhodes Must Fall, and innumerable other efforts.

The "unfreedom" that characterizes the wake has been structured into our institutions and ideologies, but we believe the everyday and extraordinary freedom stories shared in this publication will inspire us to act as if injustice is not inevitable. *In Slavery's Wake* encourages readers to define liberation anew, realize their unique freedom-making potential, and breathe possibility into the wake. If we, as global citizens, are attuned to the concept of freedom as an ongoing process, then we can chart new constellations of freedom by continuing to tap into joy, struggle, refusal, and activism. We can refashion a set of tools forged by past freedom-makers, whether enslaved, colonized, or free, to build a future beyond the unfulfilled promises of legal emancipation, civil rights, and independence. Black educator Anna Julia Cooper instructed in the aftermath of the American Civil War and amid the rising tide of new forms of racial segregation and inequality that: "The cause of freedom is not the cause of a race or sect, a party or class—it is the cause of human kind, the very birthright of humanity."

This project, then, is meant to foster an active reclaiming, remembering, and stewarding of the stories of named and unnamed people in their full humanity. We also seek to highlight the challenges and visions that they voiced, which are, in so many ways, greater than, and yet akin to, our own. The stories of these everyday people deserve our profound and careful attention, as the memories of *what was* might spur a radical hope of *what can be*. How can we, in their name, actively seek a more just world for future generations? Or as the writer Alexis Pauline Gumbs evocatively asks, can we remember that will surround us in oceans of history and potential? And how?" The culminating provocation of this exhibition, this publication, and the work of the GCP is an invitation to reflect on and learn from the past in order to understand today, as we envision a different tomorrow.

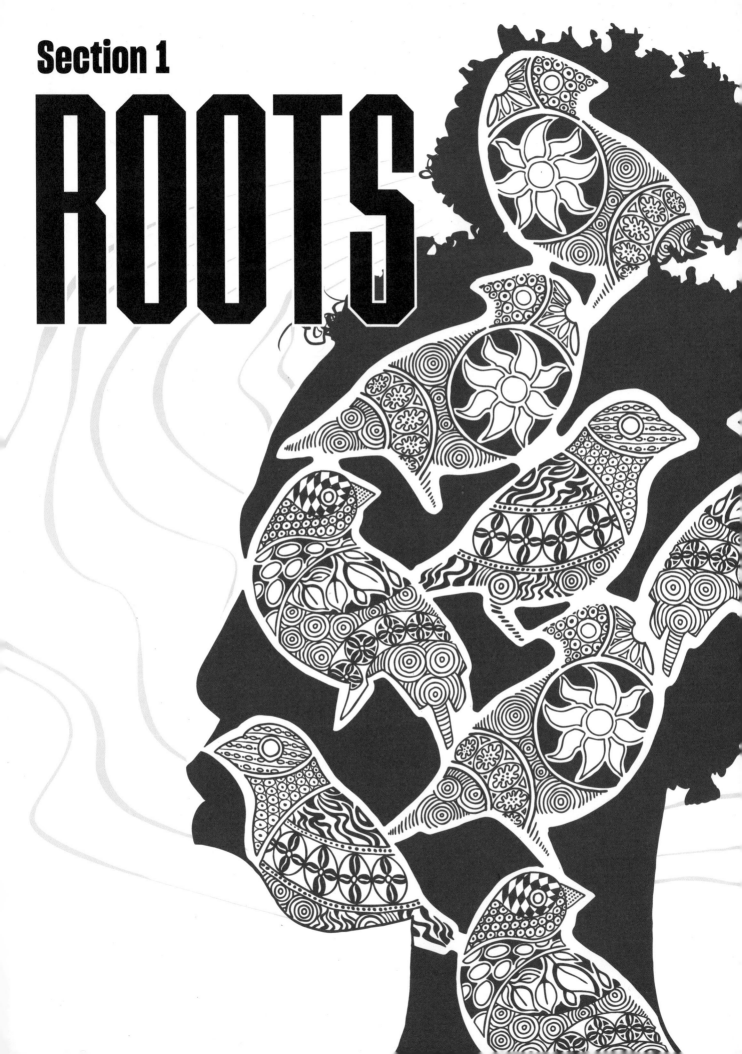

Section 1
ROOTS

In the fifteenth century, European states began maritime expeditions in pursuit of new resources and trade routes, establishing colonies in the Americas and parts of Africa and Asia. Over several centuries, colonizers violently displaced Indigenous peoples and built mines and plantations dependent on enslaved labor. Unlike other forms of slavery in Europe, Africa, and the ancient world, which were often based on religion or war, this form of slavery was catalyzed by capitalism and came to be based solely on skin color. Millions of Africans were trapped in this cruel institution of hereditary enslavement and treated as commodities to be purchased and sold like the products they were forced to cultivate and craft. Together, colonialism and racial slavery created a world that benefited certain people and nations at the expense of others, laying the uneven foundations of modern economies, our natural and constructed environments, and our understandings of race and difference.

Centuries before European colonial expeditions to Africa, Africans and Europeans were already connected through an overland network of trade centered on many commodities, including West African gold. Later, in the 1440s, Portuguese and West African traders connected along the Atlantic African coast for the first time. In exchange for African commodities such as ivory and gold, Europeans brought iron bars, cloth, cowrie shells, and copper for trade, all of which were used as currencies in West Africa. Europeans in West Africa created trade monopolies, and by flooding local markets, they caused rampant inflation of local currencies, disrupting African economic power. Meanwhile, the gold that Europe acquired in Africa was rising in value on the international market, increasing European economic power and fueling colonial expansion. As Europeans developed colonial projects in the Americas, human labor became even more valuable than any other African trade commodity. The growing European demand for captives, paired with the devaluation of local currencies, placed a set of complex pressures on African societies, leading to their destabilization. By the 1600s and increasingly over the next two centuries, the primary commodity of trade between Europeans and Africans became captive African people.

The Transatlantic Slave Trade was a global trade market and the largest forced migration of people in world history. On custom-built ships and multipurpose vessels, captive Africans were trafficked from their homelands to European colonies across the broader Atlantic world. The slave ship was a floating prison and an engine of the trade. Packed tightly in filth-ridden holds, captives endured unimaginable suffering. The grueling voyage from West Africa to the Americas lasted up to eighty days, without sufficient ventilation, sanitation, or food. An estimated 1.8 million African captives died at sea.

Racial slavery and colonialism also shaped landscapes and the way people engaged with each other and the environment, which resulted in people and the environment being treated as disposable resources with which to build colonial empires and wealth. Capitalism did not begin with the factory system and wage labor, but was founded upon the slave plantation, stolen slave labor, and a network of credit and debt arrangements. The plantation system formulated by the Portuguese in the late fifteenth century off the coast of Africa, on small Atlantic islands such as those of modern-day Cabo Verde, São Tomé, and Príncipe, was replicated in European colonies worldwide, creating societies reliant on a majority Black underclass and a European white ruling class, establishing racial hierarchies whose legacies reverberate today.

With the introduction of African enslaved labor, the plantation became the most important economic and social system in the Americas, with profound effects still being felt today on coastlines threatened by rising waters and soil stripped by hundreds of years of monoculture farming. In England, it was the model for the colonization of Ireland. In the Mediterranean, the plantation was used to grow sugarcane. In what is now South Africa, Dutch and British colonists used the model to force thousands of enslaved laborers to work on vineyards and grain farms. In the Americas, plantations relied on a large labor force and the clearing of vast areas of land for crops, disrupting ecosystems and natural habitats, as well as centuries-old knowledge that was central to sustainable environmental practices. This knowledge had been maintained by Indigenous peoples who

were enslaved within systems of forced labor, dispossessed of and displaced from their lands, and subject to both literal and biological warfare, leading to the genocide of millions for profit, power, and conquest.

Major crops such as cotton, sugar, rice, and tobacco grown and processed by millions of enslaved laborers in the Americas helped launch and sustain European industrialization and consumerism, as well as the banking and insurance industries. Cash-crop profits fueled industries such as shipping, trade, and manufacturing, which connected urban centers and consumer markets across the globe. For the first time in history, abundant clothing, due to plantation cotton, and calories, due to plantation sugar, were widely available to European consumers. By the mid-eighteenth century, sugar—the majority of which was produced on Caribbean-island plantations—became the most valuable

commodity in European trade. The mass production of sugar relied on the destruction of ecosystems across the island archipelago and the abuse of enslaved African labor. The life span for enslaved laborers working on sugar plantations, was, on average, twelve years.

Another staple, rice, was transformed from a significant subsistence crop in West Africa and converted by the plantation economy in the Americas into a source of profit and one of the largest commercial crops in the world. Africans with prodigious skill in rice cultivation were actively sought by enslavers looking to maximize their profits. Work on rice plantations was brutal, exhausting, and dangerous. Enslaved men, women, and children cleared timber from millions of acres in the United States alone. They engineered and constructed a vast system of canals, dikes, floodgates, dams, ditches, and drains. It was a landscape of pain cut by shovels, worked with hoes, and carried in baskets. If laid end to end, the ditches dug for these rice fields would measure tens of thousands of miles. In the nineteenth century, cotton would come to supersede rice by far, with profits from its sale massively elevating the United States' role in the global economy.

Extraction and exploitation were central to the growth and intersection of slavery and colonialism, and the birth of modern capitalism. Within this system, various new financial institutions also emerged—from bond markets to brokerage houses. Following that, there was the emergence of major companies—the Dutch West India Company, the French Compagnie de Guinée (Guinea Company), and the British Royal African Company—whose chief functions were linked to the slave trade, including financing plantations, and other aspects of the European colonial project.

European companies, nations, and monarchies joined forces to expand beyond the plantation into businesses

that included the massive mining industry on both sides of the Atlantic, which used the labor of enslaved Indigenous and African workers to extract valuable metals from the earth. Gold, silver, and minerals—along with millions of African captives—were traded and transported for sale internationally via port cities constructed along the Atlantic Ocean. Mining also caused deforestation, water pollution, and habitat destruction. Colonial infrastructure was developed to facilitate the exportation of mined resources to enrich colonial powers at the expense of local communities and ecosystems. The expanding worldwide consumption of slave-produced commodities such as sugar, cotton, and rice, as well as the silver—and gold— mining industries later supplemented by industries that produced cobalt, bauxite, and other precious minerals, generated enormous wealth while inflicting massive degradation on the health and existence of enslaved laborers and ecosystems.

The connections between emerging cities around and beyond the Atlantic world further facilitated trade. European cities such as Lisbon, Liverpool, Amsterdam, and Nantes were hubs for shipping, manufacturing, and trade. Slavery shaped cities across the Americas, from Baltimore and Charleston in the United States to Kingston, Jamaica and Havana, Cuba, in the Caribbean; to Rio de Janeiro in Brazil. Many cities that trafficked human beings also became influential centers of culture and trade. Some African cities, such as Luanda, Angola and Ouidah, Benin, grew as slave-trading centers, with elite residents accumulating wealth. However, European colonialism in the nineteenth and twentieth centuries severely impoverished these cities as well.

Enslaved and colonized Black people were made to be producers of consumable products as well being commodities themselves. This fact brings to the fore issues of the meaning of property, possession of self, and individual rights that formed a paradox in a Western world espousing the rights of life, liberty, and brotherhood. The foundation of the Industrial Revolution, futures markets, banking and insurance

Top
Vergelegen farm, eighteenth century. Willem Adriaan van der Stel, the governor of the Dutch Cape Colony, claimed thirty thousand hectares of land on the Western Cape of what is now South Africa, where he built this estate. Enslaved laborers were imported from present-day Madagascar, India, and Indonesia to develop the farm and maintain its wine stock, fruit orchards, and thousands of heads of livestock.

Bottom
View of the Port of Liverpool, artist unknown, 1680. Vessels constructed in Liverpool, United Kingdom, carried at least 10 percent of all African captives brought to American ports. The massive profits from this trade enriched local merchants and businesses and grew the city's shipbuilding and banking industries.

industries, and national wealth were based on enslaved Africans and the commodities produced on plantations and extracted from mines, as well as goods produced in Europe and Asia. The web of entanglements that emanated from the slave trade and its deeply intertwined connection to the construction of colonial, national, and transnational economies and polities has affected history in unprecedented ways and continues to produce inequality and injustice in our contemporary lives.

Within these expansive and enduring geographic, political, and cultural landscapes of contradiction and exploita-

tion recorded within the cold calculations of ledgers, runaway notices, and auction listings, we also find great humanity, love, and beauty. Despite the brutal conditions on plantations and slave ships and in mines, cities, auction houses, and households, generations of millions of enslaved people found ways to keep themselves and others whole—one of the most important legacies of humanity that we in the twenty-first century can embrace and reenact in our collective and public memory today.

Thousands of Africans were trafficked to Europe via the Transatlantic Slave Trade.

Up to **FIVE MILLION** Indigenous peoples of the Americas were enslaved by European colonizers.

More than **TWELVE MILLION** Africans were forcibly removed to the Americas between 1514 and 1866.

European colonial expansion that began in the late fifteenth century was undergirded by the Transatlantic Slave Trade. Between 1514 and 1866, more than 12 million captive Africans were forcibly removed to American colonies and nations in the largest forced migration in human history. Colonial expansion also relied on the dispossession and enslavement of Indigenous peoples of the Americas, the exploitation of indentured laborers and servants, and the subjugation of peoples in the Indian and Pacific Oceans.

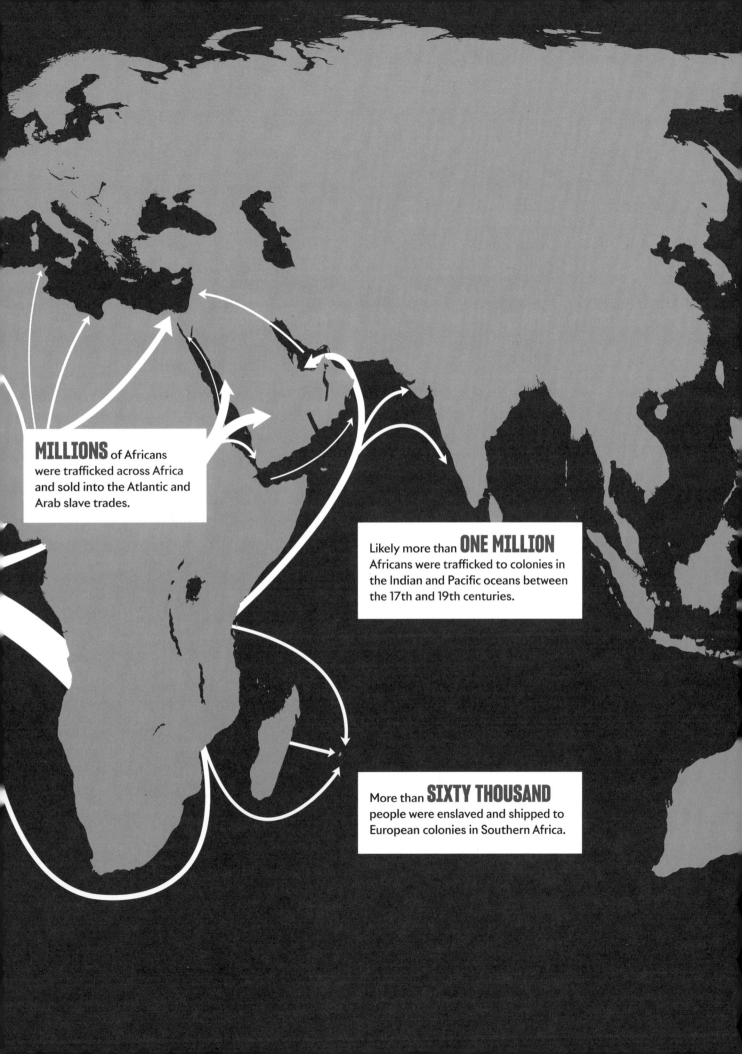

MILLIONS of Africans were trafficked across Africa and sold into the Atlantic and Arab slave trades.

Likely more than **ONE MILLION** Africans were trafficked to colonies in the Indian and Pacific oceans between the 17th and 19th centuries.

More than **SIXTY THOUSAND** people were enslaved and shipped to European colonies in Southern Africa.

THE MANY IMPACTS OF THE TRANSATLANTIC SLAVE TRADE

Jennifer L. Morgan

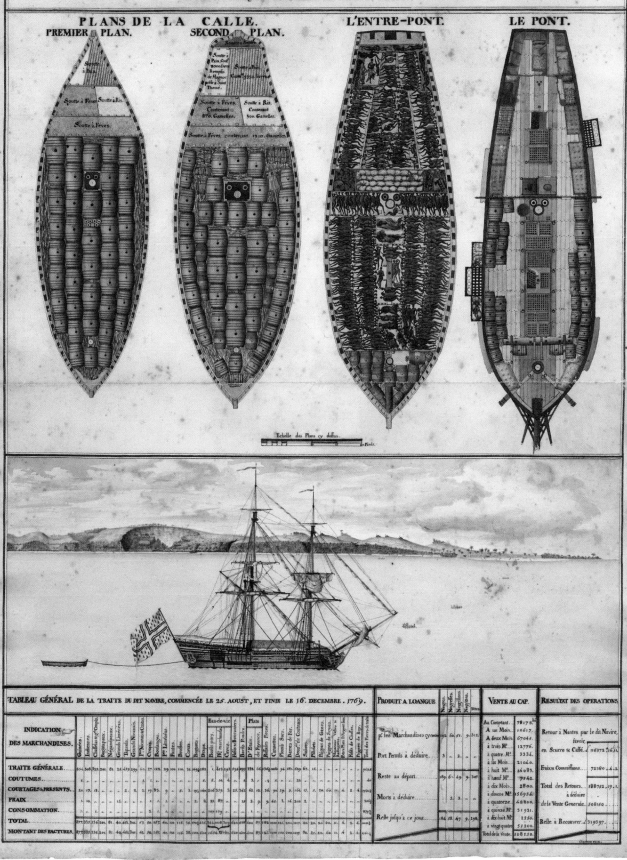

The history of slavery, its victims, and its impact might appear to be unconnected to the present. We tend to relegate slavery to a long-ago past and consider it an unfortunate episode set in motion by people living at a time distant from our own. It is hard to accept a trade in human beings. It is hard to come to terms with the dungeons on the West African coast, or the slave quarters in Louisiana, or the history of slave ownership on the part of Ivy League universities and Fortune 500 companies. Slavery shapes the ways we assess incarceration and liberty, immigration and citizenship, value and insurance, and travel and home. Slavery normalized what, in hindsight, we can agree were universally abhorrent practices. The story of slavery is powerfully at odds with logic, justice, and democracy, but lurking just beneath the surface of the institutions and experiences that shape contemporary life are the legacies of violence, racism, and dispossession of the "peculiar institution." There, we find the origins of colonialism, extractive long-distance trade, and capitalism.

For historians of slavery, the origins of the modern world and the origins of the Transatlantic Slave Trade are one and the same thing. They are so deeply interwoven that, beginning in the sixteenth century, one could not exist without the other. They gave rise to the core concepts associated with "modernity" and with the ideas of the eighteenth-century Enlightenment: capitalism, democracy, and the belief that all individuals possess natural and human rights. Ironically, each of these concepts emerged during the ascendency of the slave trade. However, the late sociologist and theorist Cedric Robinson, borrowing from debates about the relationship between apartheid, race, and class in South Africa, introduced the concept of "racial capitalism" in 1983 as a critique of scholarship that suggested slavery was no more than a primitive economic stage in the unfolding of capitalism. Robinson argued that the development of capitalism required slavery. He didn't view racism as a regrettable side effect of class but rather explained that capitalism arose from the alienation of workers, the logistics of long-distance trade, and the extractive project of colonialism. These were the outgrowths of historic racial, ethnic, and economic antagonisms among Europeans, which led to the development and embrace of hereditary racial slavery.

Today we live in the aftermath of slavery—and thus in its wake. In her book *In the Wake: On Blackness and Being*, the theorist and philosopher Christina Sharpe encourages us to consider the multiple meanings of the word "wake," because it evokes many aspects of the aftermath of slavery. A wake is the path left behind a ship; the aftermath of a ship's passing. In the case of a vessel transporting African captives across the Atlantic, the wake would include captives thrown overboard, and sharks that fed on them. The migratory patterns of sharks were transformed by the slave trade, as bodies lured sharks from the coast of Africa to the other side of the Atlantic. The word also moves us to contemplate the effects on the lives of the families left behind, as Sharpe reminds us that a wake is a gathering that marks the death of a loved one, where mourners share memories of the departed. Black people in the Diaspora have always mourned the histories that can't be accessed, the violence in communities from Montreal to Montenegro generations after the end of the slave trade, and myriad other conditions and situations that arise when one tries to navigate the grief associated with slavery. The word *wake* also signifies a return to consciousness, opening one's eyes in the morning, seeing all that is around us—bearing witness. As a historian of the early modern Black Atlantic, *wake* enables me to understand the impact of slavery on so many aspects of our current world.

Histories of Slavery

From the beginning, the history of slavery in the Americas was mired in efforts to minimize its impact. Even before the end of the slave trade and of slavery, a robust and profoundly destructive, layered narrative about African culpability in the trade developed in Europe and the United States. Before we can begin to assess slavery's impact on the modern world, we need to understand the barriers that have stood in the way of scholars' efforts to write that history. Telling the history of slavery is not neutral. Unearthing it is an act of

Blueprint

Previous page
Diagram of the *Marie Séraphique*, 1770. Considered one of the most accurate representations of conditions aboard slave ships, this visual testament to the horrors of the Transatlantic Slave Trade depicts a French slaving vessel off the coast of Loango, Angola, with more than three hundred African captives packed tightly in the hold.

Top
***Blueprint*, Terry Boddie, 2017. This work juxtaposes an image of a housing development in Harlem, New York, with an illustration of the hold of a slave ship, suggesting a connection between the treatment and organization of captive Africans and their descendants today.**

scholarship and intention that exposes the mistaken assumption that archives are straightforward repositories of factual information. Europeans struggled to make sense of their encounters on the African continent and, in the process, produced narratives and archives that excluded Africans from knowledge and civilization. Europeans viewed African systems of thought, computation, storytelling, record keeping, and religion as inferior, and Europe came to know itself in contrast to the fictions it told about Africa's lack of history, social structures, civility, and polities. In this context, the history of slavery and the slave trade was fostered by those who sought to justify or minimize the horror of the institutions: Under the veneer of "scholarship" or "education," they situated slavery as benevolent, paternal, and civilizing. As the historian and author Hasan Kwame Jeffries has shown, in the immediate aftermath of the American Civil War, scholars revised the story of bondage to erase its impact on the lives of Black and white Southerners. Rather than present the war as one that was fought over slavery, the scholars crafted

a story that the American Civil War was a conflict over states' rights—provoked by the federal government's intrusion into the "Southern way of life." These same scholars did not admit that the Union won because Black people fled slavery and joined the Union Army. Instead, the official line was that Black people worked on bucolic cotton plantations, and that they were well fed, musical, and surrounded by family. Missing from a bloodless story is the recounting of the internal slave trade that sent a million people from the upper to the lower South, the brutal slave patrols, the starvation, the whips and chains.

These conditions and behaviors were not confined to North America. They occurred throughout the Americas, across the Atlantic and ultimately informed Europe's nineteenth century colonial occupation of Africa. This rewriting of the past would come to justify the "urgent" call of European powers to bring a halt to the alleged savagery of African slave traders, thereby providing moral cover for their next stage of extracting wealth from the continent. They shifted the blame for four hundred years of

Cortejo da Rainha Negra na festa de Reis (The Black Queen's Procession at the Feast of Kings), Carlos Julião, ca. 1776. This watercolor illustrates an annual procession arranged by the brotherhood of Nossa Senhora do Rosário (Our Lady of the Rosary), a religious organization that supported free and enslaved Africans in Brazil. Afro-Brazilians forced into Catholicism adapted the religion's traditions and rituals to reflect African beliefs and spiritual practices.

extraction onto those who were the trade's victims. These justifications deflected responsibility for slavery onto African tribal incivilities, anointed the United Kingdom and the United States as global abolitionists, and authorized colonial transferring of territories in the name of halting the alleged atrocities committed by African or Arab slave traders. Europe became depicted as the driving force behind the abolition of the trade, which was driven not by Europe's rapacious economic growth, but by the alleged despotism of African leaders.

The shift from slavery to colonialism was accompanied by a re-narrating of the histories of Africa. These stories, built on German philosopher Georg Wilhelm Friedrich Hegel's claim that Africa and Africans had no history at all defined much of the scholarship on the trade. Few European or American universities recognized African history as a discipline until the pressure of anti-colonial and civil rights activism pushed for educational reforms. The first African Studies Association was founded in 1958, but Hegel's nineteenth-century claim held sway well into the twentieth century, despite the efforts of Black scholars like George Washington Williams and W.E.B. Du Bois, who were among those researching and writing histories of African peoples and civilizations.

This rewriting of the past had a tangible effect. The Transatlantic Slave Trade enabled an epic transformation of European economies and territorial possession. It established trading companies, financed shipping magnates, shaped supply networks, fed desires for sweetness and caffeine, contributed to intra-European wars of territory and trade, and provided elite Europeans with the luxury goods and services that made their households both beautiful and horrific. It also introduced and then solidified race as a marker of human difference. As a result, men, women, and children were violently wrenched into the Atlantic. Their labor produced wealth for their enslavers. But Black people in the Diaspora shaped cultural and political responses that rejected the founding premises of early modern capitalism—the violence and violations at the heart of an economy fully capable of reducing people to property.

The Black Atlantic has generated powerful refusals. When enslaved people planned revolts, ran away, or established new communities on the outer edges of Europe's colonies, they were articulating a very specific notion of freedom and belonging. When they maintained their languages and cosmologies, they were illustrating the depths of their cultures in the face of accusations that they had none. When they loved one another and cared for their own children and those whose birth parents were taken from them, they asserted the reality of their kinship ties in the face of the legally defined right to buy and sell people as though they had no family, no feelings, and no connections.

The system of slavery was built on the claim that Africans would provide docile and controllable labor in the Americas, and that they wouldn't rebel or complicate labor arrangements with demands for family or freedom. And yet, in every instance when enslaved men and women articulated the complexity of their lives and communities—through cultural practices, through collective efforts at refusal, through the labors of their heart—the falsehood of the slave owners' claims that Black people were reducible to brute laborers was made evident.

One can examine the hundreds of slave revolts, beginning in 1526 and lasting through to slavery's final days, to see the impact of Black peoples' demands for freedom. Thomas Jefferson believed that the animus between Black and white people in North America was so extensive that free Black people could never be allowed to stay in the United States. Rather, he supported efforts to transport free Black Americans "back" to Africa, whether they wished to go or not. In *Notes on the State of Virginia*, he wrote:

> Why not retain and incorporate the blacks into the state, and thus save the expense of supplying, by importation of white settlers, the vacancies they will leave? Deep rooted prejudices entertained by the whites; ten thousand recollections, by the blacks, of the injuries they have sustained; new provocations; the real distinctions which nature has made; and many other circumstances, will divide us into parties, and produce convulsions which will probably never end but in the extermination of the one or the other race.

But Black Americans, both enslaved and free, were actively articulating the terms of citizenship in ways that would come to define the very concept. Through their revolts and rebellions, through their demands to preserve and protect their families and their children's future, they defined a freedom unrestricted by race, creed, or sex. They refused the notion that simply by virtue of the color of their skin they were excluded from the categories that defined Western modernity—they claimed the rights of citizenship, the rights of representative government, the right to have and maintain autonomous families, the rights to worship, to congregate, and to move freely from one place to another. Whether as theoreticians or practitioners or protesters, the men and women delivered to the Americas through the slave trade produced a way of understanding the world that continues to shape our lives.

Black communities outside the African continent were shaped by the slave trade and by their refusal to be destroyed by it. Diasporic peoples are at modernity's core, beginning with their ideologies of freedom: Frederick Douglass, Harriet Jacobs, Toussaint Louverture, and Phillis Wheatley all embraced Enlightenment ideals of citizenship and natural rights and were in full disagreement with the racial slavery endorsed and practiced by men like Thomas Jefferson and Robespierre, even as they wrote extensively on the virtues of modernity and Enlightenment.

The Slave Trade

So what are the histories of slavery that underpin our contemporary work? We need to begin more than five-hundred years ago to start to answer that question. In 1441, a Portuguese ship slowly made its way up the river Gambia. The Portuguese crown had sent the captain to make inroads for trade goods with local people, as he searched for gold. He was also told to bring back evidence regarding wealth on the coast. The notion that trade goods could include people was, by then, not a strange idea. Enslaved laborers were found throughout Europe and Africa during the Middle Ages, a natural consequence of incursions and wars, so it shouldn't come as a surprise to learn that crew members from that ship, upon

seeing a woman with her child on the riverbank, decided to capture her. She struggled mightily, proving to be far stronger and more difficult to subdue than they had anticipated. In the end, they realized that if they simply grabbed her small child and carried him to the boat, she would follow. They used her motherhood to deprive her of her liberty. The woman and her child were a drop of water in the ocean that would become the Transatlantic Slave Trade. Later, reflecting on the effect of bringing captives to the Portuguese ruler, a writer speculated on how happy it would make the king to know that Gambia was full of potential slaves. In *The Discovery and Conquest of Guinea*, Gomes de Zurara, the royal chronicler to Prince Henry of Portugal, Eanes wrote:

> I cannot behold the arrival of these ships with the novelty of the gain of those slaves before the face of our Prince, without finding some delight in the same. For me seemeth that I behold before my eyes that pleasure of his, of what kind it would be . . . O holy prince . . . seeing the beginnings of some recompense, may we not think thou didst feel joy, not so much for the number of the captives taken, as for the hope thou didst conceive of the others thou couldst take?

In this regard, the chronicler, captain, and crew were prescient. They understood that the foundation of Iberian wealth would be enslaved women and men.

Later, in the same account of the early Portuguese efforts to obtain wealth from West Africa, there is a description of a large group of African men, women, and children who had been taken to Europe for sale. More than 250 people disembarked and were divided into lots for market. They tried desperately to maintain connections to their kinfolk, spouses, and parents, straining to remain together in a strange new land. Despite their efforts to hold on to their children, mothers and fathers endured this loss, in addition to what the shipboard passage had already cost them. What they might not have fully understood at the time was that their reproductive futures would become embedded in the imperial designs of European princes. As racial hierarchies came to shape and justify

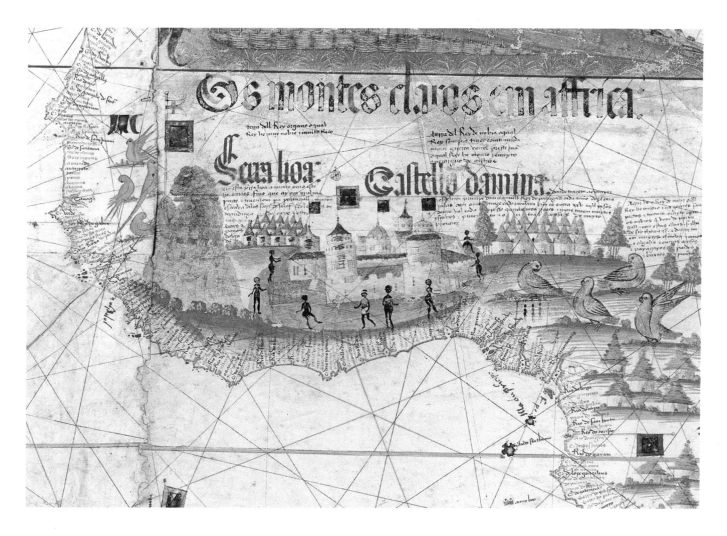

Os montes claros em affrica

Cara boa.   Castello damina.

Detail of the *Cantino Planisphere* (Cantino world map), 1502. This map depicts Elmina (The Mine), a Portuguese fortress built on the coast of what is now Ghana. Originally constructed to facilitate the gold trade, it was used by the Portuguese, Dutch, and English during the slave trade. More than thirty thousand African captives passed through Elmina's doors.

slavery and the trade in human beings, the status of enslavement would become indelible and inherited. Enslavement would be a process that subverted the usual expectations of kinship or innocence—the acts of capturing and transporting set in motion a series of fundamental transformations. The narrator of these episodes described the people as "negro," using a word that would ultimately distinguish them from any victims of enslavement who had come before. This gave rise to a radically new system of hereditary racial slavery. When the story of capturing human beings was told, the individuality of African women and men needed to be subverted in a language of racial distinction. And a sovereign polity was reduced to a source of raw materials—gold first, then humans, rubber, oil, and, later, minerals.

Fueled by the search for gold, silver, and spices to expand royal coffers, the Spanish made contact with the West African coast in the first half of the fifteenth century. Well before then, Africans and Europeans had been familiar with one another through incursions, exchanges, occupations,

and enslavement, which took place around southern Europe and northern Africa, in the Mediterranean. Therefore, prior to Columbus's voyages, the groundwork was laid for what would become a reliance on forced labor to extract wealth from the Americas. The pathway toward the Transatlantic Slave Trade was strewn with decisions not usually traced in grand historical narratives but rather found in small and intimate experiences like that of the woman whose child was used to lure her on board a Portuguese vessel.

The enslavement of Africans and people of African descent lasted for 444 years, beginning on August 8, 1444, when the slave trader Lançarote de Freitas sold 235 Africans captured in Senegambia in the Portuguese coastal city of Lagos. Slavery ended on May 13, 1888, when Brazil became the last nation in the Americas to abolish it. By 1650, upward of ten thousand Africans were transported to the Americas per year, and that number didn't decrease until approximately 1840. The height of the trade occurred between 1700 and 1810, when nearly 6.5 million Africans were captured and transported by European slave traders. Some 12 million men, women, and children were taken across the Atlantic until 1888. Adult men are most associated with the slave trade, but children and adult women slightly outnumbered them. The presence of women and children among the enslaved is a key indication of how labor and culture were being transformed.

The wealth enslaved people produced was critical to the growth of the Americas: According to the economic historian Joseph Inikori, African laborers were responsible for 50 percent of the value of the commodities exported each year from the Americas to Europe between 1501 and 1600. The value of their labor grew steadily, to approximately 80 percent between 1760 and 1800. It declined to 68 percent during the period that marks the start of the decline of slavery in the Americas, from 1848 to 1850. While there were other exports from the Americas not associated with slave labor, plantation commodities such as sugar, tobacco, cotton, and rice were produced almost entirely by enslaved Africans. So, too, was gold in Brazil and Spanish America.

We should remember that enslaved people throughout the Americas were forced to perform all manner of unpaid labor. Though slavery is primarily associated with large-scale, mono-crop agriculture, there were enslaved men and women working in every sphere in the Americas—from urban households and businesses in New England, to seal and whale hunting off the coast of Chile,

to hotels in Washington, DC, to wheat farms in Pennsylvania, to blacksmithing in South Carolina. The impact of slaves on the development of the Americas is not just in the quantities of wealth that their hands produced but also in the way we think about work, autonomy, and constraint.

By the beginning of the eighteenth century, ideologies of political freedom were gripping the Americas, among both the enslaved and the free. Slave revolts became a ubiquitous aspect of life in slave societies in the hemisphere. In North America, the first slave revolt occurred in 1526, in a Spanish settlement near what is now South Carolina. On this continent, more than 250 revolts and conspiracies to revolt tell the story of Black opposition to enslavement. The largest of these uprisings occurred in South Carolina in 1739 when enslaved men, recently transported from Angola as prisoners of war, organized a military uprising. Responding to news of a free Black outpost in Florida, they attempted to join their brethren there after deserting plantations and killing slaveholders who stood in their way.

Well before the English colonists in America demanded freedom from their king, enslaved people in the Americas demanded the same from them. The very same colonists who held slaves also considered themselves to be unjustly enslaved by King George III. Historians consider this position to be an irony of American political philosophy, but the evocation of slavery as a metaphor in the ideas and documents that forged Western

Engrav'd for the Universal Magazine, for J. Hinton at the King's Arms, in St Pauls Church Yard London.

democracies, such as the US Declaration of Independence or the French Declaration of the Rights of Man and of the Citizen, is more than an eighteenth-century irony. It hints at the way slavery and freedom were entwined in modern political philosophy. Who could be free? What was the equality among men that Jefferson envisioned?

The slave trade produced new notions of how societies and economies worked that became enshrined in constitutional and other laws, in the establishment of European colonies, and in private life. Citizens would have their rights preserved in founding documents—rights systematically denied to Black people from the start—but Black people used the law to mount systematic demands for safety, representation, and protection under the law. Even after the end of the slave trade, the idea persisted that Africa's sole purpose was to provide materials with which the wealth of Europe and

the Americas would be built. Over the course of the twentieth century and into the twenty-first, to ensure that its needs would be met, Europe used military and economic force to ensure itself a supply of rubber, palm oil, crude oil, copper, diamonds, coltan, and, most recently, the minerals necessary for electric car batteries. Further, Western nations continue to be mired in economies that rely on the use of degraded labor provided by many kinds of people designated as surplus populations, and that resulted in the amassing of wealth and resources in the hands of the few at the cost of the many.

Impacts on Africa

The impact of enslavement on millions of African souls is hard to measure. Slavery accelerated and lengthened conflict and war in Africa in the service of slave trading, and left millions of Africans to deal with the loss of family members, allies, and adversaries who could never be fully mourned or accounted for. As power was consolidated by states whose military and political growth were based in the slave trade, the market for captives transformed states and polities both near the coast and in the interior. Centralized African states expanded their power, and decentralized ones adopted slave trading in order to protect themselves. The Kingdom of Dahomey (in present-day Benin) is but one example of a state that grew rich and powerful in the eighteenth and nineteenth centuries through its capacity to conquer small states in the region and deliver large numbers of captives to European slave traders.

In the long term, as the economist Nathan Nunn illustrates, the economic under-performance of some African countries in the twentieth and twenty-first centuries is definitively linked to the extent to which they supplied captives to international slave traders. Even as Black labor created wealth in the Americas, the promise of modernization on the African continent or in the Diaspora was not realized until well into the twentieth century. As anti-colonial movements led to the independence of African countries, beginning with Britain's departure from Ghana in 1957, many of them faced criticisms for failing to modernize quickly enough. Economies that had been shaped in order to enrich Europe required time to reorganize, but were instead subjected to Cold War demands for allegiance and imperialist interference. The destruction of Congolese independence, including the involvement of the CIA in the assassination of Patrice Lumumba and the subsequent United States investment in propping up the dictator Mobutu Sese Seko, are examples of the obstacles facing emergent African states in the twentieth and twenty-first centuries.

The postcolonial landscape is fraught with the competing expectations of modernity and the notion that the failure to achieve modernism should be laid directly at the doorstep of countries whose development was hampered because they were harnessed to the growth of Western economies. Newly sovereign nations were expected to immediately realign centuries of extractive economies and despotic rule into efficient capitalist economies. Failure to do so is labeled backwardness rather

than evidence that such struggles exist because the needs of the citizenry have been systematically denied for generations. African nations and Africans in and out of the Diaspora are considered the antithesis of modernity.

Impact on Kinship

From the earliest years of their efforts to capture Africans, Europeans mobilized kinship even as they destroyed it. Recall the fifteenth-century Portuguese chronicle of the sailors who forced a woman to board a ship by grabbing her child. In the first decades of the slave trade to North America, reproduction was rare for enslaved women. On the sugar islands of the West Indies and in Brazil, mortality rates vastly outpaced birth rates. Severe work regimes, diseases, and malnutrition all had an impact on the fertility of Black people. However, this reality did not interfere with slave owners identifying the possibilities of reproduction as part of their long-term investments in amassing and expanding their labor force. From the beginning, economic gain was premised on a fictional claim that the African family didn't exist. Still, the kinship ties of African people, while ignored or weaponized by slave traders and slaveholders, persisted in defining the interior and collective lives of Black people in the Diaspora.

Simultaneous to denying the existence of family ties, slave traders used enslaved children to control their parents. In 1647, the Dutch West India Company granted the freedom

Top
Coronation of the King of Whydah, 1725. Ouidah, or Whydah, was one of the most active slave-trading ports in Africa. Located on the Bight of Benin, termed "the Slave Coast" by European traders, it was the departure point for more than one million African captives over the course of two centuries. The sale of captives in the Kingdom of Ouidah, and in the succeeding Kingdom of Dahomey, was managed in part by the state but evolved over time to become largely run by private merchants.

Right
Lucinda and Frances Hughes with their children in Virginia, United States, Peter E. Larkin, ca. 1861–62. Under racial slavery, which broke family ties, the formation of other kinship connections was crucial to survival. Enslaved people often practiced collective child-rearing, forming networks of support in the case of parental death or sale.

petition of a group of enslaved men and women in New Amsterdam (later day New York) but kept their children in bondage. In doing so, they maintained a palpable degree of control over those emancipated even in their freedom. This was a practice utilized across time and geographies to either yoke freed people to their enslavers through the love and care for their kin who remained enslaved or to sever those ties, replicating a perverse myth that slaves did not feel or love as fully as their enslavers did. The exploitation and manipulation of women's fertility also demonstrated good investment practices by the slave holder across various places and times. For example, in Virginia in the early nineteenth century, Thomas Jefferson wrote, "I consider a woman who brings a child every two years as more profitable than the best man of the farm, what she produces is an addition to the capital." This is a stark example of how the intimate lives of Black women and men came to suppose the households of slave owners. But dismissing the

kinship bonds of the enslaved did more than simply make Thomas Jefferson a rich man.

Hundreds of years prior, in the fifteenth century, the market for enslaved laborers was dominated by demands for girls and women to serve in Iberian and Mediterranean households. Writing to her banker in Portugal, Isabella d'Este, a Florentine marchioness, asked to purchase another African girl to join the one she already had working in her home—"the blacker the better." The servant girl purchased by the marchioness marked the elevated status of her private household. The concepts of the "public sphere" and the "private sphere" emerged slowly, but a clear division of what is understood as the domestic, familial, or private came into view as the Transatlantic Slave Trade and the settlement of the Americas began. The idea of the public sphere started to solidify in politics and law in the seventeenth century. The association of the public sphere with government derived from English land law, which

differentiated between land that the king held privately and land that he ruled over but could not sell, otherwise known as public lands. The idea of the private sphere—the household—was fully cemented by the turn of the nineteenth century, and it became associated with patriarchal authority. The patriarchal head represented the household, a place where family members were shielded from politics, the market, and matters of public life. The ability to own, or aspire to own, property became the foundation for Western notions of freedom, and the autonomy of the family was a cornerstone of that freedom. For people of African descent, the intrusion of the market into family relationships came simultaneously with the onset of the slave trade. Therefore, for enslaved people, family life was never protected and certainly never free. Black families were always at risk of being separated by sale or death from overwork and abuse, with little or no capacity to keep themselves and their families safe.

In 1675, the English captain of the slave ship *James* noted in his logbook, in the running tally called "Account of Mortality," that one of the female captives on board, "Being very fond of her Child, Carrying her up and downe, wore her to nothing by which means fell into a feavour and dyed." The crew had been loading men and women on board the ship for months. Death came even before it left the African coast. The captain didn't recognize her connection to her child as more than his calculations of loss, but we can understand the agony she felt over the loss of her child.

In theory, childbirth and child-rearing are deeply personal and domestic matters, and they historically occurred away from the public eye and under the supervision of women. This notion of a domestic sphere applied primarily to women whose economic and racial identity gave them the capacity to hire or appropriate other women's labor inside the home to protect themselves from work. The ideal private home could not exist without the material, wealth, and leisure produced by slave labor. The restorative morning tea and coffee, the sweet pastry and chocolate, the clean hearth, the well-hemmed garment, the children fed (sometimes on a Black woman's breastmilk) and put to bed so

spouses might sit by a fire chatting about their day—all depended upon the labor of enslaved people either working in fields or tending to the comfort of others. For enslaved women, the domestic work of a home of their own was brutally shattered by the demands placed on their labors and by the reality that their childbearing potential was locked into the marketplace by the men and women who enslaved them.

The appropriation of Black people's futures through transforming enslaved women into "generative forms of capital" was the ideological foundation of hereditary racial slavery. As slave societies developed, they did so by legally distinguishing childbearing from kinship. The fact that enslavement and "enslavability" were passed down as an inherited status meant that this most vulnerable and personal aspect of human life engendered financial speculation, boundless estates, and the idea of expanded wealth for generations. Racial slavery relied on the intimate lives of enslaved women. Racial slavery also introduced the idea that Black women and men were racially and thus biologically marked to be slaves. The origin of modern biology and genetics is rooted in the claim that Europeans could scientifically prove the legitimacy of their rule over others. With the 1839 publication of Samuel George Morton's *Crania Americana*, the belief that racial hierarchy was biological and scientifically ascertainable took hold. Morton argued that human skulls proved each race of humans is a different species and that in the order of rank, "negroes" are at the bottom of humanity. This kind of pseudoscientific thinking lent itself to the degradation of all women of color, as women passed on the racial order from parent to child. Because these women were identified as part of a distinct species, the inheritance of race could be disconnected from the feelings of family. The claim that centuries of racial slavery were justified by the scientific discovery of multiple strands of the human species was, for some, deeply satisfying. Race built a context within which the economization of the enslaved made moral and financial sense. Slaveholders maintained a fantasy that Black people had few or no strong or legitimate ties to one another, so Black people have historically been at pains

UNDER DECREE IN EQUITY.

SANDERS vs. SANDERS, et al.

On *Tuesday, the 11th January*, 1859, will be sold at the *Court House*, in Charleston, at 12 o'clock, M., under direction of James W. Gray, Master in Equity, the following Slaves.

TERMS.—One-third Cash ; balance in one, two and three years, secured by bonds and mortgages with approved personal security. Purchaser to pay for Papers.

NAMES.	AGE.
1 London,	55 yrs.
2 Nelly,	50
3 Dick,	15
4—4 Rosy,	4
5 Cuffy,	35
2—6 Becker,	19
7 Caroline,	29
8 Martha,	4
9 Bull or Frederick,	12
4—10 Infant,	9 ms.
11 Charity,	30 yrs.
12 Susan,	17
13 Floride,	2
4—14 Infant,	6 ms.
15 Ned,	60 yrs.
16 Silvy,	35
17 Frank,	11
18 Harriet,	14
Easton,	3
19 Infant,	3 ms.
20 Billy,	65 yrs.
21 Lucy,	50
22 Binah,	14
23 Phillis,	12
7—24 Jack,	11
1—25 Thomas,	26
1—26 Toney,	30
27 Becky,	30
28 Sammy,	5
29 Fed,	2
4—30 Infant,	7 ms.
1—31 Isaac,	30
1—32 Moses,	25
1—33 Morris,	21
34 Billy,	45
35 Hagar,	50
36 Joe,	35
37 William,	20
5—38 Rose,	15
39 Martha	70
40 Nancy	45
41 Rachel,	22
42 Ben,	16
5—43 Lot	10
44 Betty,	25
2—45 Plymouth,	2
46 London,	26
47 Grace,	22
3—48 Harriet	2
49 Hester	25
50 Amos	21
3—51 Elsey	5

NAMES.	AGE.
52 Jacob	55 yrs.
53 Mary	45
54 Emma,	21
55 Rose	15
56 Aelie	18
57 Simon	13
58 Francis	6
8—59 Mary	3
60 Hardtimes	70
61 Sary,	30
3—62 Anne,	18
63 Old Peter	70
2—64 Old Nancy	60
65 Old Hester	68
66 Maggy	40
67 Edward,	19
68 Susan	17
69 Robert	13
70 Martha	7
7—71 Sarah	2
72 Peter	28
73 Venus	25
74 Henry	8
75 Hamilton	4
5—76 Cornelia	1
77 Lydy	25
2—78 Hannah	6 ms.
79 Hannah	30 yrs.
80 Nero	10
81 Rachel	7
82 August	4
83 Henry	2
6—84 Infant	1 mh.
1—85 Old Frank,	60 yrs.
1—86 Toney	30
87 Jake,	35
88 Eliza	30
89 Pleasant	12
90 Sukey	10
91 Amanda	8
6—92 Catharine	3
1—93 David	36
1—94 Jim	39
1—95 Binah,	60
1—96 March	40
1—97 Bob	35
1—98 Sarah	12
1—99 Harriet	14

to both protect themselves and amplify their kin ties to the wider world. Under racial slavery, family became imbued with the violent intrusion of the public into the private, and modern life became inextricable from the resulting contradictions.

Making Race

The slave trade, the reliance on slave labor, and the justifications that were developed to make both of those things appear to be rational and moral produced more than just anti-Black racism. They also produced a category of identity in opposition. European nations long had contentious relationships with one another, but over time, the claiming of one's identity as white began to take increased status alongside national, cultural, ethnic, or religious identities. Thus, hostilities decreased between those who previously saw themselves as French, not English, or Swedish, not Italian. Over time, the investment in identifying as white, in addition to and sometimes over, and above one's nation, culture, or religion, began to allay some antagonisms rooted in the long history of European conflict. Similar factors were at play in United States history. As the historian Noel Ignatiev has shown, when Irish immigrants first arrived in significant numbers in the United States at the start of the nineteenth century, they were treated as degraded and unworthy. It was later, as some collectively embraced anti-Black sentiment, that they were seen more positively and became more accepted as a dominant culture receiving its privileges.

Throughout the slave societies in the Americas, there was never more than a minuscule elite of settlers, colonists, and landowners who had the financial means to own other people—and an even smaller number owned more than five. But whether or not they actually accumulated the considerable wealth necessary to purchase land or laborers, many white people who were not part of this elite also perceived the legitimacy of their presence on the land and their access to the labor of others as an unquestioned part of social and political life.

Slavery not only produced new identities for Europeans, whether wealthy enough to purchase people at markets or not. In the Americas, it introduced new forms of wealth, new commodities, new ways to access trade, and new aspirations. Racial identity became understood as part of a set of overlapping communities and identities: congregations, guilds, counties, and nations in which racial provenance was increasingly associated with access to, or exclusion from, possibility. Across the Americas, the elites accumulated wealth through other people's labor and came to dominate national political economies in ways that enshrined and normalized massive structural inequities—inequities that are not confined to Black people.

The unequal distribution of wealth that grew out of the slave trade was by no means unprecedented. The accumulation of economic power in the hands of the very few may indeed be as old as human history. However, the Transatlantic Slave Trade coincided with the emergence of the modern nation-state and with the financial, scientific, political, and legal instruments that have come to define contemporary economies. As previously stated, slavery introduced a profoundly new way of conceptualizing human hierarchy. Rather than dividing allies and enemies, true believers and infidels, civilized and savage, race became a central determining factor in dividing the world. This set in motion the rationalization that some humans were inherently made for brute labor to serve the needs of others, and destined to lose their land to colonizers who intended to "civilize" them. In the United States, we have both inherited and produced generations of ideological justifications for Black poverty that circle back again and again—in both policy and culture—toward blaming Black people for producing their own condition.

Damages

To measure the impact that slavery has had upon modern life, historians turn tragedy into evidence: We count the number of bodies thrown overboard from a slave ship; the number of bodies hanging from trees in Indiana; and the 5.4 million dead as a result of wars in Congo since 1998 over access to minerals needed to manufacture cell phones and video games. We analyze the death rates of Indigenous communities exacerbated by European arrivals, death rates in the Middle Passage, and population counts of enslaved laborers in the American South or the Caribbean. We do so because, in part, we know that to be modern is to

Bottom
Enslaved laborers at a coffee farm in São Paulo, Brazil, 1882. As the development of American colonies intertwined with European economic growth, enslaved labor began to saturate every industry. In Brazil, coffee became one of the main exports. This industry's development not only promoted slave labor but depended on it.

have a rational relationship to information that we are able and willing to quantify accurately and honestly. But quantifiable data can only be part of the path to knowledge, to comprehending the impact of what we study. When we aggregate, we lose the specificity of each life lost to war or disease or the ravages of a changed climate. We lose the understanding of the pain of addiction, despair, and loneliness.

The story of how the capture and sale of human beings became embedded in the production of other merchandise is a terrible one. The story of how those human beings were made to work without end to enrich those who stole their labor is another terrible tale at the heart of our modern world. Slavery and the slave trade deserve to be mourned. The stories deserve our grief. They deserve a wake. They also must be understood as the source of current disparities in financial standing, incarceration rates, health, and life expectancy.

The damages that are at the heart of our modern world exceed those that I've charted here, of course, but my presumption is that the only way to understand today's realities is to understand the

history of race and racism that began with the Transatlantic Slave Trade. The historian Walter Johnson writes that if you don't start with the history of slavery, many of our contemporary problems simply don't make sense. Thinking about history by starting with slavery does not congratulate those of us who are looking back on that history for how well we've done, how far we've come, how hard we've tried. Indeed, it's a pretty sad place, and it means starting with a methodology that is steeped in melancholy. A melancholy born in the realization that human suffering has always been at the heart of economic growth.

I spent some time imagining that my work as a scholar was objective and disinterested, but I have increasingly come to know that this claim was an effort to mask the sadness and anger I feel when I confront the history of slavery and its wake. Once I accepted that sadness, I became interested in using it to draw attention to the fact that the never-ending echo of the Atlantic graveyard must be silenced, we lose the possibilities for reframing liberation. The men and women who were the victims of the Transatlantic Slave Trade were

Nuit de Noël. (HAPPY-club) 1963   Malick Sidibé 2008

caught in circumstances outside of their control, yet they responded by developing a set of critical strategies: theories of power and plans for rebellion and opposition. This tradition of Black radical response transformed Black life in the aftermath of slavery. The Black radical response set in motion powerful counter-narratives through which communities were formed, intellect was shaped, opposition was mobilized, music was made, style was deployed, love was experienced, and children were born. All this might be a compass with which we find a better, more just and humane future.

However, global political engagements are still organized around the vestiges of European colonialism, whereby the raw materials of empire are taken, by force or by sleight of hand, from the Global South in service to the economic and military demands of the Global North. While there are moments of collective refusal, such as the organization by non-Western nations of alliances like CARICOM (Caribbean Community and Common Market), there is also a long history of denying the autonomy and sovereignty of the people and polities of Africa and Latin America. The connection between long histories of slavery and dispossession on the one hand, and current global economic, social, and political inequities on the other continues to pose challenges in how we might bring about new ways of understanding modern life.

We need to grapple with the ways that the foundations of modern economies are built on the disenfranchisement of the majority. When we move forward in time, out of the period of hereditary racial slavery in the Atlantic world, we still see structures of racial inequality, which have persisted into the twenty-first century. The wealth gap between white and Black families in the United States has continued and grown over the past four decades. In 2022, the average wealth of white families was seven times higher than the average wealth of Black families. Worse still, median white wealth (wealth for the family in the exact middle of the overall distribution—wealthier than half of all families and less wealthy than half) was twelve times higher than median Black wealth. More than one in four Black households have zero or negative net worth, compared to fewer than one in ten white families, which explains the large differences in the racial wealth gap.

There is a set of normalized conditions whereby the individual freedom and capacity for economic success of some inevitably hinge on the dispossession of others. Unpacking the history of the slave trade is not about casting blame or offering absolution. Rather, it is an opportunity to closely examine two things: the structures of normalcy that have followed the economic and social development of the Atlantic world, and the ways in which new structures and assumptions are normalized in the here and now. We are confronted with questions about the ethical response to wealth. If we have inherited a set of structures that legitimize the accumulation of wealth through the violent dispossessions of slavery and colonialism, we must ask whether it is possible to align our desire for material comforts with our desire for social justice. As we confront the massive rise of wealth in the hands of the few, we can reimagine its limits.

We live in a moment when a desire for easy access to consumer goods and material comfort quite frequently comes at the cost of living wages, environmental justice, and peace. Much of the growth of the technology industry is rooted, for example, in the extraction of the mineral coltan from Democratic Republic of Congo. This extractive process is embedded in the colonial relationships that have defined the region since the onset of the Transatlantic Slave Trade and have left it mired in warfare with no end in sight. All in the service of cell phones and laptop computers, of producing goods cheaply, of the belief that the rewards for developing new methods to move faster and more efficiently through our world justify the refusal to fully calculate their costs. All too often, the blame for political and economic chaos is laid at the doorstep of its victims. The long histories that shape the present fade and, indeed, become impossible to see. What is it impossible for us to see? Or to imagine? We live in slavery's wake. The struggle to envision a different set of values and comforts—of freedoms and responsibilities—is crucial.

CONTROL AND RESTRAINT

The two restraints featured here, iron ankle chains and handcuffs commonly used by police forces on both sides of the Atlantic, reveal connections across geographies and through time, linked together by the materiality of coercive control and restraint—and by the business Hiatt & Company.

Hiatt & Company was founded in Birmingham, United Kingdom, in 1780, as a maker of handcuffs, leg irons, and collars for enslaved people and prisoners. It continued to supply slave traders across the Atlantic World into the nineteenth century, well after the abolition of the slave trade in the British Empire. In the centuries following the abolition of slavery, Hiatt & Company continued to pioneer new means of restraint, when, in the 1990s, it developed the rigid handcuff design that is now the standard used by British police.

The use, abuse, and deprivation of power were integral to transatlantic enslavement, particularly because enslaved people resisted the attempted control of their bodies. Those who enslaved other human beings used visual and material signifiers intended to dehumanize them, such as collars, badges, brands, and shackles.

While the United States' experience of racialized enslavement happened within its borders, the United Kingdom's colonial subjects were located out of sight, at its periphery. Products intended for the plantations of the British Empire, such as Hiatt & Company shackles, traveled thousands of miles across the Atlantic to restrain and control enslaved people. This happened largely out of

Left
Ankle shackles, 1780–1850. This pair of ankle shackles was produced by Hiatt & Company, a Birmingham, United Kingdom business that supplied restraints to traders and slaveholders across the Atlantic.

Miles Greenwood

the sight and minds of the British public until the abolitionist movement in the United Kingdom in the eighteenth century, which used shackles as evidence of the brutality of slavery.

Following the abolition of slavery across the British Empire in 1838, the United Kingdom retained its overseas colonies and continued to use restraints as part of the control of their inhabitants. In Jamaica, people practicing African-based religions were punished with imprisonment and hard labor, as were those who "stole" produce from land owned by another. The formerly enslaved, once deemed to need controlling physically and mentally for fear of their uprising and seizing their freedom, were now criminalized for asserting their identities, practicing their religions, and obtaining food from land they and their ancestors had forcibly worked for centuries. Even contemporary accounts identified this criminalization as an attempt by the plantocracy to maintain a form of racialized slavery when legal slavery—the foundation of their livelihoods—was abolished.

It wasn't until the large-scale arrival of people subjugated from across the British Empire that the legacies of slavery and coercion would coalesce within the boundaries of the British Isles. From the 1940s to the 1970s, hundreds of thousands of people from the Caribbean answered the call to rebuild the "mother country" following World War II. Named after the passenger liner, HMT *Empire Windrush*, that brought people from Jamaica to London in 1948, the Windrush Generation was directly descended from people enslaved by white Britons a little more than a century before.

Birmingham, a city built for centuries on the industry of metalworking, was a popular destination for migrants. In the eighteenth century, manillas (currency used in the slave trade), weapons, and restraints smelted in Birmingham and surrounding areas made their way to the slave ships of the United Kingdom's Atlantic ports, such as Liverpool. Metalworking was still a major industry and employer in Birmingham when the Windrush Generation arrived, with Hiatt & Company still operating there. Some of those who moved to Birmingham, who embodied the legacies of British colonial violence and whose ancestors might have been restrained by shackles manufactured by Hiatt & Company, even came to work in the metal industries, finding jobs "beating iron."

Many of that generation and their descendants would be criminalized by a police force and legal system that sought to equate their Blackness with criminality in the same way the colonial Jamaican government did in the nineteenth century, thus contributing to the disproportionate incarceration of Black people in the United Kingdom. Hiatt & Company continued producing and supplying a variety of restraints to police forces in the United Kingdom until 2008, when its UK operations closed, eliciting a reported fear of handcuff shortages. The production of Hiatt-branded shackles was moved from Birmingham to the United States under a company called The Safariland Group. Many handcuffs produced, like the cuffs pictured here, still bear the Hiatt name.

SURVEILLANCE AND SEGREGATION

Ivie Orobaton

A close look at seemingly different items—slave badges and apartheid-era passbooks—provides a powerful view into a long history of practicing control and surveillance on Black communities a century and an ocean apart. Enslaved people have always been tightly monitored. As work opportunities for enslaved people expanded outside of the confined environment of rural plantations, slave owners' control became increasingly tenuous. To protect their property, planters created a visual language to differentiate between free and unfree Black people and mobilized local governments and the landowning public to monitor their human property. Urban enslaved people experienced greater mobility, and this increase in freedoms within slavery jeopardized the entire system, and so slave passes were created. They ranged from paper notes to badges and buttons that marked enslaved bodies—reaffirming the subjugation of the enslaved and the control of the slave owner.

In 1860, Charleston, South Carolina, ended its sixty-year legal practice of requiring enslaved laborers to wear badges, which monitored their movement and marked their status as unfree. This faded blue-green slave badge, an oxidized copper square, is stamped with a single word, "SERVANT." Each badge was customized with a yearly registration number. The wearer of this badge, issued in 1860, was number 2938. The simple, utilitarian style belies the dehumanization and terror of surveillance and control embodied within this small square of metal. A second button, stamped "TPORTER," denotes ownership by Thomas Porter II of Paradise plantation in Guyana from 1815 to 1834. Designed in and imported from the United Kingdom, these diminutive buttons were sewn onto the clothing of the enslaved. Across the Atlantic Ocean, the practice of issuing slave identification badges was also used in the Cape Colony of Southern Africa. This practice emerged and readapted in the post-emancipatory landscape of apartheid. The roots of apartheid—meaning "separateness" in Afrikaans—can be traced back to slavery in the Cape Colony. The exploitation and disenfranchisement of Blacks and other people of color were at the center of South Africa's white-supremacist government that ruled from 1948 to 1994. Under apartheid, the National Party

Left
A group of women demonstrate against pass laws in Cape Town, South Africa, in 1956. Under South Africa's apartheid system, Black, "Coloured," and Indian people were forced to carry an identification document—a passbook—to move within a segregated society.

Top
Slave badge, 1860. In Charleston, South Carolina, enslaved people hired out as part-time skilled laborers were required to wear copper badges issued by the city. While slaveholders took most of these enslaved laborers' earnings, the workers may have been able to save funds to buy freedom for themselves or their families.

Bottom left
Slave button, ca. 1820. This button, marked "TPORTER," was likely created as an identification tag for an enslaved person from the plantation of Thomas Porter II in the British colony of Guyana. Means of identification varied across slave societies, sometimes including an assigned number or the wearer's occupation.

Bottom right
Passbooks like this one were required for people of color living under apartheid rule in South Africa. Similar practices involving state-issued passes and identification were implemented across colonial Africa in places like Rwanda, the Belgian Congo, and Kenya. These identification tools were used to control movement and mark social and economic status.

expanded the purview of the government into every aspect of Black life, governing who Black people could marry, where to live, and where to work, all under the threat of arrest or death. The intentional alienation of the majority population laid bare the prejudice that Black bodies should be used only for labor.

In 1952, the National Party passed laws mandating that Black, "Coloured," and Indian people carry passbooks, which restricted their movement and limited their work under the apartheid regime. Closely resembling passports, these passbooks were emblazoned with the national crest of South Africa and the words "travel document" in gold lettering. The palm-sized booklet contained personal information, such as the bearer's name, a unique identification number issued by the South African government, a black-and-white image of the bearer and an official magistrate stamp. This document of the modern state was issued expressly to segregate, demoralize, and demean: Its bearer did not have full freedom of movement or freedom to choose the kind of work they desired.

Enslaved and colonized people defiantly reclaimed their humanity within such systems of oppression in individual and communal practices of self-empowerment. Under the slave-hire system in Charleston, enslaved workers retained a small portion of their earnings, while their owners took the remaining sum for taxes and payment. This small

but meaningful income provided financial independence, affording laborers the opportunity to purchase their own or their families' freedom in an attempt to end the generational trauma of chattel slavery.

In South Africa, people used their passbooks to draw attention to the abhorrent practices of apartheid and fight for their freedom. In a defining moment of the anti-apartheid campaign, twenty thousand men, women, and children protested the pass laws by burning their passbooks in Sharpeville, South Africa, in 1960. Despite the threat of incarceration and physical violence, Black South Africans brought attention to the hypocrisy and brutality of white minority rule and reaffirmed their human rights, declaring, "With passes we are slaves."

The afterlives of practices such as badges and passbooks are found in systemic institutional racism and persistent hypervigilant surveillance of Black bodies, especially those of Black men. In the United States, Black Americans are more likely than whites to be stopped by police and three times more likely to be killed during such encounters. In post-apartheid South Africa, race is the main indicator for persistent economic, social, and spatial inequalities, which predominantly affect the Black population. Despite these lasting inequalities, however, people across the Atlantic world continue to fight the afterlives of slavery and colonialism.

IRIPHABLIKI YETRANSKEI
REPABOLIKI YA TRANSKEI
REPUBLIC OF TRANSKEI

ISAZISI
LENGOLO LA BOITSEBISO
IDENTITY DOCUMENT

(Abantu abaneminyaka elishumi elinesithandathu ubudala nangaphezulu)
(Bakeng sa batho ba dilemo di leshomet-shelela le ho feta)
(for persons of sixteen years and older)

FIGHTING BACK

Alexander Scott

A man and a woman of African descent fight off a pack of dogs. Broken manacles hang from the man's left hand, implying that he is in flight from slavery. His shirtless upper body is muscular, bearing marks that may have resulted from corporal punishment, branding, or dog bites. He is positioned as if protecting the woman, presumably his fellow runaway. The man lifts a hatchet to strike at the dogs, one of which lies incapacitated. The painting's runaways actively and forcefully resist capture—a far departure from the passive representations of runaways in slaveholders' "wanted" notices. The dogs act as surrogates for enslavers: they appear to be Cuban bloodhounds, a breed commonly used to hunt escaped enslaved people. Water reeds and a snake (possibly a cottonmouth) are visible, suggesting a wetland setting.

When *The Hunted Slaves* debuted at London's Royal Academy in 1861, the exhibition catalogue included lines from Henry Wadsworth Longfellow's 1842 poem "The Slave in the Dismal Swamp." Longfellow was inspired by stories of enslaved people escaping into the Great Dismal Swamp, a vast wetland spanning parts of Virginia and North Carolina. Contrary to Longfellow's description as somewhere "hardly a human foot could pass," the swamp was, in fact, home to permanent settlements of Black freedom-seekers. Generations of African American Maroons adapted to, and thrived in, its semiaquatic terrain. They

raided surrounding plantations and welcomed fugitives from slavery into their communities. The Dismal Swamp was more than a transitory refuge; it was a space of Black freedom making.

Yet *The Hunted Slaves* offers an outsider's perspective on the practice of marronage. The painter, Richard Ansdell, was a white Briton born in Liverpool, and there is no evidence he ever visited the United States. The Dismal Swamp likely entered Ansdell's consciousness through abolitionist literature by white authors such as Longfellow and Harriet Beecher Stowe, whose follow-up to *Uncle Tom's Cabin* (1852) was a novel about Maroons: *Dred: A Tale of the Great Dismal Swamp* (1856).

Ansdell may also have drawn on African Americans' first-hand testimonies. Reminiscent of *The Hunted Slaves'* depiction of a man and woman fleeing slavery together, two married couples, Ellen and William Craft, and Julia and John Andrew Jackson, toured the United Kingdom as abolitionist campaigners during the 1850s and 1860s. Paintings of the Dismal Swamp were also featured in traveling shows staged by two prominent fugitives, William Wells Brown and Henry Henry Box Brown. Ansdell's painting also mirrors narratives by survivors of the Underground Railroad. Addressing a Liverpool audience in 1858, one escapee, Tom Wilson, described fleeing a plantation into swamplands and showed scars inflicted by bloodhounds that "tore at [his] legs and body with their teeth."

The American Civil War increased the political significance of The Hunted Slaves in Britain during the 1860s. The war's consequences demonstrated how slavery structured the economy of Liverpool and the surrounding region. Lancashire's textile industries were halted as the Union Navy blockade prevented exports of enslaved-grown cotton from American plantations. With unemployment rife, Ansdell raffled *The Hunted Slaves* to raise money for the Lancashire Cotton Districts Relief Fund. Gilbert Winter Moss won the raffle and donated the painting to the Liverpool Town Council. The painting was eventually exhibited at Liverpool's Walker Art Gallery, where it was visited by the most famous ex-fugitive, Frederick Douglass, in 1886. Today it is displayed at the International Slavery Museum, Liverpool.

The Hunted Slaves, Richard Ansdell, 1862. This abolitionist painting, created by a British artist, depicts an enslaved man and woman making a daring escape from slavery. Unlike the typical abolitionist imagery from the period, which positioned enslaved people of African descent as passive and docile, this painting's couple is armed and actively resisting oppression.

The abolitionist sentiments associated with *The Hunted Slaves* were a counterpoint to the support of many Liverpool merchants for the pro-slavery Confederacy. The painting's provenance also illustrates how wealth derived from slavery permeates Liverpudlian history. Whatever its antislavery intent, *The Hunted Slaves* exemplifies how museum collections continue to benefit from historic patronage by individuals who accrued fortunes from enslavement. Gilbert Winter Moss was the son of an enslaver, and Ansdell's patrons included Jonathan Blundell, the heir to another Liverpool slaveholding dynasty.

Nonetheless, the cultural significance of *The Hunted Slaves* reaches far beyond Liverpool. The National Museum of African American History and Culture in Washington, DC, owns a copy of the painting (dated 1862). Engravings of it were sold throughout the Victorian period, allowing buyers to hang versions in their own homes. The image is still widely reproduced, including on the cover of the Martinican author Patrick Chamoiseau's novella *L'Esclave Vieil Homme et le Molosse* (1997; translated as *Slave Old Man* and *The Old Slave and the Mastiff*).

The Hunted Slaves has enduring resonance because it both challenges and aligns with conventions that were used consistently by white abolitionists in the nineteenth century. The man and woman defy their pursuers: They are armed, and they fight back. Consequently, *The Hunted Slaves* remains a compelling emblem of Black resistance.

RECLAIMING VALONGO

Mônica Lima e Souza

In the nineteenth century, Valongo Wharf in Rio de Janeiro, Brazil, was the main port of entry to South America for Africans. An estimated 900,000 enslaved Africans arrived at Valongo over several decades, making Brazil the country that received the most enslaved peoples in the Americas. In 2011, the site was uncovered during construction work. It is the most significant remains of a landing point for enslaved Africans in the Americas, carrying enormous historical and spiritual importance for Afro-Brazilians, Africans, and other people around the world.

When Valongo Wharf was recognized as a World Heritage Site in July 2017, it was acknowledged as archaeologically and historically sensitive. This means that the United Nations Educational, Scientific and Cultural Organization, better known as UNESCO, deemed the pain and suffering endured by enslaved Africans who disembarked there, as well as the ways in which they resisted and survived, to have exceptional universal value. I can say that I am both an heir to and a part of this history, because my great-great-grandmother Honória landed there. Many times,

Left
Lavagem do Cais de Valongo (The Washing of Valongo Wharf), Tomaz Silva, 2021. In 2011, the remains of Valongo Wharf were rediscovered in Rio de Janeiro, Brazil. The stone wharf, originally built for the disembarkation of enslaved Africans, is one of the most significant physical sites connected to the arrival of enslaved Africans in the Americas. In 2012, descendants began an annual symbolic ritual of washing or purifying the wharf in honor of the African ancestors who arrived there.

Bottom
Beads recovered from Valongo. These materials provide a glimpse into the presence of thousands of captive Africans who landed at Valongo Wharf in the nineteenth century. These beads, likely fragments of jewelry, prompt questions of who these people were and what materials they held close to them.

I have found myself wondering, what was the level of her fear? Did she cry or have nightmares during the journey? What did she hope for? What enabled her to survive and endure it all, and still have love to give?

As a historian, I participated in drafting the World Heritage Site nomination dossier for Valongo Wharf. As part of this process, I delved deeply into the histories of the region through historical documents and conducted interviews with the local community, who still find direct ancestral lines of connection with those who were forcibly brought, bought, and sold there. I read accounts from nineteenth-century travelers describing the horrors of the slave market and the somber spectacle of the arrival of those who survived the crossing Through this experience, I could palpably feel the pains of the past in the present.

Articles in nineteenth-century newspapers about *zungus*—meeting and gathering places for the Black population in the Valongo region—relayed the life and energy of Africans and their direct descendants. There were many reports of escapes and resistance, and articles covered the fears of people who claimed to be "owners" that their "property" and free Black people would come together to revolt.

Beyond the textual evidence, most often related through the lens of

slaveholders, material culture also offered information about what happened in Valongo. The objects found in archaeological excavations at Valongo Wharf and in its surroundings are physical expressions of the stories of these people who, even when treated inhumanely and regarded as commodities, never ceased to manifest the strength of their humanity. Through the creation of culture in a new land, based on African retentions, they filled Valongo with the beauty of their adornments, the strength of their faith, and their rhythmic and sonorous ways of celebrating and communicating with the spiritual world. I could hear, through these objects, the sounds of drumming, chants, laughter, and the narratives of many experiences.

Glass bead bracelets and necklaces served as adornments and protection: These two functions complement each other, as beauty and the defense of the body and soul against evil. Not a single bead was strung on the thread without a reason or a prayer to give it meaning. While viewing these artifacts, I heard the jingle of bracelets on the streets of Valongo from centuries ago and felt the pride the ancestors must have experienced when wearing these ornaments. I held the amulets close to my body to ward off evil. Clay pipes, used in daily life, pulled out of pockets or purses during breaks or rituals, were adorned with intricate designs, of which some were protective magic words and others celebrated the spiritual world. The sweet smell of tobacco enveloped me, and I heard the laughter of an elder mixed with a throaty cough, connecting me even deeper to the ancestral realm. The pipes were more than instruments for enjoying tobacco, however. They connected living souls to the universe of the divinities.

I am proud of my work researching and rescuing the stories of the enslaved at Valongo Wharf because of its significance in the struggle for the right to remember slavery and the ongoing quest for freedom by Africans and their descendants in Brazil. This work was also a path to discover my history through the history of my ancestors—those ordinary people who lived without great prominence. They were survivors, who shape and give meaning to my heritage and to my life and work.

FROM NO RETURN

Paul Gardullo

December 1794 marked the final leg of the voyage of the Portuguese slave ship *São José Paquete d'Africa*. Named with cruel irony after a saint, like many of its sister vessels named for saviors, martyrs, and ideals such as benevolence, prosperity, and salvation, the *São José* set sail at the end of the century that witnessed the peak of the slave trade, one that trafficked more than 7.2 million Africans to the Americas.

The *São José* departed Lisbon, Portugal, in 1794 for the Island of Mozambique, in one of the first attempts by European traders to bring East Africa into the broader Transatlantic Slave Trade. In early December 1794, the *São José*, laden with 512 captive Mozambicans, likely from the interior of the country, set out for its destination: Maranhão, Brazil. Caught in a storm off Cape Town, South Africa, just after Christmas, the ship was wrecked about one hundred meters from shore. A rescue was attempted and the European captain and crew and approximately half of those enslaved were saved. The remaining Mozambicans perished in the waves. The captain submitted his official testimony before court, describing the wrecking incident and accounting for the loss of property, including enslaved humans. The surviving Mozambicans were most likely brought to the fortification

known as the Slave Lodge and resold into slavery in what is now the Western Cape of South Africa, where they were lost to history until the ship was identified in the twenty-first century.

The São José remained, battered, for more than two hundred years, unassuming and incomplete: The wrecked fragments were long buried below the sand and surge of the sea. Having come to light, they are an extraordinary impetus for reflection, knowledge, and repair for people around the world. Through them we can reckon with the past and refashion our relationships in the present.

To those reclaimed historical items, a modern object was added: a simple cowrie shell basket created by local artisans in Mozambique at the site where the São José set sail in 1794. On May 30, 2015, during a solemn ceremony aimed at commemorating a significant story, Evano Nhogache, a traditional community leader from Mossuril, filled a basket with soil from the region. He then entrusted members of the Slave Wrecks Project, hosted by the National Museum of African American History and Culture, with the task of placing the enclosed soil as close to the wreck site as possible. This symbolic act was intended to reconnect with the Mozambicans who were once

Left
Members of the Slave Wrecks Project scatter soil from Mozambique near the site where the wreckage of Portuguese ship *São José Paquete d'Africa* was found, as part of a unification ceremony in Cape Town, South Africa, 2015.

Top
Iron ballasts, eighteenth century. These iron ballasts recovered from the wreck of the *São José* were used to offset the weight of the 512 Mozambican captives aboard the vessel, allowing the ship to maintain its balance at sea.

Bottom
Ceremonial basket, 2015. This cowrie shell basket was created by artisans in Mozambique. Soil from the region was carried in this basket and later deposited at the site of the *São José* shipwreck during a reunification ceremony in South Africa.

lost, as Mossuril is believed to be the likely site of the enslaved people's last footfall in their homeland.

"Once the ancestors direct you to spill the soil over the wreck, it will be the first time our people will have slept in their homeland," Nhogache said to the community leaders who had gathered. He continued, "Look into our faces. Do you see us? Surely amongst the fallen were those who were guardians of these same communities. Tell our ancestors that their people are still being cared for by those of us here who are standing here today." He then asked the founding director, Lonnie Bunch, to add the basket to the Museum collections.

Days later, at a second memorial, at Clifton Beach in Cape Town, the soil was carried in the cowrie vessel and poured into the ocean adjacent to the wreck site by three members of the Slave Wrecks Project: an African American diver, Kamau Sadiki; a South African marine archaeolo-

gist, Tara Van Niekerk; and a Mozambican student, Yara de Larice. The beautiful beach where the *São José* wrecked has become one of the most restricted and expensive places to live in Cape Town. Its history of violence, oppression, and pain that began long before apartheid was submerged right offshore.

Evano Nhogache, the leader who entrusted the Museum and the Slave Wrecks Project with the task of depositing the soil, was both a refugee and a freedom fighter during the Mozambican War of Independence against Portugal in the 1960s and 1970s. He finds deep resonance with the history of the slave trade and the historical roots of injustice and inequality that are connected to the enduring legacies of colonialism, forced migration, poverty, environmental degradation, violence, and xenophobia in the present. When representatives returned in 2018 to meet with Nhogache, he thanked them, finding solace in knowing that one part of the task was complete, with more work to be done. Because of that shared labor, he claimed, "We are now family.... The tears that you shed there, fall on us as rain here."

For hundreds of years, the slave ship, an engine used for dehumanization and degradation, helped make our modern world. Only by grappling with the resonance of slavery, colonialism, and the reality of their continuing histories and with the lives lived in their wake can we hope to deliver ourselves, find repair, and fight for justice.

"MY NAME IS FEBRUARY"

Diana Ferrus

my naam is Februarie	My name is February
ek is verkoop	I was sold
my borste, privaatdele, my oë	my breasts, private parts and eyes
my brein	my brain
is nog nie myne	are not mine yet
soos die São José	like the *São José*
loop ek opgekap	I am walking ruined
word ek telkens gesink deur 'n ander storm	often sank by another storm
geen Jesus wat op die water loop vir my	no Jesus walking on water for me

my naam is Februarie	my name is February
ek soek nog die stang van die stuur	I still search for the rod of the steering wheel
want onderwater lê die familie	because the family lies at the bottom
die kind aan ma se rokspant	the child stitched to mother's dress
die ma aan pa se hand	mother's hand locked in father's fist
hoe diep lê hulle, aan watter kant	how deep down are they, on which side

my naam is Februarie	my name is February
opgeveil, verkoop, die hoogste bieder	auctioned, sold, the highest bidder
het ontslae geraak van my regte naam	disposed of my real name
geen vergoeding betaal	paid no compensation
vir dit my naam, gesteel, gesink	for that, my name, stolen, sunk
onderwater lê dit nog	underwater it still lies
saam met die familie	with the family
wrakstukke van die São José	wrecks of the *São José*
ten gronde geloop deur 'n wind	ran aground by a wind
briesende branders wat die buit	furious waves that decided
se hele toekoms besluit	the future of the loot
die profyt teen die wal uitsmyt	smashing the profit against the embankment

my naam is Februarie	my name is February
die Masbieker op die São José	the Masbieker on the *São José*
so was ek genoem	that's how I was called
toe my hierse moedertaal gestalte kry	when my mother tongue of here came into being
toe tonge met mekaar begin te knoop	when tongues started to form a bond
en letters 'n vrye gang begin te loop	and letters started walking freely
in 'n desperate poging in hoop	in a desperate attempt at survival and hope
dat magte ook nie hierdie identiteit moet stroop	that forces should not strip this identity too
word ek die Masbieker, net 'n naam	I became the Masbieker, only a name
onder 'n ander lug gekraam	born under a different sky
en diep gevul met skaam	and deeply filled with shame

My naam is Februarie	my name is February

I rearranged this landscape
my hands wove the patterns of the vineyards
my feet pressed the grapes
and I was paid with the wine
I carry Alcohol-Foetal Syndrome children on my back
my name is February
I still march on the eve of December first
I walk the cobblestones of this city
when I cry out in desperation
"remember the emancipation of the slaves!"

My name is February
two hundred years after the *São José*
I was given the vote
they said I was free

but don't you see how often I am submerged
weighed down
I am the sunken, the soiled
forgotten
and yet memory will not leave me

My name is February
stranded at Third Beach
but no one comes to look for me
no one waves from the dunes
no bridges back to Mozambique

my name is February
I will be resurrected
brought to the surface
unshackled, unchained, unashamed
My name is February.

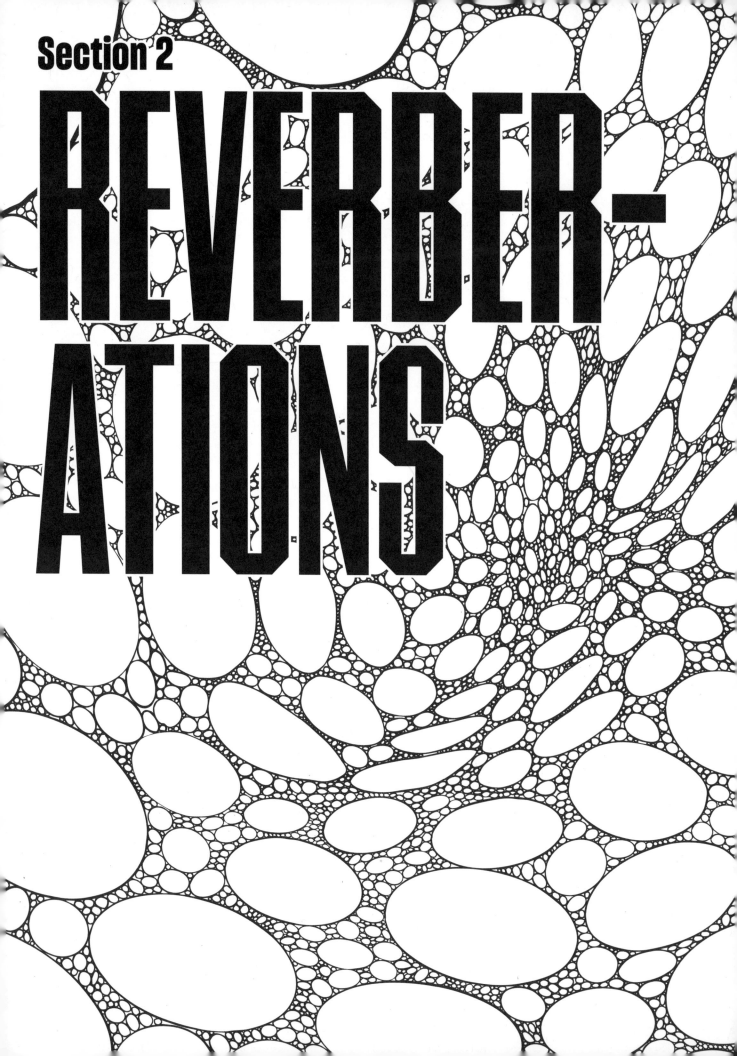

Section 2

REVERBER-ATIONS

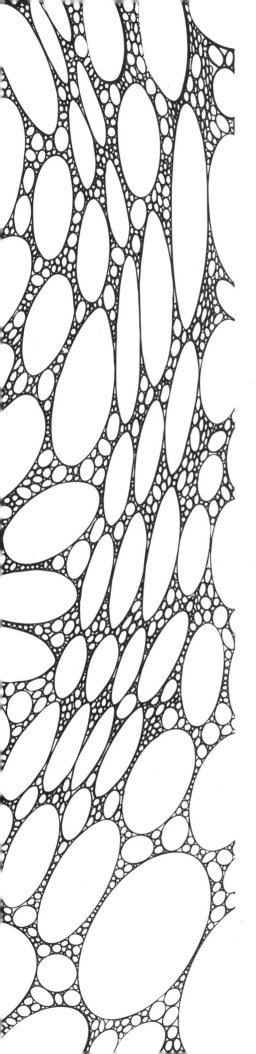

Racial slavery and colonialism are linked not just by the construction of a world of enormous economic inequality but also by a long-lasting set of violent practices enacted by individuals and institutions. At the center of the business of slavery was the African captive who became an enslaved person. The African abolitionist Ottobah Cugoano called this global system of trade a "commerce of flesh," and it was unlike anything the world had ever seen, because it operated on the transatlantic or transoceanic level as well as in the intimate and mundane aspects of daily life. This commerce of flesh was driven by violent, dehumanizing systems implemented to strip humanity from Indigenous peoples, enslaved Africans, and their descendants.

The violence of both slavery and colonialism was practiced for more than four hundred years. Enslavers and colonial authorities attempted to deny Africans and people of African descent their social identity, humanity, and autonomy by trying to control the enslaved physically and psychologically, to instill in them a sense of hopelessness. Torture devices such as gags, bits, whips, and chains were used by enslavers to silence, punish, and control the enslaved, who were people of all genders and ages. Many were subjected to horrific acts of sexual violence by their captors: Rape, coerced relationships, and forced reproduction were tactics to assert dominance. The systematic use of sexual violence aimed to undermine self-worth and maintain power dynamics that reinforced the institution of slavery and the racial hierarchies of colonial societies.

Symbolic acts of violence also characterized the interpersonal politics of slavery and colonization. These took the forms of racial stigmatization, a denial of human rights, and socioeconomic exclusion. Disrespect for African religions, cultural expressions, and languages was normalized, later influencing the psychological brutality of colonial rule in Africa in the nineteenth and twentieth centuries.

Violence was embedded and replicated in myriad scientific, social, political, and philosophical forms that shaped art, culture, law, natural science, medical practice, and religion. The concept of race as we understand it today was constructed over hundreds of years, at the intersection of slavery, colonialism, and capitalism, to justify the cruel system of slavery and the mistreatment of the enslaved. Colonial powers and slaveholders wielded religion, science, and law to legitimize and justify the enslavement of Africans and other groups, such as Indigenous peoples throughout the Americas, based on the fallacy of racial inferiority. By establishing a caste system, European colonizers positioned themselves as superior to non-Europeans, fueling violent discrimination against Africans and people of African descent and laying the foundation for the anti-Black racism and white supremacy in our world today.

Colonization led to new encounters between diverse peoples. These encounters and the colonization of environments unfamiliar to Europeans birthed the development of natural science. Naturalists sought to understand the physical differences between plants and animals, as well as the differences between people. In the search for a classification system for humankind, they created scientific theories, categories, and hierarchies of racial difference. These theories developed into some of the hallmarks of Enlightenment thinking. In the mid-1700s, the Swedish scientist Carl Linnaeus subdivided humans into four races: American, European, Asiatic, and African. Linnaeus's system of taxonomy was the first to categorize humans within the animal kingdom and laid the foundation for generations of scientific racism that worked to categorize Africans as subhuman. His systems were also adopted within the developing science of botany to bring standardization of names and a vision of control to the natural world, which could thereby be systematized, ordered, and fit into a global economy for easier trade.

Violence against the enslaved and colonized, who were stripped of their names, was thus linked to the order of the natural world that developed in tandem with the growth of the Enlightenment and the birth and institutionalization of Western democracies. In 1785, Thomas Jefferson recorded information about the natural history, inhabitants, and political organization of his home state of Virginia, including an extensive argument of his views on race. Not ten years after writing the Declaration of Independence, which declared all men equal, Jefferson advanced that "the blacks, whether originally a distinct race, or made distinct by time and circumstances, are inferior to the whites in the endowments both of body and mind." These invented racial categories and hierarchies were also put into practice through law and imagined through forms of art and writing in colonial society. While each colony around the world defined race differently, they all created racial classification systems to exploit labor in the pursuit of profit. Racial hierarchies were enforced by legal codes put in place to restrict the political autonomy and physical and social mobility of enslaved laborers and other non-Europeans.

The Code Noir was a legal decree from King Louis XIV that outlined the conditions of slavery in French colonies, beginning in the late 1600s. It defined slavery as an inherited condition passed through the mother, making enslavement a life-long status to be continued indefinitely across generations. In the 1700s, Spanish *casta* paintings illustrated an idealized racial hierarchy in the Americas, positioning "pure" Indigenous people and Africans at the bottom of society. *Casta* paintings reflected colonial elites' desire to establish racial divisions and social classes. In colonial Virginia, a series of laws instituted in the early 1700s, known as the slave codes, transformed the indentured servitude of Africans and African Americans into forced, lifelong slavery, thereby differentiating the status of white indentured servants in the eyes of society and the law.

Religious institutions such as the Catholic Church also profited from colonialism and slavery. In 1455, Pope Nicholas V authorized the enslavement

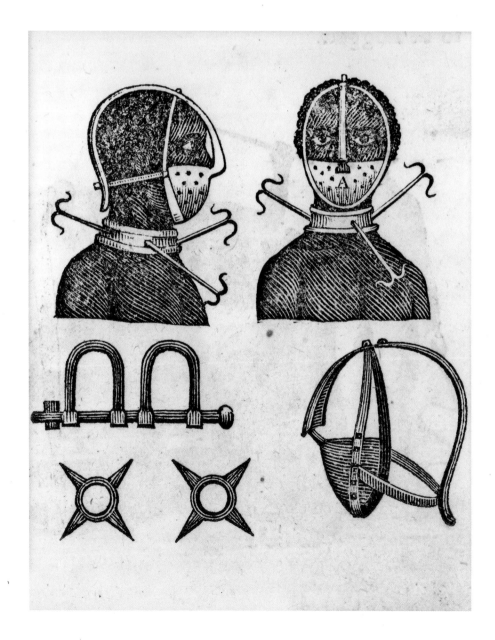

Español con India,
Mestizo.

Mestizo con Española
Castizo.

Castizo con Española
Español.

Español con Mora
Mulato.

5

6

7

Mulato con Española,
Morisco.

Morisco con Española
Chino.

Chino con India.
Salta atras.

Salta atras con Mulata,
Lobo.

9

10

11

12

Lobo con China
Gibaro.

Gibaro con Mulata
Albarazado

Albarazado con Negra
Canbujo.

Canbujo con India
Sanbaigo.

13

14

15

16

Sanbaigo con Loba
Calpamulato.

Calpamulato con Canbuja
Tente en el Aire.

Tente en el Aire con Mulata
Note entiendo.

Noteentiendo con India
Tornaatras.

of non-Christian people encountered during colonial expeditions, with particular emphasis on sub-Saharan Africans. The decree, which was repudiated only in 2023, effectively sanctioned the Portuguese slave trade and helped establish a moral framework justifying the enslavement of African people. Supporters of slavery explained the differences between Africans and Europeans through biblical interpretations that associated Black skin with sin and white skin with purity. Some slaveholders believed that Africans were not fully human and therefore did not possess a soul in the same way as Europeans, while others propagated the idea that Africans were "heathens" who needed to be "saved," although religious conversion did not result in freedom. With profit and power in mind, kingdoms, nations, popes, priests, scientists, lawmakers, and businesspeople looked for new ways to understand and order the world and did so through the construction and concretization of ideas about race—that

is, categories of who would be considered human—and philosophies about freedom and human rights.

Even entertainment around the Atlantic world had a devastating impact on Black people. For example, Sarah Baartman was a South African Khoikhoi woman forcibly taken from her homeland in the early nineteenth century and displayed in European "freak shows" as the "Hottentot Venus." She was subjected to medical experimentation for "scientific research" in France, where she stayed for the remainder of her life. Upon her death, Baartman was dissected, which shaped European medicine, especially in the field of comparative anatomy. Her sexual reproductive organs were put on display in the Musée de l'Homme in Paris. It wasn't until 2002 that her remains were returned to South Africa. Joice Heth was an enslaved woman from Madagascar owned by the infamous showman P. T. Barnumas as a part of his "freak show." Heth was said to have been 161 years old and to have served as the nursemaid of

Flagellation of a Female Samboe Slave.

the first president of the United States, George Washington. At the time of Heth's death, in 1836, Barnum organized a last show: a public autopsy to confirm her age. She was eventually dissected in front of a group from the New York College of Physicians and Surgeons, today's Columbia University. To the surprise of everyone there, Heth's organs indicated that she was likely in her seventies.

These instances of dehumanization and brutality were part of a long chain of systematized anti-Blackness, developed over time to justify and uphold white supremacy. Heth's and Baartman's lives, deaths, and afterlives must be remembered on their own and as part of a larger history, in which Black people were used as unwilling subjects for medical experimentation, and, even after death, Black bodies were executed, sold, given away, stolen, or exhumed for medical dissection in various American universities. Enslaved people's remains were—and still are—held in research institutions and museums, including the Smithsonian Institution. Even in death, Black bodies remained a commodity, viewed as the property of enslavers or white institutions for the "benefit" of knowledge and lure of fascination. In the twenty-first century, this legacy takes many forms, from racial stereotyping and blackface to medical practices based on gender and race, to racial profiling and other forms of anti-Black violence.

ATLANTIC SLAVERY, COLONIZATION, AND SHATTERED MODERN SOVEREIGNTIES

Ibrahima Thiaw

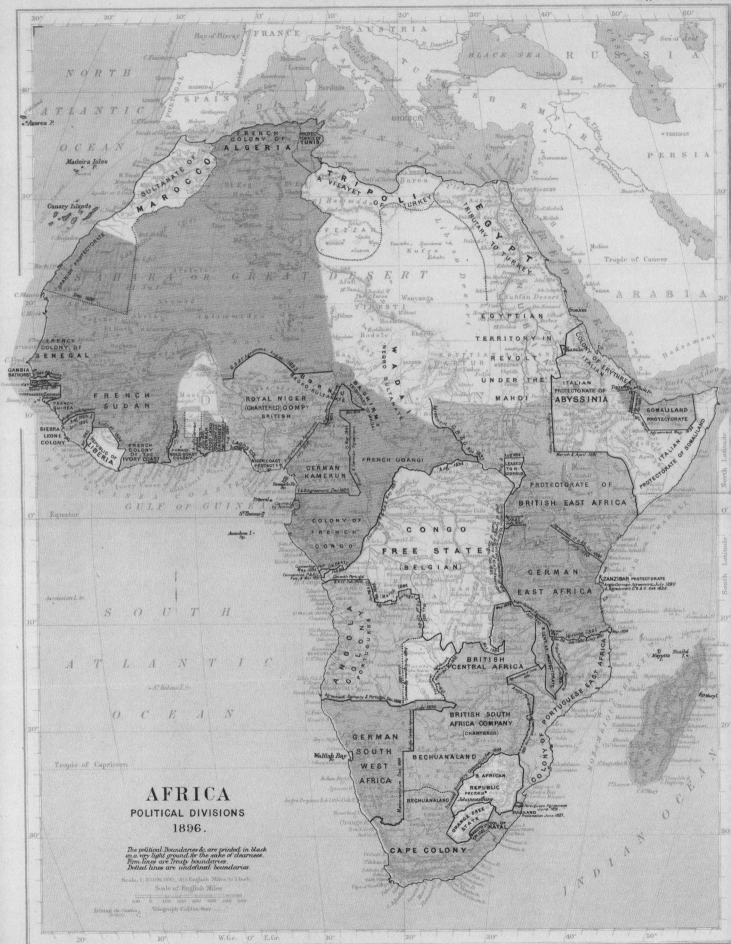

AFRICA

POLITICAL DIVISIONS
1896.

*The political Boundaries &c. are printed in black
on a very light ground for the sake of clearness.
Firm lines are Treaty boundaries.
Dotted lines are undefined boundaries.*

Scale. 1: 20,036,000, 415 English Miles to 1 Inch.
Scale of English Miles

Telegraph Cables &c.

Drawn & Engraved at Stanford's Geog. Establishment

Previous page
SOWETO, Adger
Cowans, 1983. In
this etching, Cowins
features the phrase
"SO WE TO," empha-
sizing unity in the
global struggle against
racism and oppression.

Left
Map of European
colonial divisions in
Africa, 1896. In the late
nineteenth century,
European powers
divided the African
continent among them-
selves, disregarding the
existing political and
cultural boundaries.
This devastating wave
of colonialism was
supported by profits,
as well as technological
advancements and
advantages, derived
from racial slavery.

Colonization is the appropriation of territory for the purposes of control and exploitation. Histori-cally, whether forceful or peaceful, colonization is coercive. With extortion and dispossession as its modus operandi, it usurps land and other resources and forcefully disposes of human bodies and its labor force. Colonizers devise and skillfully deploy ingenious strategies to control political offices and religious and educational systems and to impose unequal power relations that are, generally, based on discriminatory practices. The ultimate goal of the colonizer is to extract the economic resources of the colonized. Over the past five hundred years, European colonial empires were constructed on these foundations. Since 1492, the world has lived with various permutations of this basic model, which reached full swing during the height of the Transatlantic Slave Trade in the eighteenth century. Since then, it has taken new trajectories over the centuries, mutating constantly, in complex ways, shaping government, thought, culture, and identities in distant colonies and European capitals. The abolition of slavery in the late nineteenth century and the success of independence movements that shaped the African continent in the mid to late-twentieth century did little to hinder the impact of colonialism.

Even in the current decade, during the COVID-19 outbreak, the specter of colonialism revealed itself. The devalua-tion of life in the Global South during the pandemic was rampant. In 2020, as partners from the Global Curatorial Project met in Dakar, news of the spread of COVID-19 was disseminated at the speed of modern communication technologies that abridged distances, no matter how wide. No place in the world was spared the disease, but many Western discourses and attitudes on the pandemic were cloaked in paternal-istic, unequal power relations that resulted in hierarchies that granted privileges to some and denied them to others, most often those in the Global South. On *France 24* news, the United Nations Secretary-General expressed the sentiment that "inferior" Global South health systems would collapse within days and that populations there, particu-larly in Africa, would die by the millions. This did not happen the way he predicted it would. On another French program,

various top public health researchers and officials recommended using Africans as guinea pigs to test a vaccine, as had been done in other studies, including those related to AIDS or, in earlier generations, syphilis. These perceptions of Africans were painful reminders of racist colonial medical practices upon which twenty-first-century medical policies are based. The arguments were founded on colonial imaginations and representations of people of African descent as somehow lesser humans than others and with limited problem-solving capacity. The colonial mindset appears to be an everlasting pathology that still infects our lives.

Beyond political rhetoric, pharmaceu-tical companies engaged in opportunistic practices colored by the economic, sociopolitical, and imperialistic beliefs in place throughout the world. Access to vaccines in the early stages of the pandemic was structured in the Global North by discriminatory legacies founded on economic privileges, which are intrinsically intertwined with race and result in a clear divide between "the haves" and "the have-nots." In the wake of the pandemic, just as in the colonial scramble a century prior, the international ventures of the world's most powerful nations (and their pharmaceutical companies) appeared to have the end goal of spreading their influence and amassing wealth, as opposed to curing or caring for all of humanity.

Although slavery has long been abolished and colonization dismantled or widely decried, their initial premises, based upon greed and power, are subtly woven into the fabric of contemporary life. Atlantic slavery and colonization rearranged and reorganized landscapes, disturbed local places of meaning and memory, and memorialized impositions of colonialism's own power, literally through the construction of, and monuments to, European colonial figures and practices. I write from this place of knowledge, living in slavery's wake. As a Senegalese, Black, African man who lives and works at home in Senegal, but has visited various places across Global Africa and the Global North, I was never directly exposed to formal colonization but nevertheless have witnessed its modern reverberations in various forms, such as ethnic and racial discrimination at home and abroad. My political subjectiv-ity, as an African scholar, is shaped by my formal training in Western academic canons and tastes. With this sense of self, I assess the history of Atlantic slavery and colonization to comprehend a past that refuses to fade away but instead, like the coronavirus, transforms continually, unfolding into more complex forms.

Building Capital and Power

The economic growth of Western Europe from 1500 to 1850 was deeply indebted to slavery and the theft of monetary wealth, culture, and knowledge from Africa and Africans. The hallmark of this accumulation of wealth was the massive, forced exile and loss of millions of people from Africa. This violent process ruptured family ties and communal, ethnic, and national integrity, resulting in torn landscapes and disrupted social networks. Because their humanity was negated and the ownership of their bodies taken away from them, enslaved Africans were exposed to humiliation, oppression, and exploitation.

European expansionism, arising from Atlantic slavery, capitalism, and colonization, did not develop out of nowhere, or start with European voyages of conquest

in the fifteenth century. Its growth was facilitated by preexisting institutions, trade networks, and labor-organization systems. European civilizations, prior to 1500, were largely rural and not technologically more advanced than similar societies in China, India, and Africa. Socially and politically, European medieval institutions were notably unequal, with sharp distinctions based on wealth, birth, and status. Peasants were serfs, living in financial distress and socially vulnerable positions, because feudal elites exercised control over land and labor. But, with the rise of trade and commerce, the European elite, over time, obtained new riches and social status. With colonization, Europeans brought with them a brutal facsimile of the same inequalities from home.

During the era of Christopher Columbus's journeys, there were also major changes in many parts of Africa, causing empires to fall. Ghana, Mali, Sosso, Songhai, Takrur, Jolof, and the kingdoms and trading cities of Benin, Dahomey, Ashanti, Begho, Old Oyo, and Igbo-Ukwu experienced major political and economic changes. These

Bottom
Slave Trade (Execrable Human Traffick, or The Affectionate Slaves), George Morland, ca. 1788. This painting depicts a scene of an African man being torn away from his family by European slave traders on the western coast of Africa. The slave trade violently ruptured familial and communal ties and disrupted social and political structures.

Top
La Semia (Sowing), ca. 1515–20. When the first modern colonial voyages took place, much of Western Europe was under a feudal system whereby elites controlled land and labor. This practice of inequality and exploitation was imposed on new lands, people, and nations through colonial expansion and the development of racial slavery.

sites of art and cultural development and trade, sophisticated technologies, and longstanding trade networks were destabilized. They were also involved in long-distance transactions based on the flow of various commodities, including enslaved Africans. This era set in motion the formation of new elites both in Africa and outside of it and the introduction and imposition of new religious ideologies across West Africa, including Islam and Christianity, resulting in major societal and cultural shifts. Previous conflicts between ethnic nations that predated contact with Europeans helped set the stage for racial slavery and the European imperial governance on the African continent, which continues today. The creation of a global capitalist economy grew from sugarcane, tobacco, coffee, cacao, rubber, cotton, gold, iron, and silver procured by enslaved laborers. During the Industrial Revolution in the nineteenth century, mass-produced goods required even more access to new markets, new trade networks, and new systems of accumulating wealth. These developments led to an even greater fervency for European expansion and were the basis for the "Scramble for Africa" during the late nineteenth century. This long arc of destabilization and intervention, coupled with the swiftness of industrialization, allowed European powers to build immense global economic and political influence, by commercializing and removing natural resources from the conquered territories of Asia, Africa, and the Americas and tying that system of resource extraction to the extraction of people from their homelands. These European ventures were funded by a system of banks, insurance firms, and, eventually, stock markets that had been developing for well more than a century.

Making Race and Knowledge
The growth of capitalism across this period was built on coercive power, unequal racial distinctions, and social pseudoscience. While the practice of human beings owning other human beings reaches back to well before the second millennium CE and has included forms of slavery in the Mediterranean world (in the Roman Empire, for instance), the Indian Ocean and Asia, and the trans-Saharan world of Africa, it was the growth of the Atlantic slave trade, coupled with colonialism, that

helped undergird scientific and religious ideologies that posit that Black people are lesser humans. Philosophers such as René Descartes theorized that there exist beings who are capable of thinking and beings who are not, who are closer to the lower animals. This conceptualization, shared by other Western thinkers, situated Black people at the bottom rung of humanity, if not altogether below it. The systemic degradation of Black Africans went hand in hand with the elevation of Europeans as the apex of humanity. Subsequently, any suffering inflicted on Black people was acceptable and promoted as an acceptable aftereffect of ensuring the accumulation of wealth and power. Although racial slavery was a process that involved Europeans, Africans, Indigenous peoples of the Americas, and Asians, the Europeans had an obvious advantage in these transactions from the fifteenth century forward but it was not the result of a superior intellect or godly gift: Economic, political, and scientific hegemony was achieved by violence. Colonization and imperialism were supported by educational institutions such as schools, universities, and museums that collected data in order to study, classify, and represent others, often in demeaning ways. The imperial production of knowledge was thus a reflection and a product of martial, extractive, and discriminatory history, as well as an engine for creating the conditions that continue to shape our world today.

Moreover, arguments that African participants were full agents in the horrors of the slave trade with Europeans put forth this false equivalency that does not reflect the dynamics of power that developed within historical relationships. While it is true that Black Africans participated in the diabolical enterprise of the slave trade, their reasons for enslavement were not from racist ideologies but rested on differences of religion, ethnicity, territoriality, and nationhood. These social distinctions were certainly discriminatory, but not in the same sense as race-based theories of Eurocentric pseudoscience. Africans knew that slaves, although uprooted, were people with souls, thoughts, feelings, and skills, like any other human beings. Thus, distinctions were made among equal human beings who were ascribed to specific political statuses, roles, or socioeconomic activities within society.

This is asserted very strongly in the Kurukan Fuga, or Mande Charter, a constitution enacted in the Mali Empire in the first half of the thirteenth century and transmitted via oral tradition. The Charter's application spread across most of West Africa, following the expansion routes of the Mali Empire. It classified people into three main categories: free, unfree, and *nyamankala* in Mandingo or *nyeenyo* in Wolof. Free people included aristocracy, peasantry masses, and, to some extent, clerics. Prior to European contact, enslaved Africans were generally captives of war, part of the social category of the unfree. The unfree included two main groups: those born in captivity, who were generally well integrated into families as kin and therefore enjoyed a great deal of freedom, and recent captives, who, like political prisoners, could be exposed to extremely harsh treatments but were nevertheless human beings, albeit with restricted rights. The last category is referred to as "caste" in the colonial archives, an incorrect translation of local terms to designate endogamous craftspeople and musicians who were defined by their socioeconomic activities. Noble manual fields of activity included agriculture and military service, blacksmiths, leatherworkers, potters, weavers, and woodworkers. Musicians, and entertainers like griots, were grouped in the social category of *nyeenyo*. With the race-based development of the Atlantic slave trade and later of European colonization, these sociopolitical institutions underwent major changes.

Through translation and feedback, colonial archives too often interpreted social distinctions in racial terms, resulting in deep antagonisms between groups. Elsewhere in Africa, in Rwanda, similar colonial practices resulted in some of the worst genocides of the twentieth century. In West Africa, so-called people of caste were largely regarded with disdain and marginalized, much like descendants of the enslaved. All of this violated the spirit and ethics of the Kurukan Fuga, which asserts the diversity of human experiences, the importance of and the inviolability and dignity of human life, the right to the pursuit of education, and champions living together

Left
Enslaved people planting and tilling sugarcane on Antigua, 1786. More than half of all African captives trafficked to the Americas were forced to work on sugar plantations. Cultivating and processing sugar was grueling and deadly work; most enslaved laborers survived for an average of only seven years.

Right
De Humana Physiognomonia, Giambattista della Porta, 1586. This engraving from a book on physiognomy, a pseudoscientific study of facial features, matches human faces with animalistic traits. Various forms of racist scientific beliefs tied physical differences between people to moral characteristics like good and evil. Science, along with other practices like religion and law, was used to legitimize constructs of race and justify racial slavery.

in social cohesion and peace. The charter also addresses the territorial integrity of the Mande and includes a commitment to food security, the abolition of slavery by conquest, and the rights of freedom of expression and trade.

Reverberations

The reverberations of slavery and colonization are manifest in contemporary society in the form of race, class, and economic disparities. The resurgence of white supremacist movements in the United States and Europe is produced by the same legacies. To bring an end to these forms of oppression, Black militancy and political activism, alongside legal assertions for reparations, are on the rise. Global political instability is the result of centuries-long extraction from and impoverishment of the Global South. This North-South polarization

is increasingly defined by sociopolitical chaos, environmental disasters, economic precarity, disease, and a lack of basic resources like food, clean water, health care, and shelter. Those seeking to migrate from the Global South to the Global North face terrors and threats of imprisonment, forced labor, torture, hunger, exposure to inhumane and undignified conditions of life, involuntary returns, and even death. For the lucky ones who make it to the other side, there are often unexpected realities. While the possibility of economic enrichment or social freedom beckons, new challenges appear, including harsh living conditions, exposure to new forms of discrimination, and unforgiving prison systems that disrupt dreams for a better life.

Today's flows of human beings are inseparable from colonial legacies. Diasporic communities challenge existing colonial imaginations by disrupting monolithic national, racial, and ethnic identities. These communities' resolute resistance, resilience, and struggle for freedom and dignity represent an ongoing desire to address the horrors of the past and to make visible their legacies in the present. Their demands and the reaction to them shape the conceptions of borders and nation-states and will ultimately determine if the world—both north and south—can achieve peace, justice, and equity. Even amid hopes for a better future, colonialism is still enshrined throughout modern institutions, including governance and administration, security and policing, and above all, religion and education. These institutions were used to conquer the minds, wills, and bodies of the colonized but, paradoxically, became highly contested. The resulting quests for self-determination are modes of resistance to colonial and imperial power that have always been present. Abolition and emancipation in the nineteenth century were forced by the demands and rebellions of the enslaved. But even as they fractured, powerful undertakings like slavery and colonization were not removed completely. They reappeared in new complex guises that continue to plague the world's social, economic, and environmental health.

The unequal power relations that were at the foundation of global capitalism and racialized slavery continue to privilege some at the expense of others. Throughout Africa and the African Diaspora, the legacies of slavery and colonization fall most heavily upon the most vulnerable. Many social conflicts and uprisings in Africa, Europe, and the Americas are rooted in legacies of racial and economic exploitation. Global capitalism and the international policing of human mobility have caused, over the past few centuries, the loss of countless Black lives in the abysses of oceans and deserts, through the slave trade and subsequent migrations forced by poverty, war, and climate change. People have been killed by violent policing and prison systems that break apart families and keep youths behind bars. Ongoing violence perpetrated by military police in Brazilian favelas, for instance, reveals how racialized forms of governance and policing practices regurgitate ancient modes of slavery and colonialism.

Global capitalism has generated both enormous wealth and enormous crises of sovereignty, democracy, and the rule of law. In the Sahelian belt of West and Central Africa—a territory that lies between the southern fringes of the Sahara and the northern savanna—criminal gangs are growing in number and voracity, in large part driven by the combined effects of climate change and food insecurity, and sharpened through religious intolerance and political instability. All of this is exacerbated by the poor management of national resources by corrupt and undemocratic regimes supported by multinational companies and former colonial powers more eager to defend their economic and political interests than to invest in economic equity and sociopolitical justice for all.

Modern media have become another locale for the transmission of stories that deny the human dignity of the formerly colonized. In the way they imagine, create, and air differences, media sites cultivate and broadcast Eurocentric world views. This includes, for instance, the coverage of the recent collapse of the Haitian state. Hundreds of years of economic exploitation and the accompanying social and economic insecurity have forced thousands to seek refuge through risky migration ventures. Paradoxically, it is also at these media sites that Eurocentric world views are increasingly contested, making the media world a multistakeholder platform where colonial and decolonial projects are simultaneously played out and thwarted.

Brewing Anger and Global Decoloniality
Through high-speed information technologies and social media, anger and outrage can spread quickly. Since 2015, the Rhodes Must Fall movement in South Africa was sparked by the collective effort to remove the statue of Cecil Rhodes, a British mining magnate and colonial prime minister of South Africa's Cape Colony in the late-nineteenth century, from the University of Cape Town. This movement has expanded to include the removal of other monuments to colonialism and also seeks to change the educational systems embodied by Western universities that perpetuate an unequal vision of knowledge production, resources, and power. In the process, it has become a global phenomenon,

Asylum seekers traveling by boat on the Mediterranean, 2014. Violent conflicts, poverty, and environmental disasters have pushed people to risk their lives on the world's deadliest migration route: over the past few years, unprecedented numbers of people have crossed the Mediterranean Sea on a perilous journey to seeking refuge and opportunity in Europe.

inspiring numerous protests against racism and social injustice.

Such protests were spread in France by the Parti des Indigènes de la République (Indigenous Party of the Republic) and in the United States and the United Kingdom by Black Lives Matter (BLM). In Bristol, BLM protesters threw a statue of the slave trader Edward Colston into a harbor. The May 2020 killing of George Floyd, an African American, in the United States and the June 2023 killing of Nahel M., a teenager of North African descent, in France, led to widespread protests and solidarity across the globe and, sometimes, violent upheaval. In Winnipeg, demonstrators from Indigenous groups toppled statues of Queen Victoria and Queen Elizabeth II during rallies in protest of nineteenth and twentieth-century assimilation schools. In Senegal, the Place de l'Europe on the island of Gorée, known for its history in the Transatlantic Slave Trade, was renamed Place de la Liberté. Also in Senegal, Place Faidherbe, named for the infamous French colonial administrator and general in the former colonial capital of Saint-Louis, was renamed Baya Ndar, reclaiming the Wolof term for the place.

In Carlos Julião's 1770s illustration from Rio de Janeiro, Brazil, two enslaved people transport an upper-class woman in a *palanquin*, or sedan chair (*top*). The image bears a resemblance to this 1912 photograph taken by Emile E. O. Gorlia in the Belgian Congo, in which Congolese porters carry a colonial official by hammock (*bottom*).

Squares and avenues long dedicated to French figures are being renamed across Senegal.

From calls to respect and return the cultural patrimony of African nations and cultures, to questions of currency, efforts to address the colonial legacies within Africa resound. Beneath these seemingly disparate arenas are the question of profit, the definition of wealth, and the exercise of power. In 2020, Musée du Quai Branly Jacques Chirac was attacked by a group of African-diasporic activists. They asserted that cultural collections in the museum were stolen from their home countries during colonization and demanded that they be returned. This is asserting sovereignty and patrimony for African nations.

Similarly, many African nationals also denounce the colonial agreements under which the West African CFA franc is tied to French economic and political interests. This currency and the colonizers' holding of cultural and historical artifacts taken from Africa outline the connections between culture and economics and illuminate the continued marginalization of Africans and people of African descent in world affairs.

The West African Sahel has experienced activities that exemplify the continuum linking our current era to the long-standing practices of African slavery and colonization: global terror movements, religious proselytism, extraction of African resources, and struggle for influence among world powers. The Sahel has recently been shaken by a series of military coups in Mali, Burkina Faso, Guinea, and Niger. There have also been intense local protests against France's colonial and neocolonial governance practices. These protests will, inevitably, expand and grow louder in the years to come. Demands for greater recognition, repair of past wrongs, and the acceptance of difference will continue to spread worldwide. These protests question the double standard of justice inherited from European colonialism and raise novel questions. How can the Western world take responsibility for correcting past and present wrongs that challenge its proclaimed universal beliefs in justice, equity, and fairness? How do we preserve places of memory without inflicting symbolic and psychological violence on Indigenous and African Diasporic communities? In the face of colonial institutions so profoundly enshrined in the fabric of modernity, what strategies and actions are needed to build new futures for better living together?

The End of "Independence"

Within my own field of study lies the promise to record, recognize, and enable some of the strategies and actions for positive change through the possibility of unearthing usable pasts for present communities and cultures. A critical element of anthropological work in Africa must focus on ethically engaging communities to establish new archives that live and work on a basis of shared authority and outside of the historical violence of the colonial archive. This means reinventing the practices and authority of museums and research institutions. Part of that work is taking place in collaboration with the global partners of the *In Slavery's Wake* project. The collection of oral histories of Senegalese descendants of the enslaved in the Unfinished Conversations series has challenged us, as scholars, to listen with new ears to the language that everyday people use to describe their worlds lived in the wake of slavery and colonialism. One of our interviewees in Saint-Louis, Senegal, posed a troubling question during an interview: "When will independence end?" This questions the dominant conception of independence and the sovereignty of the post-independence nation-state that continues to serve primarily the interests of the former colonial power. Embedded within the question is a realization that nominal independence, as experienced so far, is no radical departure from colonialism or break from the past. For everyday people in Senegal whom we spoke with, persistent structures of coloniality in practices of governance give the impression that the more things change, the more they remain the same. This is perceptible in the continuous practices still in the hands of multinational companies domiciled in the Global North that extract natural resources from the Global South to feed their unquenchable greed for wealth at the expense of Indigenous communities, which they thereby expose to unmitigated environmental disasters, diseases, and chronic poverty. Worst of all, this is done under the guise of a law-and-order system informed by colonial authority and exploitation that privileges accumulation, competition, and the rule of force and violence over cooperation and sharing, environmental preservation, and a more sustainable future that cares for the well-being of Indigenous communities.

Despite twentieth-century movements that resulted in independence, colonialism remains neatly disguised in African nations and was still operational, not only in economic systems but permeated in modern science and education, art and language, philosophy and intellectual life. Colonial languages, education systems, other modes of knowledge transmission, and tastes are promoted in ways that stifle Indigenous worldviews and identities. This dilemma of recognizing the Indigenous while reaching for a common global language is at the heart of the collective work to establish a decolonial paradigm that searches for alternative forms of sovereignty and governance outside of how European imperialism has defined them.

The decolonial project consists primarily of identifying, denouncing, and dismantling any vestige of colonialism. It seeks to restore hope by repairing all forms of injustices that debase others and will bar all forms of coercion designed to perpetuate the exploitation of the disenfranchised and formerly colonized.

However, neocolonial institutions are not equipped to heal the legacies of slavery and colonialism, nor are they able to reimagine or reframe global capitalism. Building new ethnic, racial, national, and international relationships requires a radical, anti-colonial approach. Rather than using the master's tools to destroy the master's house, which might yield the same negative results, we must look into the everyday lives of the formerly colonized to inform our actions that will refashion all aspects of societies across the globe.

Over the past few decades, several organizations have demanded the transformation of postcolonial societies. Groups such as BLM and the Collective for the Renewal of Africa work from a Pan-Africanist/Black solidarity viewpoint. Then there are organizations that focus on Indigenous rights, including the Parti des Indigènes de la République (Indigenous People of the Republic) in France. Muslim brotherhoods focus on religious freedom. Civil society movements are committed to the institutions of genuine indepen-

Bottom
Protestors in Mali demonstrate against France on the sixtieth anniversary of Malian independence, 2020. Across Francophone Africa, a movement for greater economic and political sovereignty has emerged. Protestors have called for the removal of French military forces, businesses, and diplomatic presence.

Top
British looters pose with artifacts from the Kingdom of Benin, 1897. British forces led a punitive expedition to Benin, destroying and looting many of the kingdom's cultural artifacts and burning Benin City. This brutal episode was part of a broader practice of violent cultural theft during the colonial period.

dence, social and political justice, human dignity, equitable access to economic opportunities, and sustainable development. They include the Front for a Popular Anti-Imperialist and Pan-African Revolution (FRAPP) and France Dégage (France Get Out) in Senegal.

Despite much promise, the results have been slight, because the subtle and not-so-subtle qualities of colonialism may rest quietly for a while but reappear when least expected. Therefore, the struggle to eliminate subjugation is ongoing and requires constant readjustment. The transformation and reformation of the institutions of slavery and colonialism requires diligence: Attention must be paid to how various education techniques, museums, archives, writing practices, memorialization processes, linguistic approaches, and economic investments have become deeply and skillfully imbued with Eurocentric ways of thinking. The challenge is not simply to denounce and deconstruct such influences but instead to renegotiate them in ways that eradicate the theory

and practice of all forms of discrimination, racialization, and stereotyping. The goal is to destroy, once and for all, every idea of graded degrees of humanity and the devaluation of human life. Since education is a true force in the transmission of knowledge and values, curricula must be transformed. Museum exhibitions that raise awareness of the histories and legacies of slavery and colonization, such as *In Slavery's Wake*, might also help break the mold and open new possibilities of thinking about and experiencing cultural differences.

Decolonial practices must explore alternative narratives to cultivate a Black aesthetic. In such an endeavor, there are voices from the past and present that require us to listen with new ears. They include revolutionaries, musicians, scientists, historians, and heads of state, such as Toussaint Louverture, Harriet Tubman, Olaudah Equiano, Frederick Douglass, Bob Marley, Martin Luther King Jr., Malcolm X, Cheikh Anta Diop, Thomas Sankara, Nelson Mandela, Patrice Lumumba, Aline Sitoe Diatta,

Patrisse Cullors, Nonhle Mbuthuma, Guy Marius Sagna, Ousmane Sonko, and Obiageli "Oby" Ezekwesili.

The construction of credible alternatives to post-slavery and postcolonial sovereignties at both the state and individual levels is one of the biggest obstacles for African and African-diasporic people. Efforts to decolonize must be situated in active engagement rather than mere political and academic discourse. Like the seeds of a farmer or the mineral ores of a blacksmith, efforts to decolonize must be cultivated or minted to take new forms. Decolonial projects should be grounded in the knowledge, experiences, and habits of formerly enslaved and colonized people who are hungry for epistemic justice, political freedom, human emancipation, and reparative history. In the academic world, we must open new venues for alternative societies rooted in the relational connectivity that existed in premodern societies within and beyond Europe. We must dismantle fallacious ideas that global connections that characterize the modern world were solely a production of European oceanic voyages beginning in the fifteenth century or that those voyages were a golden age of discovery and enlightenment. For thousands of years, *Homo sapiens* have long been moving, adapting, interacting, exploring, and experimenting with various forms of societal cooperation and exchange for their well-being, peace, and stability. In premodern archives predating Columbian voyages, we might find models of societal governance to help us imagine and craft a world of post-slavery and post-colonization that celebrates heterarchy over hierarchy, cooperation over competition, and promotes and values cultural diversity and differences rather than using them to classify and hierarchize. This is why embracing a view of history with a more expansive definition of archives in all their forms must be fostered in all societies.

Removal of Cecil
Rhodes statue in Cape
Town, South Africa,
2015. The Rhodes
Must Fall movement
began in 2015, when
protestors at the
University of Cape
Town demanded the
removal of a monu-
ment to the English
colonialist Cecil
Rhodes. The move-
ment gained worldwide
attention, sparking
global conversations
and actions around
decolonization.

MARÈME: FOOTSTEPS TO FREEDOM

Fatoumata Camara

The work of uncovering archaeological sites and conducting oral histories in Senegal, as part of *In Slavery's Wake* and the Unfinished Conversations initiative, led to the discovery of several lesser-known histories. One of the most compelling is the saga of Marème Diarra, whose life has been reconstructed through archaeological findings and interviews with residents of Diel Mbam in northern Senegal. Stories of people like Marème still hold significant lessons for her descendants and for people around the world who believe in freedom. She was a captive who sought freedom for herself and a wider society in the late nineteenth and early twentieth centuries even after self-emancipating. Today, Marème is a model of resilience, resistance, and leadership for the entire community, which celebrates her memory every year.

Marème was born in the middle of the nineteenth century in French Sudan, then a vast territory spanning from Senegal through Chad. The region was racked by wars of conquest and resistance, inflamed by the European slave trade. This environment led to the widespread displacement, capture, and sale of vulnerable people, including Marème, who was taken to Mauritania.

In the 1890s, when she was approximately twenty, Marème fled, walking two hundred miles to Saint-Louis, Senegal, with her three children to secure freedom. She was aware that any enslaved person who set foot there became free, because settlements in the French colonies had abolished slavery. Marème, like many thousands of others fleeing slavery in West Africa, remained there and married. But, while the French had technically abolished slavery, the pathway for those seeking full freedom was incomplete and led to other forms of bondage. The colonial capital of Saint-Louis was like many French "liberty" villages, which were established in wider francophone West Africa to welcome people who had self-liberated. Despite the promise of freedom, these communities began to function as labor camps for the French colonial government, which used villagers as a key labor force to support colonial expansion. During this era, the French vied against North and West African leaders for control of territory and resources in the shadow of slavery.

Left
Portrait of Marème Diarra, Angoka, 2023.
For the Unfinished Conversations oral histories series, the Senegalese artist Angoka created this portrait of Marème Diarra. Captured in Mali and enslaved in Mauritania, Marème fled slavery and settled in Diel Mbam, Senegal, a haven for newcomers whose rights remained restricted in the colonial capital of Saint-Louis.

Top
Festival honoring Marème Diarra, 2023.
For the past two decades, community members in Diel Mbam, Senegal, have gathered to offer prayers and celebrate the life of Marème Diarra. Remembered for her leadership and moral courage, Diarra is regarded as a central figure in the community's history.

Through oral accounts collected in Unfinished Conversations, researchers learned that Marème resettled outside of Saint-Louis in an attempt to avoid "unfreedom." The place where she lived was identified, and archaeological excavations on the house were carried out in 2021, establishing a chronology of the site's use. The unearthed material traces tell us about her daily life. We now know that Marème cultivated a piece of land that was granted to her in an insalubrious area. She transformed it into a welcoming place for formerly enslaved people, most of whom were also migrants from Sudan. Their presence has been confirmed by the archaeological discovery of buttons from soldiers' uniforms: enslaved men often joined the French military as infantrymen, to attain freedom.

Marème and her husband created a new community, whose members were connected by a shared past and aspirations to live free and equitable lives. Drawing on her resourcefulness and experiences during exile, Marème was able to cut, process, and sell lumber to escape the marginal economic position caused by her former enslavement.

The reclamation of Marème's story demonstrates the crucial role that African archaeology and memory can play in reconstructing the history of enslaved people, whose voices rarely appear in written documents. Artifacts and oral histories help confirm the individual struggles for freedom on the African continent that were waged to end racial slavery and to navigate the colonial oppression that continued to grow in the wake of slavery.

Today, Marème's descendants remember her as a woman with a strong personality, who was brave, welcoming, and generous, with a deep commitment to sharing with others. As her descendant Mamadou Ba stated in one of our interviews, in a combination of Wolof and French: "*Donc c'est ça Mareem Njaay li muy incarner ci man kuy bañ la, kuy bañ, nanguwul kenn ku ko dominer. Mais nag elle était genereuse.*" "That's Marème Ndiaye, [also known as Marème Diarra], who, for us, represents a figure of defiance who doesn't accept in any way to be dominated, despite her generosity."

AN ANTHEM OF IDENTITY

Amadou Thiam

In Senegal, the end of slavery within French colonies in 1848 did not systemically lead to a reconfiguration of the relationships between the formerly enslaved and the former slaveholders. Even today, social discrimination between various communities persists, underscoring the disparities inherited from the slavery era. Descendants of enslaved people in Senegal, known as *maccube*, still experience social stigma through naming practices, societal roles and positions, and unequal interactions with families of former enslavers. At present, *maccube* are not allowed to speak out in village meetings, nor can they enter certain professions, including that of imam.

Today, a transnational organization in West Africa called Endam Bilali, meaning "descendants of Bilal," is working to end these prejudices. Bilal, who was formerly enslaved, was a companion of the Prophet Muhammad. The group's members, from across Mali, Mauritania, and Senegal, are *maccube* and speak Haalpulaar. The organization advocates for access to jobs, education, and land, and increased political power and religious leadership. The members proudly share their histories and claim their place in society. In the words of one member, Ousmane Mbodj, "*Tilim keen gënul keen, bo fotté mu sett*" (No one is better than their neighbor; anyone who washes becomes clean).

One of the most important ways of honoring, sharing, and laying claim to history and a collective identity in West African society is through the creation of anthems that are revealed to griots who record and carry the history of a community and the exploits of ancestors. For the noble classes in society, griots are keepers of knowledge and oral tradition. The griot assumes the role of genealogist and historian of events, mainly praising the great warriors who have marked history. Because the *maccube* are at the bottom of the social ladder, they have no such keepers of tradition, since griots prefer to limit their services to the upper classes. Endam Bilali, however, was able to engage the griot Mamoudou Dembel Guissé in the city of Orkadiéré, near Senegal's border with Mauritania, where a special anthem of the *maccube*—the "Maa kari"— was discovered. Guissé performed this

Left
Mamoudou Dembel Guissé with his *khalam*, 2020. Interviewed as part of the Unfinished Conversations oral history series, Dembel Guissé discussed his practice as a griot in the Fatou region of Senegal: "I learned to sing from my father, I learned to play the *khalam* from my father, who inherited it from his father."

Bottom
This *khalam* was used by the late griot Mamoudou Dembel Guissé to perform the "Maa kaari," a special anthem of the *maccube*, descendants of enslaved people from across West Africa, who still experience social stigma. This anthem gives strength and confidence to the *maccube*, and to the members of Endam Bilali, an association working to end this prejudice.

anthem at gatherings of the organization until his passing in 2023. The song awakens and inspires feelings of belonging and pride, giving the group's members confidence and strength in their history and hope for a better future.

Guissé was a weaver, but his ability to sing and play music, especially the "Maa kari," filled a gap left by traditional griots. He was a unique and valuable presence in the life of the Endam members, inspiring a deep connection with their musical and cultural heritage. Generally, *maabo sudu paate* are griots who specialize in the genealogies of the *subalbe* (fishermen). Guissé played his traditional guitar-like instrument, the *khalam,* which he constructed himself, which added a special resonance to each note played. He was known for producing a distinctive *lebbol* (tone) when playing the "Maa kari." According to Guissé, the melody is a breath of life, a link between the generations of the past and the future. "This hymn has been acquired by blood," he claimed. When he surrounded you with the music of the "Maa kari," you felt the emotions of the *maccube* community resonating through every syllable that was sung. Guissé explained that the "Maa kari" came about through an enslaved woman, who was said to have acquired this melody for the community of the enslaved at the cost of her life.

The "Maa kari," importantly, celebrates an enslaved heroine. It transcends simple musical notes, for it embodies the painful history of slavery and the struggle for dignity. In a society where, according to some Endam members, slaves such as Mbori, Bafi Ba Dembele, Sarr Teïba, Molo Sarr, Denguel Wela Khore, and Saloma Djambour were hidden and sometimes even kidnapped by the nobles, the "Maa kari" represents a place in the collective memory of the broader society. This song inspires Endam members to accept who they are without apology. The stories in the music that honor the enslaved demonstrate that the struggle for freedom and equality and for claiming identity is an ongoing process which can take on complex forms. But the power of history felt through the "Maa kari" is an essential, if intangible, component of that struggle. In the words of an Endam member, Thierno Ablaye, "If the griot plays this anthem, we have more courage in everything that we do; it makes us stronger."

IRONWORK AND SPECULATIVE WORLD MAKING

Michelle D. Commander

As one traverses Charleston, South Carolina, passing cobblestoned streets, markets, and rainbow-colored row homes, one marvels at the beauty of the historic vestiges that remain. Forged by enslaved blacksmiths and artisans or by their steady-handed descendants to whom the knowledge had been passed down, intricate wrought-iron gates adorn many properties, providing a visible signature to the city and compelling passersby to pause and admire them, and then memories of slavery-era atrocities come flooding in. They tend to haunt and persist here—in the wake.

On the coastlines of Africa over four centuries, ships awaited the boarding of captured Africans who would then be carried across the expanse of unknown waters and into unknown futures. The captives were often bound together with iron shackles and fitted into small compartments in an immediate attempt to dim their willfulness and restrict their movements. Packed as human cargo into these cramped spaces for much of the six-to-eight-week journey, they were mired in human waste and struck by unimaginable levels of grief, confusion, and anger at their circumstances. This sustained turmoil prompted untold numbers of enslaved captives to take flight in individual and collective suicidal leaps from ships—their intent was to return spiritually to their homelands. Others refused to eat or rebelled violently to take some measure of control over their lives. The captives were connected by this defining event physically and psychically, sharing linked fates through-out slavery and its aftermath.

The utilization of iron to collectively punish and limit the movements of enslaved people must have felt like an affront to those affected, for obvious reasons, but given the deep role that the metal long played in how people worshipped, self-actualized, and maintained cultural and spiritual connections to their belief systems, the shackles were another level of insult. Once at their destination, the enslaved captives discovered that their experiences aboard the slave ship had been an unfortunate precursor to life in slavery, which was marked by similar and sometimes even more extreme levels of cruelty, physical restriction, and constant surveillance. In his 1789 personalnarrative, Olaudah Equiano recounted the mundane insidiousness of the violence that undergirded slavery from the ship to the plantation societies across the Atlantic world: "Slaves [were] branded with the initial letters of their master's name; and a load of heavy iron hooks hung about their necks. On the most trifling occasions, [enslaved people] were loaded with chains; and often instruments of torture were added. The iron muzzle, thumb-screws, &c were sometimes applied for the slightest faults."

Enslaved people's embrace of Kongo cosmologies and those found in syncretized religions such as Haitian Vodou, Cuban Santería, and Brazilian Candomblé would prove central to their survival. They forged kinship groups and created subversive ways to maintain

Left
Ceremonial sword, sixteenth or seventeenth century. In the Kingdom of Kongo—a historic kingdom covering parts of present-day Angola, Democratic Republic of Congo, and Republic of Congo—large iron swords like this one came into prominence with the introduction and expansion of Christianity. Artisans crafted these swords for political elites, blending traditional styles with European iconography.

Top
Mordaça (iron muzzle), Brazil, nineteenth century. Torture devices, such as this iron muzzle from Brazil, were used to silence, punish, and control enslaved people. In *The Interesting Narrative of the Life of Olaudah Equiano*, the formerly enslaved Equiano writes of the pervasive use of such objects, "The iron muzzle, thumb-screws, etc. are so well known, as not to need a description, and were sometimes applied for the slightest faults."

Bottom
Candomblé iron altar piece, late twentieth century. Candomblé is an Afro-Brazilian religion that developed during the era of slavery. Altar pieces, like this one, merge sacred practice with artistic tradition and represent the presence of orixás, or spirits. The design of this work may signify its use for Oxóssi, a deity associated with hunting and prosperity.

elements of their cultural and spiritual backgrounds via the fusion of their traditional beliefs with the Christianity of their European slaveholders. Archaeological unearthings have turned up myriad artifacts that offer evidence of the centrality of African ironwork traditions to enslaved communities across time and space. Two examples here—a Congolese ceremonial sword and a Brazilian altarpiece—give insight into the ways that Africans and their descendants were able to maintain their spiritual practices and connections to the ancestral realm, as well as to the peoples and cultures from which they had been separated. Admired for what was believed to be their supernatural gift of rendering freedom-making tools and sacred ceremonial objects out of malleable metal, blacksmiths and artisans of African descent, who had often been enslaved to exploit this very skill set, fashioned sacred materials with which members of enslaved and descendant communities could protect their bodies and minds. Enslaved people leaned on significant tenets that would help them heal, center, and sustain themselves as they negotiated their realities. The production of iron objects also armed self-liberated formerly enslaved people and their compatriots with weapons as they embraced postures of resistance and sought to fortify the Maroon and *quilombo* settlements that they established in swamps, mountains, and other landscapes of freedom.

Blacksmithing was an art and technology that enabled new cosmological possibilities and aided the world-making imaginations of African captives and generations that followed, particularly as they were forced to make and remake their lives. Indeed, they reoriented their religious and spiritual practices and European iconography in ways that suggested a reverential posture even as they often endeavored to subvert outside knowledge of their collective sensibilities and desires to escape their circumstances. This speculative philosophy for living full lives under enslavement endures in the wake of slavery, as certain cruel elements of the past continue to reverberate against these shores.

TAHRO: SHAPING SPIRITUAL VESSELS

Johanna Obenda

In November 1858, under the cover of night, a retrofitted racing yacht named *Wanderer* reached Jekyll Island, Georgia. More than fifty years after the United States had outlawed its Transatlantic Slave Trade, the *Wanderer* arrived at the island with more than four hundred captive Africans on board. Many of the captives smuggled aboard the vessel were Bakongo, including Tahro, a twenty-seven-year-old man from the Madimba Valley of the Kongo Kingdom, one of the powerful states of West Central Africa.

Tahro and the other *Wanderer* survivors were a part of the millions of Africans trafficked to the Americas during the trade's illegal period, between 1807 and 1867. To avoid detection and legal consequences, the crew of the *Wanderer* dispersed the captives, placing them on trains and barges headed to purchasers across the American South,

Left
The *Wanderer* was one of the last known slave ships to arrive in the United States. The vessel landed illegally in 1858 with more than four hundred captive Africans aboard. This photograph from the 1930s, captured in Edgefield, South Carolina, features *Wanderer* survivors, from left to right, Cilucängy (Ward Lee), Pucka Geata (Tucker Henderson), and Tahro (Romeo).

Top left
Face cup, unidentified enslaved maker, possibly Tahro (Romeo Thomas), ca. 1861–62. Following the arrival of African captives from the slave ship *Wanderer*, enslaved potters in Edgefield, South Carolina, began making face vessels like this cup. These potters were seemingly influenced by their heritage and Central African *minkisi*, sacred objects of protection and healing.

Top right
Nkisi figure, late nineteenth century. *Minkisi* (plural) are ritual vessels used by spiritual practitioners for healing and protection. This *nkisi* figure is styled as a Kongo chief, likely signifying its power. At its center is a mirror-covered medicine box, which may have been used to hold important medicines and other spiritual items.

from Florida to Texas. One large group, which included Tahro, was sent up the Savannah River to Edgefield County, South Carolina—a hub of industrial pottery driven by enslaved labor.

In Edgefield, Tahro was renamed Romeo Thomas and labored as a potter at Palmetto Fire Brick Works. The alkaline-glazed stoneware produced in the Edgefield District directly supported the region's plantation economy. Along with smaller wares like bowls, jugs, and pitchers, enslaved potters produced massive jars for food and water storage to meet the needs of local plantations and homesteads. Enslaved potters such as Tahro were involved in every part of the manufacturing process, from gathering clay, to mixing glazes, and firing the ceramics in the industrial-sized kilns. They joined thousands of other enslaved people whose labor spurred growth in American manufacturing industries like metalworking, mining, and lumber.

With their arrival in Edgefield, it's likely that Tahro and his fellow *Wanderer* survivors ignited a resurgence of African spiritual and artistic customs. Beyond crafting utilitarian pottery for sale, enslaved and liberated potters in Edgefield produced pieces for personal use, notably distinctive face vessels. These vessels—small cups, jugs, and jars—featured intricate facial details created with white kaolin clay. Scholars

believe these ceramics echo Bakongo traditions. In particular, the facial characteristics of the Edgefield pottery resemble the design of some Central African *minkisi* (singular *nkisi*) ritual objects, especially the white kaolin eyes. *Minkisi*, spiritual containers, often incorporated kaolin to facilitate ancestral connections, which is significant, given the abundance of kaolin in both the Kongo region and the southeastern United States.

Across the Americas, Kongo culture shaped a variety of mediums and practices, such as religion, language, music, and art. In Edgefield, it appears that the survivors of the *Wanderer* found a new way to cultivate and express their heritage and beliefs through the creation of face vessels. While there is much still unknown about their uses, we can surmise that these multipurpose vessels were important objects. Possibly set at the threshold of a home, placed lovingly at a grave, or gifted between kin, face vessels evoked protection and healing. Evidence even suggests that some were carried north along the Underground Railroad. These face vessels point to the ways that Tahro and millions of other Africans used art to make and remake their culture, creating meaning and understanding that transcended the brutality of enslavement and reconfigured African identity on American soil.

INDUSTRY AND EXTRACTION

Ivie Orobaton

Reshaping nature was a project central to colonization. While reshaping landscapes through the plantation model was, perhaps, the most visible type of terraforming, mining was, and remains, just as significant in its impact on both transforming and extracting wealth from landscapes around the world. The search for precious metals—silver and gold—drove Atlantic exploration and conquest by European powers. Beginning in the 1500s, the Spanish and Portuguese established mines across Central and South America. Because of the rapid growth of mining operations and new demands from the global economy, land and laborers suffered. Forests were razed, hills were cut and demolished from the inside out, and miners were exposed to noxious air and unsafe working conditions.

In 1693, gold was discovered in Brazil in an area that encompasses modern-day Belo Horizonte, Ouro Prêto, Congonhas, and Santa Bárbara d'Oeste. Over time, expeditions of *bandeirantes* (prospecting pioneers) organized in cities like São Paulo to search the interior for gold, silver, diamonds, and topaz. These expeditions seized land and enslaved Indigenous communities, putting them to work in new mines. Ouro Prêto, whose name

Left
Congolese workers in a cobalt mining pit, 2022. Democratic Republic of Congo sits on over half of the world's cobalt supply. Cobalt is a central component in nearly every modern battery—from cell phones to electric cars. The global dependence on cobalt brings both enormous profit as well as human and environmental cost, with local laborers facing low wages and extremely dangerous working conditions.

Bottom
Topaz mine, 1823. The British mineralogist John Mawe traveled through the interior of Brazil, where he recorded mining operations in regions like the gold-rich Minas Gerais. In this illustration, Mawe depicts a topaz mine, emphasizing its impact on the natural environment.

translates to "black gold," was established during the first gold rush in Minas Gerais. Surrounding the city, the rolling hills of the Serra do Espinhaço (Espinaço Mountains) were embedded throughout with veins of crystallized ores: gold, iron oxide, and other metals.

The artist and mineralogist John Mawe is credited as the first foreigner to depict and publish accounts and observations of mines in the state of Minas Gerais. His illustrated book *Travels in the Interior of Brazil* was published in 1816 and captured the destructive nature of the industry. To reach the gold buried deep in the mountains and hills, miners meticulously stripped soil and rock to expose the ore. Mountain faces were sheared off, changing lush landscapes into massive pits. Miners used the natural landscape to their benefit: small streams were used to wash the metal and send it down the mountain to the laborers at the base. The region saw a massive influx of people seeking work in the mines—both free, some of whom had abandoned their positions on plantations, and enslaved. At the height of the gold rush, Ouro Prêto was the most populated town in the colony, surpassing even São Paulo.

In 1888, Brazil became the last nation in the Americas to abolish slavery. The cascading effects of abolition strained the global system of commerce as newly emancipated people attempted to take control over their lives and labor. As slave colonies dwindled across the Atlantic world, imperialists turned to Africa in

a second wave of colonial expansion in the late nineteenth century. While Black people were no longer subjected to enslavement, coercive labor practices that began under slavery, such as quotas, long workdays, and violent punishments like whipping or bodily mutilations, were routinely employed.

In 1884, at the Berlin Conference, European imperialists had divided Africa among themselves, allocating territory to different powers. At this gathering, the Belgian Congo was recognized as the private colony of King Leopold II. There, mining for cobalt and other rare minerals became a vital component of the colonial system. The Belgian Congo, which is now Democratic Republic of Congo (DRC), lies on nearly half of the world's supply of cobalt. In the 1800s, cobalt was used to dye fabric and ceramics a vibrant blue. The Union Minière du Haut-Katanga (Miner Union of Upper Katanga) controlled mining operations across Congo's copper-rich Katanga region from 1906 to 1966. Today, cobalt is an essential component of the batteries used in vehicles and cell phones. Despite advances in technology, whether in Brazil or the DRC, human labor is still the primary means of extracting metals and minerals, using methods developed under the exploitative systems of slavery and colonialism. Mines ranging in size from small and artisanal to industrial dot the landscape, and unseen tunnels extend deep into the earth.

As the world's nations have adopted more battery-powered "green" products to combat climate change, cobalt mining in the DRC has exploded. As in earlier gold and mineral rushes, like those in Ouro Prêto, thousands of people have flocked to work in the mines. As many as five thousand laborers are gathered at a Congolese artisanal mine in a photograph taken by Junior D. Kannah. There, shifts of miners descend into a network of mines, chipping away at the compacted dirt for cobalt. As endless streams of trucks remove mounds of dirt, miners reinforce the mine walls when dwindling yields force them to dig deeper in search of the mineral.

The dual exploitation of the land and human beings continues to leave scars on landscapes and lives around the Atlantic world as cycles of exploitation and wealth generation continue.

WEAVING HISTORY AND HEALING

Johanna Obenda

Artists and communities around the world are tapping into traditions of quilting, embroidery, and weaving to reflect on the past and imagine freer futures, stitching together stories of struggle and joy. The artists and collectives whose quilts and tapestries are shown here span four continents. Their works connect to histories of slavery and freedom in South America, mass incarceration in North America, colonial rule in Africa, and modern-day human trafficking in Europe. Embedded in their practice is a commitment to record silenced histories for future generations and to care for one another in the present.

The community of Mampuján is one of twenty historical palenques, or Maroon settlements, formed by people who fled slavery in Colombia. Across generations, the residents of Mampuján have faced waves of violence and displacement, from colonial extermination campaigns to a devastating attack by paramilitary groups in 2000. In the aftermath of the paramilitary attack, women from Mampuján formed a collective to work on matters of reparation and healing. Drawing on Afro-Caribbean storytelling and local textile art traditions, the Mampuján collective began to create large-scale tapestries as a medium to process their trauma and share their stories. In works like *Violencia y Esperanza en Colombia* (Violence and Hope in Colombia), the Mampuján weavers capture painful memories of their community to create catharsis, seek reparation, and ensure that these violent acts are never committed again.

Across the Caribbean Sea and past the Gulf of Mexico, another collective of textile artists gathers within the walls of the largest maximum-security prison in the United States. The Louisiana State Penitentiary, otherwise known as Angola, was built on the site of a slave plantation of the same name. It is still a working farm, and prisoners today do much of the same work as their enslaved predecessors, growing and harvesting crops like

Left
Violencia y Esperanza en Colombia (Violence and Hope in Colombia), Mampuján Collective, 2006–2008. This tapestry depicts scenes from a devastating paramilitary attack in Mampuján, Colombia, in 2000. In the aftermath of this attack, women from Mampuján formed a collective to share their community's histories and process trauma through textile arts.

Top
The Blue Print, Lawrence Jenkins, Allen Nguyen, Harun Sharif-El, and Gary Tyler, 2009. This quilt tells the story of the inmate-led Angola Prison Hospice Program. In the top corner, people from many nations and cultures come together, experiencing the same circumstances but holding different perspectives.

EPOQUE COLONIALE

corn, wheat, and cotton on the eighteen-thousand-acre property. In 1901, Louisiana began to use the former plantation as a state prison and has since faced severe accusations of sanctioning violence, enforcing prolonged solitary confinement, and providing inmates with inadequate health care. Today, the overwhelming majority of the six-thousand-person prison population is Black men serving life sentences, most of whom will die there. Recognizing the need for end-of-life care and companionship, inmates created a hospice volunteer program. As a part of this inmate-led initiative, volunteers stitch quilts to keep patients warm and sell to fund the program. Angola quilt makers tell a range of stories in their work, reflecting on themes of life, death,

and social justice and bringing a tangible source of care and humanity into what has historically been and continues to be an inhumane place.

In the DRC, the artist Lucie Kamuswekera is also using textiles to tell place-based stories. Working with reclaimed jute bags, Kamuswekera, known as Artiste Lucie, uses the practice of embroidery to illustrate moments of Congo's past. For Artiste Lucie, her work is an act of preservation, a creation of a visual record of Congolese history that can be understood and accessed by younger generations. Her tapestries cover a range of topics from the degradation of natural resources to life under colonialism, as seen in the work *Époque Coloniale* (Colonial Era).

Kamuswekera uses the income from the sale of her embroideries to support a small textile workshop, where she provides shelter and training to a group of orphaned children. Through her tapestries and through the work of the youths she mentors, she hopes the art of embroidery and collective memories of Congolese history will survive.

The Sophie Hayes Foundation in the United Kingdom is also working to process difficult histories and truths. The organization was founded to draw attention to the pervasive issue of modern-day human trafficking and to aid survivors. Placing an emphasis on mental health and healing, the foundation helps survivors learn skills needed to live independent lives and gain financial freedom through stable employment. The organization's Freedom Quilt Project invited survivors of human trafficking and modern-day slavery to create unique quilt squares, which were then assembled into large quilts. In this collaborative process, survivors shared their stories and connected with others who have lived through similar experiences. For these women and the other textile artists, the practice of this art is both a means of self-expression and a therapeutic tool for processing past and present trauma. Each artist has used their needle as a pen to record a history—personal or collective—to be shared with the world, and in the process they have created spaces for themselves and their communities to heal through creation.

Top
Époque Coloniale (Colonial Era), Lucie Kamuswekera, 2021. The artist Lucie Kamuswekera weaves together eras of Congo's history. In this work she draws connections between Swahili slave traders and Belgian colonial officials, prompting the question: What was the difference in the treatment of Congolese people under slavery and under colonialism?

Right
Detail of *Northern Freedom Quilt*, 2022. This quilt was sewn in the city of Manchester, United Kingdom, as a part of the Sophie Hayes Foundation's Freedom Quilt Project. Created by women survivors of modern-day human trafficking, each of the quilt's squares represents a survivor's past and her future hopes and dreams.

Section 3
NAVIGA-
TIONS

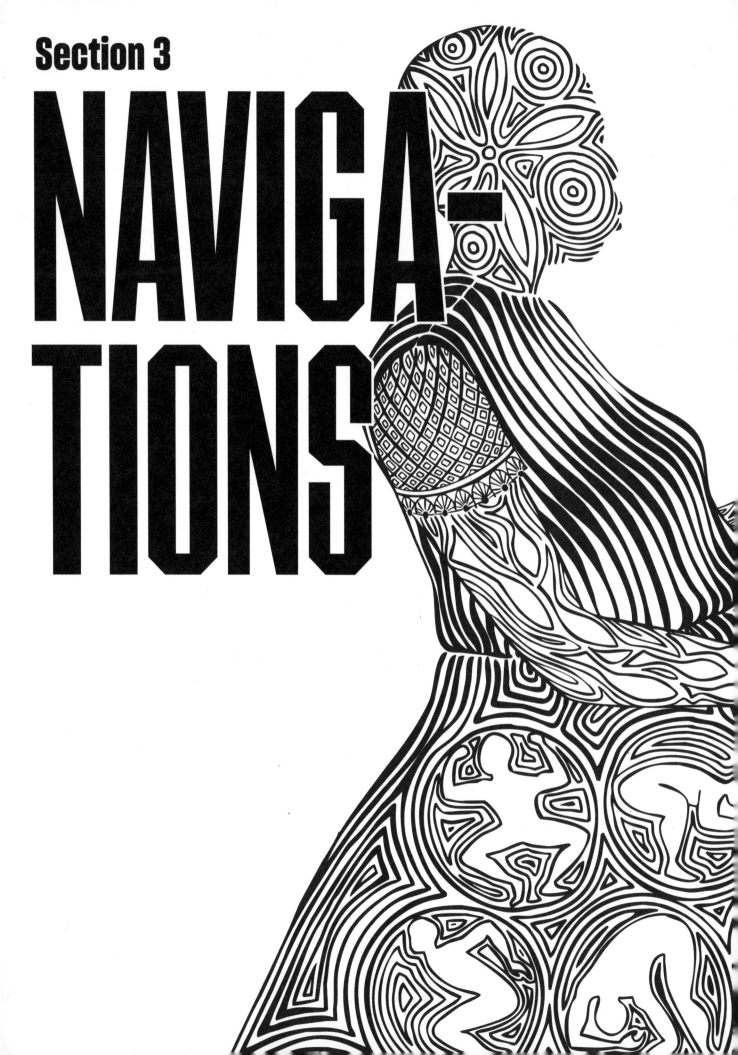

The long struggle for full freedom emerged at the very beginnings of enslavement and colonialization. On sea and land, through body and spirit, enslaved and colonized people refused dehumanization at every turn. In the most horrible of circumstances, they kept themselves whole and defined their worlds beyond the will of enslavers. They practiced care in the face of harm, formed communities out of strangers, claimed rights despite subjugation, and made culture across continents. From mounting armed rebellions to forming spiritual cosmologies, enslaved people created a universe of freedom populated by constellations of diverse actions and beliefs. Through this universe, they made freer lives for themselves and future generations in as many places and spaces as oppression subjugated them.

While the slave trade turned the sea into a site of violence and horror, enslaved and free Black people navigated those same waters to create freedom and routes of resistance. Hundreds of shipboard revolts have been documented: Even before leaving the African coast, captive Africans resisted enslavement aboard ships that were docked for an average of eight months while captives were gathered. Aboard slave ships, captives formed social bonds and community, aiding the organization of collective revolt. Black abolitionists created networks in port cities throughout the Americas, passing on politics, information, and aid to other freedom seekers. Enslaved people took advantage of these networks to make successful escapes at sea and on a variety of waterways, seeking passage and refuge in ports around the Atlantic.

On land, from cities to plantations, enslaved people asserted their individual and collective humanity. They cultivated gardens and established healing spaces. Herbalists, conjurers, bonesetters, and midwives cared for their communities, drawing on ancestral African knowledge to restore bodily autonomy stripped away by enslavement. In the face of familial separation and fracture, the enslaved built new communities and formed kinship networks that expanded beyond blood relatives. It was common for enslaved communities to practice collective child-rearing, forming networks of love and support that helped to soften the emotional pain of life under slavery.

People from various backgrounds forged new societies, merging diverse African cultures with Indigenous American and European practices. Through dance, music, artistry, ritual, foodways, and movement, they claimed their humanity in religious rituals and the practices of daily life. This immense and living archive of knowledge, beliefs, and aesthetics is transmitted beyond writing and the silences of the colonial archive. It includes movement or gesture of a body in ritual or dance, the sound of a voice raised in song or a message embedded in the pattern of a drumbeat, and the style of adornment in the way a body carries or inhabits clothing. These embodied practices bridge our past and present. They help descendants open lines of communication between the worlds of the spiritual and the physical, the dead and the living, and ancestors and future generations.

Black people forged communities of freedom across a wide geography and in a multitude of ways and forms—from settlements to townships, fortifications, and Maroon communities. Whether rural or urban, northern or southern, and hidden away from all eyes or exposed among interracial neighbors—all demonstrated people's desire to live, work, and worship freely despite racism, violence, and inequality. They also sought to end the institution of slavery. Recent scholarship illuminates the efforts of Africans who appealed to the Vatican to abolish the institution as early as the sixteenth century, offering an important glimpse into the long history of formal demands for abolition far earlier than the larger movement for abolition that coalesced at the end of the eighteenth century.

Although white and Black abolitionists worked together, Black abolitionists often took a more radical approach. In a variety of arenas, Black abolitionists looked beyond the legal end of slavery to envision and create a future that guaranteed rights and equality for all people. The multifaceted abolition movement included practices like strikes, petitions, networking, testifying, and revolt.

On plantations and in other places driven by involuntary labor, enslaved people resisted by escaping, implementing work slowdowns, and intentionally damaging property. This refusal to work struck at the heart of racial slavery by targeting the profits of enslavers. The enslaved and their allies used their economic power as laborers to press the issue of abolition across the Atlantic, engaging in a type of mass action that would be called upon by future labor movements.

Enslaved and free Black people used petitions to seek protection and demand their full rights in a legal system where they had limited political voice. Thousands of petitions were put forth by groups and individuals as part of the broader abolitionist movement. Petitions mobilized communities, spread the word about abolitionist causes, and placed public pressure on governments to end slavery.

Black abolitionists also formed and joined antislavery societies across the Atlantic, such as the Sons of Africa in London, the Société des Amis des Noirs (Society of the Friends of the Blacks) in Paris, and the American Anti-Slavery Society. Local and national organizations connected diverse groups of abolitionists worldwide. These organizations hosted public meetings, founded newspapers, and petitioned courts to end racial slavery. Other abolitionists formed more clandestine networks, working undercover to help fugitive slaves escape to freedom.

Abolitionists assisted the enslaved develop a new genre of literature, slave narratives. These detailed records of life in captivity challenged readers around the world to embrace the abolitionist cause and were expanded upon by Black newspapers and printers. These autobiographies, biographies, and other writings were a powerful medium for sharing the horrors of racial slavery and advocating for freedom.

Finally, large and small anti-colonial/antislavery rebellions and revolutions, led by free and enslaved Black people, proliferated throughout the Atlantic world in the eighteenth and nineteenth centuries. Distinct localities and cultures often differed in their demands, but they all generally focused on sovereignty and individual and collective rights. In South Carolina, there was the Stono rebellion. The Jamaican slavocracy was shaken to the core by Samuel Sharpe's rebellion. From the Grito de Lares (Lares rebellion) in Puerto Rico to the Revolta dos Malês (Muslim Revolt) in Brazil, and the Aponte rebellion in Cuba and well beyond, each was buoyed by what the historian Julius S. Scott called "the common wind" of

Black radical thought, where anti-colonial activities found great movement in the Haitian Revolution, the world's first successful anti-colonial and antislavery revolution.

This constellation of Black abolitionist practices, from legal advocacy to armed rebellion, helped bring about formal legal emancipation and the abolition of slavery across nations and colonial empires in the span of just over half a century, culminating with the end of slavery in Brazil in 1888. In the actions of Black abolitionists is the wellspring of a deeper and wider vision that hopes for full equality and justice in the world today.

DOMESTIC WORLD MAKING OF THE ENSLAVED

Geri Augusto

nslaved Africans and their descendants throughout the Americas were, in many ways, *dispossessed architects*. Theirs is a collective story that unfolded across the plantations and cities of the "New World," leaving few, if any, individual names. However, these ancestral presences have left indelible traces. Under duress, the captives built and sometimes designed much of the valuable infrastructure that undergirded regimes of racial capitalism, like roads, dams, barrages, irrigation works, ports, and train stations. Enslaved people also worked on buildings used for manufacturing, refining, milling, and other activities, including religious worship. From building this environment, the enslaved almost always received no profit or succor, although some rare, infinitesimal earnings accrued to them from being "hired out." The skilled craftspeople and artisans working in stone and wood, copper and iron, thatch and tiles, and mud and daub built the townhouses and plantation manors of the masters, as well as their own modest, often cramped cabins, huts, and *senzalas* (collective barracks) on thousands of tobacco, indigo, cotton, rice, coffee, and cocoa plantations.

These sites of confinement, surveillance, control, and dehumanization were also where enslaved women and men somehow managed to imagine, design, and create green counter-landscape architecture such as yard gardens and provision grounds, located in the interstices of the plantation and on more marginal lands some distance from it. These pieces of land provided a green supplement to the cruelly inadequate, starch, salted-meat, or salted-fish diets that slave owners provided. Early iterations of the onerous Black Codes, instituted first in Spanish and French colonies and later in British plantation societies, featured, among other stipulations, the quantity and types of rations an owner should distribute to the captive laborers.

But in actual daily practice, to a degree which varied depending on plantation size and crop harvesting and refining seasons, many plantation owners in different parts of the Americas adopted what came to be known as "the Brazil model," and flaunted outright the proscription against captives working seven days a week. Instead, on tiny plots just outside their doors, and on collectively or individually worked provision grounds situated on distant or difficult terrain, enslaved laborers were "allowed" to cultivate or raise a good portion of their own food. It was work that demanded a second—or in the case of many enslaved women—a third shift, one which could only be done at night, after a day spent laboring in fields, kitchens, and workshops, or else on the days supposedly set aside for Christian worship and celebration. But this double or triple exploitation quickly took on counter-meanings for many of the enslaved. Plots and gardens became a hard-won if precarious "right" zealously and repeatedly negotiated with plantation owners. Out of hillsides, swamps, and woodlands, or on the little patches that became important extensions of their crude lodgings, enslaved gardeners and

Top
Servants at a Pump,
Nicolino Calyo, ca.
1840. At the center of
this painting, a woman
holds a basket of fruit.
In gardens and plots of
land on the edges of
plantations, enslaved
people grew crops to
sustain themselves.
Sometimes their
harvests would yield
enough surplus to be
sold in markets or by
urban street vendors.

horticulturalists carefully tended and
coaxed crops sometimes abundant enough
to sell their surplus in weekly markets, or
through vendors plying urban streets.

Enslaved women possessed skills that
drew on the prominent role their gender
had played in farming and marketing in
West and West Central Africa before
European contact and colonization.
Selling a portion of their food crops,
flowers, and herbs fetched cash that the
enslaved used to buy foodstuffs they
could not raise, additional or better-
quality clothing, personal adornments,
and household items. Always operating
at the margins of the law, enslaved men
and women sold a wide array of goods
and services in city streets that were
heavily regulated and repressively
policed. The list of their wares includes
small implements, wood, cloth, thread,
vegetables, fresh fish, and fowl. For
enslaved, freed, and self-liberated
women, flowers, herbs, prepared dishes,
and delicacies of diverse types were their
province. However, perhaps the most

precious way to use the proceeds of
gardens and grounds was in garnering,
penny by penny, year by year, sufficient
cash to buy one's freedom, or that of
a spouse, an elderly parent, or one's own
child. For many of the enslaved, plots and
gardens became a hard-won and precarious "right," zealously and repeatedly
negotiated with plantation owners.

These dispossessed architects
valued the landscapes they designed.
Sometimes, they were compelled to
go on strike and even to rebel outright
when access to them was threatened.
One such story comes to us from the
French colonial island of Martinique,
where, after slavery ended in 1848, it
was quickly reborn in other guises, as
coerced or barely remunerated labor
on lands still retained by the former
enslavers. Greedy *habitation* (plantation)
owners set about confiscating not
just the *cases nègres* (former cabins)
of the previously enslaved but also
the adjacent yard-gardens. For many
free Black Martinicans, this was a final,
unacceptable blow, so in 1870 they
revolted against rapacious sharecropping
work contracts, public discrimination,
and lack of access to schooling for their
children. It was a short-lived uprising, in
which Lumina Sophie, a pregnant young
Black seamstress, became a formida-
ble, incandescent leader despite her
subsequent capture and imprisonment.

The gardens and plots had become
an indispensable part of sustaining self
and family. They were also the spaces
where memories of African agrarian
practices were reinterpreted under the
harshest of circumstances: Enslaved
cultivators drew on the knowledge of
the natural world, ecological and farming
practices, aesthetic traditions, and
religious beliefs of the diverse African
societies from whence they had come.
They also put to use botanical knowledge
learned from America's Indigenous
peoples and introduced African legumes,
tubers, herbs, cereals, and fruits that
also made the crossing over the Atlantic:
okra, sesame, watermelon, groundnuts,
sorghum, yams of various types,
black-eyed peas, pigeon peas, and others.

The exchanging of botanical
knowledge took place where Native
Americans and Africans were enslaved
together early on. It also happened in
quilombos, palenques, and *mocambos*
(Maroon settlements), where some of
the Africans and their descendants

boldly fled, against all odds, to inhabit a freedom that allowed them to build and defend new lives and cultures, with alternative models for self-provision and trade.

While the gardening practices of the enslaved included plants brought by European settlers to the Americas, Africans' ideas about land use and gardening were different from those of settler botany, such as that found in the slave-based agro-industries of sugar, cotton, and tobacco, which transformed islands and entire continental regions through deforestation and impoverishment of soils. The gardens of the enslaved included cropping in layers, raised mounds for tubers, and curved instead of straight, uniform rows. Multiple crops were preferred over monoculture. The green counter-landscape of the enslaved constituted a sacred, sometimes secret, geography for religious practices such as honoring ancestors, offering food to the *loa* and *orixás* (African divinities), and celebrating births. Natural medicines and kitchen herbs were also cultivated. Plant-based teas, baths, poultices, wildflowers, and sprigs from bushes were not just for physical healing but a part of rituals for spiritual sustenance.

It is not hard to imagine that rich tones of green, purple, and red in these gardens produced rare moments of solace, pleasure, or pride and provided a bit of beauty nearby. More than a few of the slave narratives recorded in the Southern United States attest to the spiritual and emotional sustenance of color and fragrance bestowed by even the smallest gardens. Indisputably, as the geographer and African landscape historian Judith Carney has argued, the gardens of the enslaved constituted "Africa's botanical legacy to the Americas," which gave rise in many societies to a delicious variety of cuisines and valuable botanical pharmacopoeia. The gardens also connected rural and urban enslaved laborers and engendered the first domestic food markets in the Caribbean and many Latin American cities. This legacy is sometimes hidden in plain sight—ephemeral but reproduced and reinterpreted century after century.

Captives in the City: Essential Workers

Viewed in its entirety, urban African

D.Blair F.L.S. ad sicc. del. et lith.   HIBISCUS ESCULENTUS, *Linn*.   M & N. Hanhart imp.

and African-descended labor was, for centuries, essential human infrastructure in many of the grandest cities of the Americas. From Baltimore to Charleston, from Rio de Janeiro to Cartagena and Lima, the world of urban enslaved and free people comprised social practices and relations, struggles and dreams, repression and mutual help, techniques and ideas, and the built environment.

Many urban enslaved people were in domestic service, toiling in physical and heartbreaking labor behind closed doors, making possible their enslavers' lives of

Okra botanical illustration, 1880. Arriving in the Americas via the Transatlantic Slave Trade, okra is an African crop with deep cultural significance. From Southern gumbo to Nigerian *akara awon*, okra links culinary traditions from communities across the African continent and the Diaspora.

leisure, fine dining, carefree child-raising, and ostentatious dressing. In some cases, at public outings, elaborately dressed enslaved men and women served as testimony to their enslavers' wealth.

A considerable number of the urban enslaved engaged in skilled occupations and in street- or market-based commerce, both of which drew a great deal on centuries of African practice. In cities, enslaved men's occupations ranged from carrying sedan chairs and hauling packages to working in sanitation. Many were carpenters, tailors, barbers, goldsmiths, tanners, wagonmakers, stonemasons, furniture makers, ritual specialists, workers in decorative iron, and builders of fine city homes and modest worker's dwellings. A few enslaved men were engineers of textile mills in Southern US cities. Some labored as sculptors whose exquisite works can still be found in some of the finest churches built in colonial Brazil, such as in the city of São Paulo, where the enslaved worker Tebas carved the foundation stone of the São Bento Monastery and designed and built the facade of Igreja das Chagas do Seráfico Pai São Francisco (Church of the Wounds of the Seraphic Father Saint Francis), and the tower of the first Catedral da Sé (See Cathedral). Enslaved women in cities across the Americas were seamstresses, dress designers, expert laundresses, herbalists, ritual specialists, midwives, hairdressers, bakers, and confectioners, though they might also have been employed in domestic service. Their work took place in multiple shifts: Many women on plantations labored in the fields by day, took care of their families in the evenings, and afterward expertly spun, wove, and sewed with wool, flax, and cotton till near dawn to clothe the enslaved and the enslavers.

Urban Scapes of the *Ganhadeiras*
Colonial Brazil provides but one example of the lives and contributions of urban enslaved Africans and Afro-descendants in the Americas. For much of Brazil's settler-colonial history, its principal cities all had substantial populations of enslaved and free Black people. They dared to live beyond the subhuman status to which they were relegated by enslavement and a globally prominent racism that, by the nineteenth century, operated under the pretense of being "scientific." These white supremacist ideas

were reinforced by the social apologetics of elite Brazilian academics such as Sílvio Romero and Raimundo Nina Rodrigues.

Salvador da Bahia was the site of the first slave market in the Americas and the first capital of Brazil, from 1549 to 1763. There, urban slaves rented or hired out by their enslavers were known variously as *escravos* or *escravas de ganho*, or *ganhadores* and *ganhadeiras*—male and female "wage-earning slaves." *Ganho* is also the term for the system of municipal regulations and surveillance that circumscribed Black people's movements and social lives. Another term for urban street vendors who crossed the Atlantic as Angolan captives is *quitandeira*. This term, still in use and economically relevant in urban Angola, derives from *quitanda*, a Kimbundu word for the portable straw mats and trays that women carry atop their heads and set down on the street while engaged in commerce.

The *ganho* system assured one essential dimension of bondage: the enslaved had to hand over the bulk of their earnings to masters and mistresses weekly, under informal verbal agreements that were often violated. The earnings in excess of the "agreed-upon" weekly amount were the means of obtaining food and lodging for those who were allowed to live away from the enslaver's town, home, or workshop. Once those payments were made, the captives put aside some of the money so painstakingly accrued.

The vast majority of the urban enslaved had few or no legal rights. Yet despite turning the bulk of their earnings over to their enslavers, they succeeded in keeping body and soul together as individuals and sometimes as families, albeit at varying levels from extreme poverty to comparative prosperity. Many such families were headed by women, who took pride in the precarious relative autonomy of street-selling. They managed to individually or collectively save a painstakingly accrued *peculium* (personal fund) with which to buy freedom for themselves and others. By the time Brazil's formal abolition of slavery occurred in 1888, more than half of the country's African and African-descended slaves had arranged their own freedom, either by self-purchase or by joining *quilombos* (Maroon settlements and communities). After abolition, Blacks who worked and sold on the city streets were still continually harassed by police; a practice finally reduced in most Brazilian cities owing to the late-twentieth-century protests of Black social movements.

Enslaved Africans and their descendants—and none more so than the *ganhadeiras*—indelibly etched a visual and sonic presence into slave society cities. Leda Martin, the Afro-Brazilian professor of literature, poet, and theorist of religious performance conceptualized *afrografia*: She posits that enslaved Black people and their descendants invented many ways to publicly manifest and transmit their knowledge, history, beliefs, identities, and aesthetics in urban spaces. And the written word was not the only way, because there were multiple forms of inscription, embodiment, and performance: Music, dance, rituals, oral recitation, symbols, images, and artifacts carried the essence of the history. In Salvador, we might extend Martins's notion to the way food was served and displayed, inside and outside, and to the traditional dress styles of some of the *ganhadeiras,* which often caught European viewers' attention.

From the simplest dress worn by the enslaved woman to the elaborate one worn by the freedwoman who had more to spend on her attire, their grace and colorful styles stand out in oil, watercolor, or sketch. The traveling French artist Jean-Baptiste Debret's 1827 watercolor from Rio de Janeiro titled *Banho de Cabellos* [sic] *bem Cheirosa* (Fragrant Hair Cream), shown here at right, shows similar contrasts in clothing in colonial and imperial Salvador. Two *ganhadeiras,* one in dress typical of enslaved women and the other in a more European style, sell their products at the doors of opposite-facing elite households. It is unclear whether these products are edible or used for hygiene and beauty. The *ganhadeiras* offer their goods to two types of customers. The first is a well-dressed white woman, just barely tipping open her latticed window. From the cool retreat of her home, she seems to delicately beckon the *ganhadeira* on the left. The second customer is a barefoot brown man, possibly a domestic servant, eagerly reaching into the tray of the *ganhadeira* on the right. She is dressed in the unique, characteristic Bahian style, which incorporated elements of African

dress that she or her female relatives and age-mates might have worn in Central or West Africa before captivity. The prominent *pano da costa* (cotton shawl), made from textiles imported directly from Africa, is gracefully slung over one shoulder; a lace-trimmed white blouse is tucked neatly into a European-style skirt; and her headscarf is made of Indian patterned textiles, which had been circulating globally, including in Africa, for many centuries before the Transatlantic Slave Trade. The *ganhadeira* on the left seems, by her dress, to be more prosperous: She is clothed in a lacy, more costly, European-style white dress and wears white pearl-like beads on her neck and ears. Each has an African style of headwear: one of the artfully tied head wraps, or ornaments of beads and flowers fastened in natural hair. However, both are barefoot, which was often a sign of bondage.

Many urban enslaved women living in wealthy white households expertly sewed the dresses that their mistresses wore. Some *ganhadeiras* made European-style garments for sale, but the profit went almost entirely into the pockets of their white enslavers, most often women. *Ganhadeiras* either made their own clothing or bought or bartered it from the many talented seamstresses in their ranks.

Hopefully, when a more complete history is revealed, it will account for the

Top
Negras Vendedoras (Market Women), Carlos Julião, ca. 1770. In urban settings like Rio de Janeiro, enslaved laborers sold a variety of professional services and goods such as textiles, fruits, and vegetables. While most of their earnings were turned over to enslavers, these laborers worked diligently to save personal funds.

presence and influence of *ganhadeiras* well beyond the confines of style and servitude, and within social and political movements for freedom, including several slave uprisings. For example, *ganhadeiras* participated in the June 1835 Revolta dos Malês (Muslim Revolt) in Salvador. Though it was aborted, the event shook Brazil's powerful slaveholders profoundly. Its shadow hung over every colonial administrative measure of Black repression that followed. The Brazilian historian João Reis analyzed in detail the profiles of the rebels who were caught, tried, imprisoned, and/or executed. He noted the prominence of Black urban workers of many professions among the defendants. Most, but not all, were male Muslims from West Africa, but there is an additional element in the defendant roster. Of the 185 people whose trial records Reis examined, 26 were women, of whom 19 were freedwomen, and almost all were *ganhadeiras* of some sort. Some of them would have, more than likely, sewn clothes for their enslavers, themselves, or both.

The two gracefully dressed *ganhadeiras* of Debret's painting represent those who sold their wares to Salvador's wealthy elites. If we consider what we see in the frame and things that may have been going on outside of it, perhaps we can perceive something more complex than the women's beauty, elegance of dress, and enticing manners. This painting shows women who were skilled laborers, who contended with the privations of slavery but did not allow themselves to abandon attention paid to personal beauty and adornment. Also, the privations did not prevent remembrance and adaptation, space-crossing, and, perhaps, the will to rebel.

Let us look at another Salvador painting by Debret, *Negresses Marchandes d'Angou* (Black Porridge Sellers). Several free Black women and a male helper are preparing porridge in huge pots. Others in the background are arriving at the space carrying fresh produce, as male customers, presumably dockworkers, and other women are eagerly lined up to buy. Those who have already purchased

their food are eating on the ground. One woman, sitting across from the other porridge sellers, appears to enjoy her own cooking while keeping a close eye on the small tomatoes and peppers that have been put out for sale on a mat. This scene bustles with movement and shows working Black people resting momentarily. If we look at it with eyes attuned to the counter-landscapes of enslaved women navigating their worlds to carve out spaces and places of resistance and freedom, we can read it as an alternative urban geography, made and remade, likely far beyond Debret's intent.

"Here, There, and Over There"

In contemporary Brazilian life, *ganhadeiras* in Bahia state, for example, may also be *pescadoras* and *marisqueiras* (women fishers and shellfishers) arriving from fishing *quilombos* who sell their catch, or those of their neighbors, in city markets. A poem by the Brazilian activist and writer Lígia Margarida Gomes de Jesus captures the lives of such women.

"*Zungueiras*, or Are They Ganhadeiras?"
Here, there, and over there
With their joyful talk, the Mamas arrive.
With much color . . . one lifts her voice and
    cries:
    Who wants to buy?
There is *mungunzá* and *lelê* . . .
There is *fungi* and *angu* . . .
Are these wage-earning women
    zungueiras or ganhadeiras?
With their babies on their backs or in
    their hearts
They *zunga* to earn a living and sustain
    their families.
Practice has a time, a lifetime
Which crossed continents and the
    Atlantic.
Yes, I am . . . a wage-earning woman,
    exploited and vilified
But . . . I keep on selling from my tray
Fried fish, coconut sweets, little cakes,
    and other delicacies.

At night, tired, she makes *fungi*
    or *angu* to satisfy her hunger
Quiets her body and falls asleep

Negresses Marchandes d'Angou, (Black Women Angú Vendors), Jean-Baptiste Debret, ca. 1834. Vendors prepare porridge for eager customers in Rio de Janeiro, Brazil. Women enslaved in urban settings had greater mobility and autonomy in their daily lives than those in rural areas. Some were even able to save money from their work and purchase freedom for themselves and their children.

dreaming of the day's toil and smiles.
The day dawns . . . wake up, *ganhadeira*,
    it is time to get moving
A *zunga* which repeats itself day after day.
Arise, *zungueira* . . . or is she
    a *ganhadeira*?
She smooths out the circle of her skirt and
    sets out gracefully to enchant the
    world with her joy.
Come, my people, buy . . . my tray has
    tapioca and *quindim*.

Lígia Margarida's poem unveils a story that deserves to be more widely known. It connects urban slavery, the skilled hands, minds, and often troubled spirits of enslaved people; the labor of enslaved and free Black women; and African material culture and economic practices reconfigured in a new space and time. They all became integral parts of many cities of the Americas. There is a bidirectional movement here: the traversing of what Brazilians sometimes call *kalunga grande* (the sea separating the land of the living from that of the dead in Kongo cosmology, and another name for the Middle Passage), implied in the poet's juxtaposition of the terms *ganhadeira* and *zungueira*. The former comes from Brazil, the latter from Angola. Like many of Salvador's majority Black population, Lígia Margarida grew up in a favela amid neighbors who were *ganhadeiras*. For her master's thesis in social development studies and management, she discussed the political action and organizing of the *ganhadeiras* and the *zungueiras*. In the Angolan language of Kimbundu, widely spoken in the capital city of Luanda (just as it was when millions of captives were shipped out from Angola to Brazil), the verb *zungu* means "to move continuously," and, by extension, to have the tenacious will to travel long distances to earn the means to sustain family. Rising early, preparing food at home, and then setting out with a distinctive, pleasing demeanor, using the voice to oscillate between melodic enticement and demanding shouts designed to capture the buyer's attention, is a lesson in Black feminist labor history. Many inhabitants of current-day Salvador and Bahia still buy from *ganhadeiras*, the prototypes for whom were the independent market women of West and Central Africa.

    The contemporary *ganhadeira* of this poem, like her enslaved and freed forebearers, sells workers the affordable, African-style foods needed to sustain hard physical labor. Her tasty porridges, such as *angu* and *mungunzá*, are made in traditional Angolan style from the maize or cassava indigenous to Brazil. They were among the American crops adapted sometime in the sixteenth century by African women living near Africa's western coast. In the poem, Lígia Margarida's *ganhadeira* eats those same dishes herself at night, at the end of a tiring day. Children are at the center of her concern; whether they go with her on her back to the streets or stay behind, they are held close only in her heart. Are they the source of the joy with which she greets the next day? Does she leave them with an older woman, part of the informal networks of solidarity first created by enslaved *ganhadeiras*? This poem speaks from the past and the present and from both sides of *kalunga grande* simultaneously.

    There is more to the history of enslaved *ganhadeiras* behind Lígia Margarida's poetry. She was the first woman head of Brazil's oldest civic organization, the *Sociedade Protetora dos Desvalidos* (SPD; Society for the Protection of the Helpless), in its nearly two centuries of existence. Founded in 1832 by a group of African and African-descended enslaved and free men, the SPD helped to secure individual and collective manumission and provided assistance to members and their families. Lígia Margarida has spent considerable time in the organization's archives reinterpreting its history to fill in some puzzling gaps. She discovered that despite the SPD's membership being all male, during the slavery era a few *ganhadeiras* were recipients of small loans from the society. This has given her a different viewpoint on the cautiously and carefully constructed lives of Black people in Salvador when it was rocked by two Bahia-based slave rebellions, both of tremendous importance to Afro-Brazilians' history of freedom struggles. The first was the 1798 Revolta dos Alfaiates (Tailors' Revolt), also known as the *Revolta dos Búzios* (Cowrie Shell Revolt), in which a cross-section of Bahia's races and classes participated, including many free and enslaved Blacks. Beyond the rebellion's demand for separation from imperial Portugal, what made the Cowrie Shell Revolt a watershed in Black history was its clarion call for the abolition of slavery and for equal rights.

Some of the SPD's founders may have witnessed this revolt in their youth.

The second rebellion was the 1835 Revolta dos Malês, in which the *ganhadeiras* participated. Margarida insists that the small group of men who founded the SPD between these two uprisings must have been profoundly influenced by these events to respond to the social demands and the increase in destitute Black women and children in their wake. A deeper purpose, she suggests, might be read into their publicly stated aims of securing the emancipation of members and protecting their widows and orphans: the securing of social rights for the enslaved. The SPD, in many ways, resembled a similar drive in the United States for mutual self-help, education, information sharing, and individual and collective socio-economic rights by Black people in the decades before and after Reconstruction. The writer Thulani Davis has called one route of this activism the "emancipation circuit."

The SPD's new strategy, inspired by the histories of enslaved and freed *ganhadeiras*, focuses on urban and rural communities, reaching out to younger women from Salvador's nearby *quilombos* and peripheral neighborhoods. Professor Regina Célia Rocha is now the second woman to head the society, and among its current projects is restoration work on the SPD's headquarters. I was honored to accompany her on a small tour of its publicly inaccessible upper floors.

The gendered shape of freedom politics under slavery in Salvador seems to have inspired not just interior decoration but something more that I can describe only as stepping onto hallowed ancestral ground. Among the *alcovas,* or small rooms, being restored are several that once served as temporary lodging for homeless enslaved and free people, *ganhadeiras* included. Other rooms were offered as longer-term shelter to elderly and irreparably injured captives summarily turned out of their enslavers' properties and dumped on the streets. These spaces of succor are not as well known as the social security payments the society gave its elderly or infirm members and their widows and orphans long before the Brazilian government had any public policy regarding such aid. The rooms

have been renamed for historically significant Afro-Brazilian women, such as the two Luizas: Luiza Mahin, who participated in the Muslim Revolt and was the mother of the famed Black Brazilian abolitionist, lawyer, and writer Luís Gama, and the late Luiza Helena de Bairros, the brilliant activist, sociologist, and former government minister.

Along the corridor, artwork and exhibit labels evoked the gamut of spiritual practices of urban Africans and their descendants in Bahia, from the Afro-diasporic religion of Candomblé to Islam. These references highlight the society's early role in providing shelter for Black adherents of religions other than Catholicism.

One small unfinished room housed an installation that had all the elements of a *mística* for *ganhadeiras*. Set up on three straw mats on the old bare wooden floor were various implements used by enslaved women working for hire. Margarida considers these items "decisive for [the women's] survival": an early sewing machine, a baker's rolling pin, tools for the heavy work of laundering, and more examples of *afrografia* suffused with enslaved women's toils and strivings toward freedom.

For me, such encounters in public city spaces are epistemic walks where one can see, feel, and have conversations about the past, because inscribed within the present are the lives of the captives of slave societies from bygone eras.

Pretas Velhas, Pretos Velhos: The Old Folks

At the center of many Afro-diasporic memories, creative practices, and religions is the ancestralization of elderly Black women and men through the *boa morte* (good death), which they achieved only after release from the toils of slavery, through rituals of respect, whether humble or elaborate. But those enslaved ancestors were and are the bearers and transmitters of knowledge. That they were people of expertise, skills, and abundant creativity rather than mere instruments of brute labor has been revealed and restated, insistently, by many scholars for more than a century now. The need to recognize these ancestors seems more urgent these days because there is a war on Black studies underway, and with it, the attempt to

Women from the *Irmandade de Nossa Senhora da Boa Morte*, the Sisterhood of Our Lady of the Good Death, lead a religious procession, 1983. Formed in the early nineteenth century as a religious society for enslaved and formerly enslaved women, the order of *Boa Morte* celebrates the liberation of enslaved ancestors through prayer and special ceremonies.

dehumanize those who endured chattel slavery and their millions of descendants.

How can we find more pathways to bring to light what the enslaved knew, both before their arrival at places of subjugation and as they reconfigured that knowledge to survive in new environments? One way might be to resignify the gardens and grounds, the urban streets and workplaces, the connections between the enslaved across these different geographies, and even the imaginaries and spirits traversing them that were such a critical part of the domestic world making of the enslaved. They tenaciously made do under extreme duress. They insistently created utilitarian objects of great beauty, just as they shaped their spaces of refuge and solace, which were often ephemeral and even stolen or destroyed. That Black world making could constitute an alternative genealogy for landscape architecture and urban design, for the social networks connecting Black geographies and territories, and for the social networks and economic practices of African and Afro-diasporic women and men was the manifestation of a hard-won, gendered Afro-diasporic futurity purposefully inscribed on the land, against all odds.

PAÁNZA: SEEDS OF MEMORY

Johanna Obenda

In the 2019 documentary *Stones Have Laws*, women from the Saramaka Maroon community harvest rice while singing about a founding member named Paánza:

> Foremother Paánza, Ma Paánza brought rice seeds to feed her people. Did she bring her wisdom from Africa?

The Saramaka of Suriname are among the hundreds of Maroon communities that were established as spaces of freedom by people who fled slavery. Maroons faced the challenge of creating new cultures with unique languages and traditions that blended their various African backgrounds with their new environments. Many of these communities persisted for generations, and some, like the Saramaka, continue into the present day. The Saramaka cite their ancestor Paánza as the person who brought them seed rice, planting a harvest that would sustain their community for centuries.

Likely the daughter of an enslaved African mother and a European plantation owner, Paánza was part of the earliest generation of enslaved people born in Suriname. Founded a few decades before her birth, Suriname was established in 1651 by the British and became a Dutch colony in 1671. The colony was a safe haven for persecuted religious groups from Europe, welcoming Huguenot, Jewish, and Protestant refugees. It was also a prolific site of slavery, with estimates placing the number of African captives brought to Suriname at around 300,000. Early in the colony's history, a group of Sephardic Jewish planters fled the Catholic Inquisition in Brazil and established plantations in the Upper Suriname River region. It was here where Paánza lived and worked.

Some oral traditions recount that in the 1730s, Paánza was approached by a Maroon leader while working on the plantation. Emerging from the forest, he beckoned Paánza to follow him. She made the daring decision to flee the plantation and join the rebels living in the rainforest that covered more than 90 percent of the colony. Before making her escape, Paánza hid several grains of rice in her hair. Upon her arrival in the forest, she planted this variety to the Saramaka. With its bounty, the Saramaka were able to feed their community

Left
Surinamese wooden comb with scorpion handle, nineteenth century. From concealing grains to expressing identity, hair held significance in the lives of Maroons and enslaved people. Today, hair remains a source of ancestral connection and immense pride for Black communities across the Atlantic.

Top
Matawai women and baby, ca. 1972. The women and infant in this photograph are Matawai, a Surinamese people who trace their origins to Africans who escaped slavery. Around the world, escapees, or Maroons, created independent communities, merging their various African backgrounds to create languages, traditions, and political structures in new environments.

and sustain themselves in a century-long war for liberation from the Dutch. Paánza's actions reverberate today in oral tradition and in the varieties of rice still used by the Saramaka that bear her name.

Paánza's story signifies the importance of rice for the survival of Surinamese Maroons and also points to the sharing of a foundational narrative by different Maroon groups. From northeastern Brazil to coastal South Carolina, descendant communities hold a common memory about a woman from Africa bringing rice to the Americas by hiding it in her hair. These stories diverge from the dominant narrative about rice in the Americas, which centers the grain as a commercial export product, in the domain of European planters.

Recent scholarship has turned its attention to actions of the enslaved—particularly enslaved women—in the arrival and cultivation of rice in colonial America. Historian Judith Carney argues that Maroon communities' memories

of African ancestors bringing rice to the Americas align with several key historical facts. As the Transatlantic Slave Trade grew, more food was needed to sustain traders and captives alike. Rice, a staple of many West African societies, became prominent in this transatlantic economy. As noted in archival records and accounts, Europeans purchased large quantities of a husked variety of African rice for provisions. On slaving vessels, African women were put to work preparing the husked rice for consumption. They would have had direct access to rice seeds, as would women on the other side of the Atlantic who were forced to tirelessly labor on rice plantations. Like Paánza, these women may have concealed seeds to be planted later.

Exactly who introduced rice to Suriname, and to other rice-growing regions of the Americas, is a contested topic. The grain's arrival includes several historical pathways, following its varied use as a commercial, subsistence, and ceremonial crop. What is certain is that African expertise played a central role in its production and cultivation. Slave traders and plantation owners targeted laborers from rice-producing regions of Africa for their specialized knowledge and skill, and in turn, African knowledge of rice-field engineering and cultivation contributed to rice's emergence as one of the largest commercial crops in the world. The significance of rice in the Americas is not limited to its economic value, however.

Beyond the plantation, rice sustained an entire way of life, influencing arts, religion, and language. By growing rice for sustenance and ritual, enslaved and liberated peoples ensured that African preferences and tastes lived on in new, unfamiliar landscapes. Today, descendants continue to uphold rice as a source of survival, and center African women, like Paánza, as the cultivators of their communities.

TÒYA: DRUMBEATS OF REVOLUTION

Sherri V. Cummings

In the ink-black slumber of night, the sudden, sharp tone of the conch shell could be heard far and wide, calling battle-worn revolutionaries to the designated gathering place. Under a large cottonwood tree, the drummers sat waiting. The lead drummer surveyed the weary faces of the group, his fingers caressing the smooth goatskin of his drum. At the right moment, he began beating a rhythmic pulse, low and deep. The invocation of the Vodou lwa had begun.

The women made their way to the center of the clearing. Many of them possessed spiritual and medicinal knowledge, as well as entrepreneurial and military acumen rivaling that of the men they supported and fought alongside.

There are many accounts of the Haitian Revolution that detail the feats of men. However, contrary to the male-centered historiography of the most successful insurrection by the formerly enslaved, in the late eighteenth and early nineteenth centuries, many of the revolutionaries who fought for freedom were enslaved and free women. Their myriad skills exhibited during the revolution reflected their abilities passed down for centuries in their homelands before being adapted to the new realities of the Americas. Despite this, their role has been diminished in the archive and many details of their histories remain unknown. Today, public historians and descendant communities are working to highlight the women of the revolution, piecing together elements of their lives from written and oral records. This work, at once an act of historical reclamation and productive speculation, has brought the actions of several people to the forefront.

Victoria Montou, also referred to as Tòya, is one of these women. Many details of Tòya's life remain unclear, and at times are contested. It's likely that she was born during the early 1700s, a time of dynamic change in both West Africa and the French colony of Saint-Domingue, where she was enslaved. While little is known about her upbringing, some narratives describe Tòya as an African-born woman who was recruited into an elite group of warrior women to defend the ruler of the Kingdom of Dahomey, now present-day Benin. After completing extraordinary tasks that challenged her physical dexterity, Tòya is said to have worked her way up the ranks to become an *adbaraya*—a general. As an *adbaraya*, Tòya would have been required to master the art of healing, as well as to balance

Left
Haitian Vodou drum, twentieth century. This drum is part of a Rada Battalion, which typically consists of three drums. Crafted by a Haitian religious society, the painted figures on this Rada drum may represent the *Marassa*, divine twins associated with the physical and spiritual worlds. In the Vodou tradition, Rada drums hold esteemed status in ceremonies.

Top
Marie Jeanne Lamartiniere, Patricia Brintle, 2012. Most of the women who fought in the Haitian Revolution remain anonymous. Few, like the woman here, have been named in the historical record. This painting depicts Marie Jeanne, a revolutionary who served in the major Battle of Crête-à-Pierrot.

the temporal and spiritual worlds grounded in the traditional custom of Vodou, practiced by the Aja, Ewe, and Fon of West Africa. Like thousands of Africans before her, Tòya was captured and taken to the French island of Saint-Domingue, where she is believed to have been purchased by Henri Duclos and brought to his estate located on the northern coast. Her name was changed to Victoria, a gesture emphasizing her propertied status and erasing her African identity.

Tòya is revered in popular memory for her strength and leadership, and particularly for the relationship she formed with a young Jean-Jacques Dessalines. The story goes that on the plantation, Tòya befriended a fellow enslaved woman who was heavy with child. Despite their language differences, the two found a way to communicate. When the woman suddenly went into labor, Tòya remained by her side. After the difficult birth, the woman handed the newborn to her friend, pleading with her last breath for Tòya to raise her son as a warrior. Grief-stricken, Tòya vowed to keep her promise. Thus it was that Jean-Jacques Dessalines grew up in the nurturing bosom of his tante—his aunt. Despite their often being separated on the plantation, Tòya taught him the principles of Vodun, the art of combat, and how to use various medicinal plants and herbs. She also instilled in her young charge the importance of radical disobedience, having organized and participated in several insurrections herself. Hence, when the revolution called for his leadership, Dessalines would be prepared for the prodigious task. That time came in August 1791 during the Bois Caïman Vodou ceremony, when, under the cover of night, attendees, both enslaved and free, made a pact to fight for liberation.

Dessalines first fought at the revolution's inception under the command of Jean-François Papillon, a Maroon who had liberated himself years before the start of the revolution. While fighting on the side of the Spanish against French forces in Santo Domingo, Dessalines became friends with and fought alongside another rising commander, Toussaint Bréda, later known as Toussaint Louverture. All the while, women participated in battles, provided food and medical care, and procured what the forces needed. In 1802, Dessalines assumed control of the revolution after the dubious arrest of Louverture by the French. Like a Vodou priestess or the sacred drum in the hands of a skillful player, Tòya opened the gateway for Dessalines to lead while she and other remarkable women fought valiantly for freedom. Napoleon's army was finally defeated in the Battle of Vertières in November 1803, the last battle of the revolution.

Adbaraya Tòya fought fiercely but was severely wounded. Nevertheless, it's believed that she lived to see Dessalines proclaim Haiti the first free Black republic in the Americas, on January 1, 1804. The following year, Adbaraya Tòya joined the ancestors. In Haitian memory, she is forever memorialized as the guiding figure who prepared the liberator Jean-Jacques Dessalines, and many others, for revolution.

JAN: NOTES FROM A HEALER

Shanaaz Galant

For more than two hundred years, enslaved people worked as farmers, seamen, and domestic laborers on the Cape Colony, at the southernmost tip of Africa, alongside the Indigenous Khoi and San people. From the late seventeenth to the early nineteenth century, more than sixty thousand enslaved people were brought to the Cape, initially from West Africa and then from locations including South Asia, Madagascar, Mozambique, and parts of East Africa.

The Cape Colony was a Dutch and later British possession. The Dutch East India Company / Vereenigde Oost-Indische Compagnie in Dutch, or VOC—established slavery there. In 1679, the VOC's Slave Lodge was founded. This was where enslaved men, women, and children, so-called company slaves, were brought and held in prisonlike conditions from 1679 to 1811. One of those enslaved children was Jan Smiesing. Jan (also known as Johannes) was born in 1697 in the Slave Lodge to an enslaved

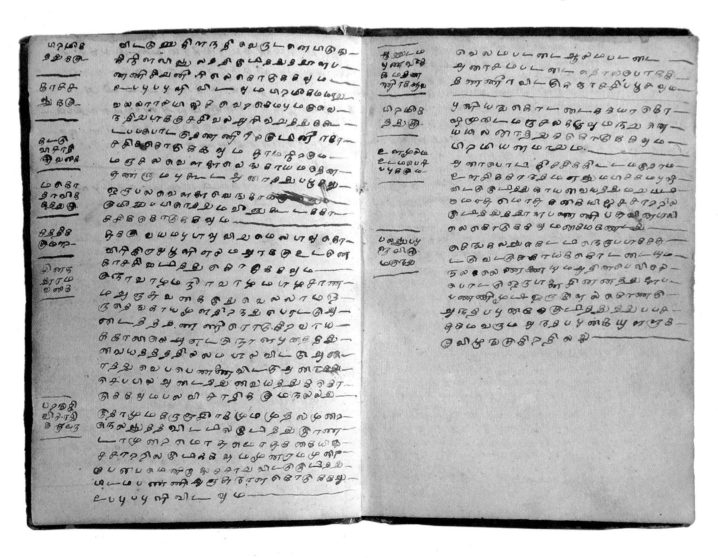

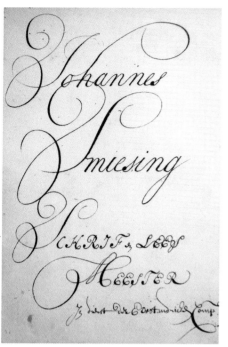

woman named Manda Gratia and Jan Smiesing, a VOC employee. He attended a school for enslaved boys and girls at the lodge. Jan's mother was a matron and schoolmistress at the lodge, like her mother, Armozijn Claasz, before her. Jan became a teacher there when he was just seventeen years old and was, later, the headmaster. In 1731, he was manumitted, yet he chose to remain, as a teacher and healer, until his death in 1734, at age 37. Between 1717 and 1732, he kept a personal journal, where he recorded his observations and drawings in Tamil, as well as Ayurvedic remedies.

The Slave Lodge held more than four hundred people at a time. Jan witnessed its daily operations. The adults worked more than twelve hours a day. Each night, the lodge opened its doors to free men (burghers, sailors, and soldiers) who raped and sexually assaulted the enslaved and Indigenous Khoi and San women living there. Needless to say, there were many ailing bodies requiring healing and rest. Jan's notebook reveals treatments and remedies for a wide range of conditions, from fevers to backaches, toothaches, headaches, and venereal diseases. Deadly physical realities and substandard living conditions contributed to many illnesses. However, enslavers provided limited, if any, treatment. Healers like Jan Smiesing used traditional African and Asian knowledges, exchanged information with Indigenous peoples, and formed

networks to pass their expertise to new generations. Treating fellow enslaved people was a revolutionary act that restored bodily autonomy stripped away by enslavement.

Through the oral tradition, researchers learned that the enslaved taught each other during the workday, and many lessons were drawn and written on the ground in the sand. This history is a powerful example of medical learning and early literacy among the enslaved population in the Cape Colony. This is a testament to the agency of free Blacks and the enslaved and highlights their pivotal role in building and maintaining what is now Cape Town.

Jan Smiesing's life and work are worth remembering and reclaiming because he brought humanity into an inhumane space. As revealed in his journal and other historical sources, Jan's life as a teacher, headmaster, and healer is inseparable from the lives of the enslaved across the entire Cape of Good Hope, where people sought ways to survive the brutality of slavery. The space where the former hospital for the enslaved was located has been renamed the Jan Smiesing Room. The Slave Lodge has been reclaimed and renamed the Iziko Slave Lodge Museum. It is dedicated to telling tales of human wrongs and rights, including the long history of slavery and racism and their legacies in South Africa.

ROSA ORDERED TO BE FLOGGED;

Berbice, 1825.

W. H..ney, d l. S. M. Slader, sculp.

ROOSJE: A MOTHER'S TESTIMONY

Candra Flanagan

An empty cradle: a haunting reminder of the daily terror of brutality and forced labor, the fierce protection of a mother, the circling of a community, and the strength to speak out.

Roosje lived in the Dutch colony of Berbice in what is now Guyana, South America. Her life symbolizes the courage of enslaved women and others in navigating systems of violence and injustice. Forced to work when heavily pregnant, Roosje and her sisters in bondage endured grueling conditions that threatened their bodies and the lives of their unborn children. In 1819, she was sent to pick the plantation's coffee crop, and she and other women on the plantation were punished for falling short of their daily quota. The plantation manager ordered that the women were to be flogged by Zondag, the enslaved driver, "until the blood starts." Roosje "received 12 strikes on her bottom, some missed and went on her loins," as her husband, George, later testified in the Court of Criminal Justice of Berbice. Bloodied and in pain, she was forced to continue to work. In the following hours, she gave birth to a child that her sister described as swollen, bruised, and broken. When the baby died, the midwife and George buried it.

Roosje, like other African-descended women in Berbice, turned to the court system to seek justice through a formal complaint against the plantation manager for beating her and, ultimately, killing her child. The Dutch colonial system was unusual because it allowed the enslaved to bring cases to court. Roosje's husband, sister, and midwife displayed significant courage when they testified about the violent treatment she had suffered. While the court pronounced the plantation manager's treatment of Roosje to be "inhuman and unwarrantable conduct," it fined him a nominal fee. Roosje's horrifying experience and case received significant attention in the international abolition movement as a miscarriage of justice and an example of the inhumane treatment of enslaved people, especially women.

Like Roosje, millions of women of African descent were doubly commodified: valued for the products of their hard labor and for the potential children they could bear over their lifetime. Historians Camillia Cowling and Sasha Turner have argued that enslaved women and their bodies were central to struggles for abolition. Enslaved women were not passive in the debates but rather claimed authority over their bodies. A large percentage of the claims brought by enslaved people to the courts, especially those in the Dutch legal system, were from women who were fighting for protection of their own bodies, their reproduction, and, subsequently, the lives of their children.

The journey to motherhood for enslaved women of African descent was navigated under the shadow of forced procreation and routine incidences of physical, psychological, and sexual abuse, all of which were normalized by practice and law. Racism and efforts to deny humanity added to this shadow in which Roosje and other enslaved women had to live, and its legacies include inadequate and biased medical care for women of color, which remains a problem today. Researchers have found evidence that racism is linked to higher levels of stress and worse health outcomes for people of color. The impact of this generational stress is reflected in the contemporary experiences of Black women and rising infant mortality rates for people of color.

According to a 2022 report from the US Centers for Disease Control and Prevention, Black infants are 2.4 times more likely than white infants to die within a year of birth, and Black mothers are 3 to 4 times more likely than white mothers to die of pregnancy-related complications. The World Health Organization states that maternal mortality in sub-Saharan Africa accounts for 70 percent of the world's cases. These statistics are stark reminders of the continuing reverberations of slavery and colonialism.

Black women's struggle for control over their own bodies is an aspect of ongoing freedom-making practices in this century. For example, Black Maternal Health Week is recognized each April in the United States to bring awareness to the precarious road that Black mothers travel to deliver healthy, precious children. Roosje's story reminds us that, over many centuries, Black women have been speaking up to protect their bodies and the bodies of their children, combating the twin legacies of slavery and colonialism with struggles for justice, protection, and recognition of their humanity in the courts and in their everyday lives.

WILLIAM: SAILOR AGAINST SLAVERY

Marcus Rediker

Colored Sailors Home, 1839. The African American abolitionist William P. Powell Sr. founded the Colored Sailors Home in New York City. The boarding house provided Black seafarers with food, clothing, and shelter, and served as a refuge for people who had escaped from slavery in the Southern United States.

Bottom
The Port of Liverpool, nineteenth century. William and Mercy Powell found work and opportunities in Liverpool. The bustling port had grown in the eighteenth century as the United Kingdom's slave-trading capital, building ships that carried more than 1.5 million African captives. When the Powells arrived in the 1850s, the city had ongoing ties to slavery but was also home to antislavery activists.

William P. Powell Sr. was an activist and organizer in the transatlantic antislavery movement from the early 1830s through the outbreak of the American Civil War in 1861. He was a man of the waterfront: a sailor by training, a builder of new maritime institutions, and a strategic thinker within the abolitionist movement. He studied "history from below," from the perspective of common, working people. He made history the same way, working with other sailors and waterfront laborers.

Born in 1807 to an enslaved African American father, Edward Powell, and a Native American mother whose name is unknown, he married Mercy O. Haskins, a ninth-generation Abenaki woman from New England. William respected his Afro-Indigenous origins while identifying as Black. One of his historical heroes was Crispus Attucks, the half Black, half Natick Indian man who led the rebelling Boston crowd into the streets to battle British soldiers in 1770, and who, for his daring, became the first martyr of the American Revolution during the Boston Massacre.

William went to sea from New Bedford, Massachusetts, in 1827, sailing around the world on merchant and whaling vessels. This was the formative experience of his life. He imbibed and embraced two of the central values of deep-sea sailors: The dangers of work at sea generated an ethic of solidarity in him, and his travels with a motley crew of shipmates gave him a cosmopolitan view of the world. Throughout his life, William promoted solidarity at sea, both among sailors, especially Black sailors, and between sailors and enslaved people seeking freedom. He would envision and wage the struggle against slavery beyond national boundaries, from New York to the Caribbean, Brazil, Liverpool, and beyond.

After he married Mercy in 1832, he left the sea but did not leave behind the seafaring life. The Powells opened a Colored Sailors Home in New Bedford to minister to the needs of his ocean-going brother "tars," slang for sailors. When recruited by the American Seamen's Friend Society, a Methodist missionary group, to open a bigger boarding house in New York in 1839, he jumped at the opportunity. William slowly built a new institution that was one part boarding house, one part union hall, and one part depot for people who had arrived in the port city seeking freedom. He fought off those he called "land sharks," the crimps and hustlers who preyed upon sailors in port. William distributed the sailors' pay to family members and savings accounts and got sailors jobs on ships that offered good wages and working conditions. The Colored Sailors Home in New York was a site of profound mutual aid and empowerment.

William slowly transformed the boarding house into a new, highly effective kind of abolitionist organization. Using Black sailors and their strategic knowledge of Southern ports, he took hundreds of fugitives into the Colored Sailors Home, where he fed and clothed them, tended to their health, and helped them to reach other free destinations, often by ship, all free of charge. In 1851, after the passage of the Fugitive Slave Act in the United States that threatened all free Black people with enslavement in Southern states, William moved to Liverpool, but continued helping freedom seekers. He assisted as many as 1,500 people to freedom over the course of his lifetime.

History was a significant part of William's thinking. He was keenly aware that African Americans had contributed much to American history—in the American Revolution and the War of 1812, for example—and that their heroic actions had been left out of the history books. He added to the missing history to bolster claims for Black citizenship. He demonstrated his understanding of history from below as he prepared to leave for Liverpool, writing a request to the New York government to pay his family's way as a form of reparations. He explained that his grandmother, Elizabeth Barjona, had been the cook who fed the founding fathers when they wrote the Declaration of Independence in 1776. Her labor had helped to create the new nation.

Combining the struggle against slavery with advocacy on behalf of Black seamen, William linked the themes of race, class, labor, and freedom across the Atlantic as he promoted maritime solidarity in the broadest sense. He demonstrated that the oceans of the world could be a place of freedom. One important outcome of his work was the establishment of the American Seamen's Protective Union Association—one of the first trade unions in US history—at the Colored Sailors Home in March 1863. Its origins lay in the Atlantic maritime circuits of solidarity and resistance.

REBELLION AT SEA

Kate McMahon

On the humid night of July 1, 1839, fifty-three enslaved Africans revolted aboard the ironically named slaving schooner *La Amistad (The Friendship)* while they were being shipped to a plantation in Puerto Príncipe (now Camagüey), Cuba. Originally kidnapped and trafficked from modern-day Sierra Leone to Havana on a larger vessel, they were transferred to the smaller *La Amistad* to reach their final destination. A captive named Sengbe led the rebels—who suffered ten fatalities in the fray but managed to kill the captain— Ramón Ferrer, and take control of the ship. They ordered the surviving crew to return them to their home in Mende country. The crew instead secretly sailed the vessel north, where it was captured in the Long Island Sound, in New York. The rebels were detained and charged with mutiny and murder. The determination to win their freedom led Sengbe and the other Amistad captives, with the support of American abolitionists, to take their fight to the US Supreme Court in February 1841. The fate of the rebels would be decided by the country's legal system. The defense team hired famous lawyer John Quincy Adams, a former American president. Adams made the argument that whatever the status of *La Amistad*, these people deserved their freedom based on the natural rights with which they were born. The majority of justices on the high court were enslavers themselves or proslavery.

Nevertheless, they voted seven to one to free the captives.

Seventeen of the rebels had died at sea or in prison while awaiting trial, but thirty-five returned to Sierra Leone.

The case of the Amistad captured the world's attention in the 1840s, provoking moral, legal, and ethical questions for people in the United States and internationally. Were the rebels "slaves and murderers" because they killed members of the crew, or were they free people and heroes who had liberated themselves from the violence of an unjust and immoral system?

A remarkable set of twenty-three pencil-drawn portraits of the Amistad rebels sketched as they awaited trial in New Haven has helped people then and now find conclusive answers to these questions. Created by the Connecticut artist William H. Townsend, the drawings provided a rare glimpse into the humanity of these individuals at a moment when they publicly claimed their right to live free. Portraits of enslaved Africans were rare in the nineteenth century because these people were often viewed as property—or as stereotypical brutes, loyal servants, or helpless victims. Townsend's intimate portraits contrast with the visual culture of slavery. His study of Fuli, one of several captives who had stolen water on board the vessel and was ordered to be flogged shows a fullyhuman individual. Fuli gazes at the viewer with a solemn, self-possessed air.

Bottom
Broadside illustrating the *Amistad* rebellion, ca. 1840. While being transported from Havana to a plantation in central Cuba, fifty-three African captives aboard the Spanish slave ship *La Amistad* revolted with hopes of returning to West Africa. Their actions and subsequent trial sparked international debate around matters of sovereignty and abolition.

Right,
following page
Portrait of Fuli, ca. 1840. After *La Amistad* was seized off the coast of New York, the rebels on board were captured and imprisoned on charges of murder and piracy. This portrait of *La Amistad* captive Fuli is one of several sketches made by the eighteen-year-old William Townsend while the rebels awaited trial in New Haven, Connecticut.

Right
Portrait of Margru, ca. 1840. Margru, also known as Marqu or Sarah, was one of few children aboard *La Amistad*. After the Supreme Court ruled in their favor, the rebels worked with American missionaries to fund their trip home. Margru was the only captive who returned to the United States, attending Oberlin Collegiate Institute (later Oberlin College) in 1846.

Margru (or Marqu) was one of the three young girls aboard *La Amistad*. Showing us her youth and personality, she gently smiles, despite living through what must have been an extremely traumatic experience both on the ship and in prison awaiting trial. Townsend highlights the individuality and dignity of each person while providing a sense of their collective determination to be agents in their own liberation. In Sengbe's words, "Brothers, we have done that which we purposed... I am resolved it is better to die than to be a white man's slave."

La Amistad rebels were part of the long, broad history of the fight for full freedom. Captive Africans are recorded to have revolted or attempted to revolt during one in every ten of the thousands of slaving journeys across the four-hundred-year history of the trade. These portraits—like the testimony in court and the revolt on board *La Amistad*—bring this massive story to a human scale, providing tangible evidence of these individuals' humanity, resistance, and bravery while reminding us that this landmark case was just one demonstration of many millions of souls yearning for freedom and sovereignty over their own lives. Their visages call upon present and future generations to collectively remember not just the horrors that the slave trade inflicted but also the power of individual dignity and collective resistance amid inhumanity. They light the darkness both in the 1840s and in our world today.

Juli

Fuliwa, 9.

"TESTIMONY"

Kevin Young

You call us rebels we were spoons
in that ship for so long the wood
dark, drowned as the men who
made it from song sold on land
like ships like us christened
out of water You call us rebels
we were thrown with schools of fish
in the stomach of that ship we slept
with the dead which is not at all
You call us rebels one day we took
the wheel from men with eyes of
water we turned the ship towards
the rising sun let the wind grace
our backs that night we slept like
anchors that night the sailors
turned us towards a Newborn
England in dawn we saw blessèd
land then felt the sun's heat
betraying our backs too late
we saw the sunless men their navy
racing to rescue us into chains
now we know the edge of setting
sun where only the dead are free
to come and go as you please

RECLAMA-TIONS

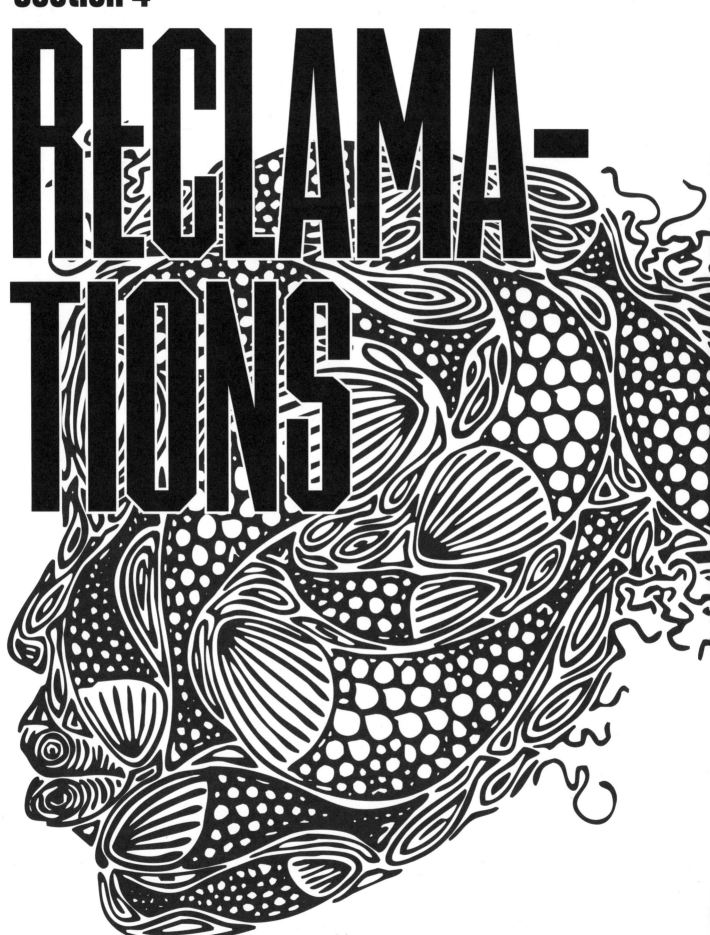

Black revolutionaries and abolitionists envisioned the end of racial slavery as a step toward fuller freedom and rights. However, even as Black freedom fighters across the Atlantic world secured the legal end of slavery in the mid to late nineteenth century, their rights and dignity remained threatened. By the beginning of the twentieth century, the structures and practices of imperialism, racism, resource extraction, conquest, and economic consolidation through monopolies, all birthed by the initial collision of racial slavery and colonialism, were reformulated across the globe through a rapid reorganization of political boundaries, landscapes, and people that was far from the promise of emancipation. New economic, political, and social systems were created or adapted to uphold old practices of subjugation and exploitation. All were set in place using physical and systemic violence and racism.

In the late nineteenth and early twentieth centuries, recently emancipated people were trapped in indentured servitude and poverty and locked into similar working and living conditions as those experienced during racial slavery, often on the sites where they had been enslaved. In many colonies and nations of the Caribbean, as well as in South America, slavery was replaced by apprenticeship or forced labor systems that required former slaves to work on plantations for several years without pay. Colonial laws prevented newly emancipated people from migrating to other islands in the Caribbean, leaving few options beyond plantation work even after the end of slavery and apprenticeships. New groups of laborers were targeted to replace enslaved Africans following the abolition of racial slavery, leading to the large-scale immigration of Chinese and Indian laborers who were brought to the Americas to work on plantations, mines, and railroad construction.

Across the Atlantic, people of African descent faced not only limited economic opportunity and social support but also terror and legalized racial segregation. New laws were rewritten over old Black Codes in various geographies, intent on upholding racial hierarchies and limiting the physical and socioeconomic movement of the formerly enslaved. For example, broad vagrancy laws criminalized unemployment, allowing authorities to arrest emancipated people for minor infractions, trapping Black communities in an unending cycle of fines and imprisonment. Under these laws in the United States, Brazil, and elsewhere, prison populations grew significantly, and predatory systems like convict leasing ensured that a large, unpaid Black labor force was readily available for working on private and public projects. Practices such as legalized racial segregation through Jim Crow laws in the United States and apartheid in South Africa, as well as other less formal but still virulent racist practices, further oppressed Black communities, thereby weaving discrimination and racism in the very fabric of post-emancipatory societies. In many ways, the anti-Black violence that developed across the arc of the twentieth century can be understood as a backlash to the end of slavery and demands for Black freedom.

The formal end of racial slavery must be viewed together with the industrialization of Europe and the rise of colonialism on the African continent. The profits and products of racial slavery spurred the European Industrial Revolution from the mid-1700s to the mid-1800s. European economies that had been based on agriculture were transformed into economies based on large-scale industry, mechanized manufacturing, and the factory system. As racial slavery was being legally abolished across the Atlantic, European industrialization was increasing. New, greater-scale industrialization created a huge demand for raw materials from Africa and Asia. For example, West African palm oil was used as a lubricant for the engines of the Industrial Revolution and replaced animal fats in products such as candles and soaps. European manufacturers, dependent on African oils, rubber, and minerals, looked to cut out African producers and extract resources directly from the continent. This led to new waves of colonialism, which expanded upon old systems of power and trade relationships, blurring boundaries between what had been slavery and what was now deemed "freedom."

The demographic and economic devastation inflicted by the centuries-long slave trade, paired with the technological advancements of the Industrial Revolution, set the stage for mass colonial expansion into the African continent in the late nineteenth

century. In 1884–85, at a conference in Berlin, the major European powers negotiated the partitioning of the interior of the African continent amongst themselves, formalizing claims to territories. European control of Africa grew from 10 percent in 1870 to 90 percent in 1914. European powers displaced African people from their lands and forced them to work in colonial farms, mines, and infrastructure projects. In spaces like colonial French Senegal and the colonial Belgian Congo, the Transatlantic Slave Trade was replaced with new predatory commercial exploits, such as the large-scale trade in peanuts and palm oil. Diamond and gold mines were established across the continent, further scarring the earth and harming people coerced to labor in the dangerous operations for colonial profit. On the Western Cape of South Africa, "Coloured" laborers were entrapped on vineyards, working the same fields as their enslaved ancestors and subjected to similar working conditions as people

who had lived under racial slavery. As the sociologist W.E.B. Du Bois explained, "The abolition of American slavery started the transportation of capital from white to black countries where slavery prevailed.... When raw material could not be raised in a country like the United States, it could be raised in the tropics and semi-tropics under a dictatorship of industry, commerce and manufacture."

Life for African people during this new era of colonization was marked by violence, authoritarianism, and discrimination. Along with partitioning the continent, European colonists imported ideas of cultural superiority and developed systems of governance to impose their will on the religious, political, and cultural sectors of African life. Western bureaucratic and educational systems were put in place to control the local populaces and replace Indigenous beliefs with ways of life deemed to be more civilized. And yet, people refused to be dehumanized and resisted colonialism. African societies

Top
Juvenile convict workers, ca. 1903. In the Americas, harsh legal codes limited the mobility of recently emancipated people. Under these laws, prison populations grew significantly, allowing for the creation of profitable convict-leasing programs, through which inmates were leased out as unpaid laborers for public and private projects.

Sunlight soap factory, near Liverpool, United Kingdom, ca. 1897. European demand for West African palm oil grew as it became essential as a machine lubricant and an ingredient in products such as soap. Bypassing African producers, British manufacturers established plantations in Central Africa to extract the raw material, which was later processed in European factories.

Rwandan workers at a copper mine in Katanga, Belgian Congo, late 1920s. In the early twentieth century, the Belgian company Union Minière du Haut-Katanga began commercial mining in colonial Africa. Operating in the copper belt of what is now Democratic Republic of Congo, Union Minière forcibly recruited local workers, who were subject to mistreatment and mining-related illnesses.

sought liberation and independence from European rule. Leaders, prophets, and everyday people led armed uprisings to topple colonial governments, from the Maji Maji rebellion against German officials in modern-day Tanzania, to the Pende revolt in Congo. People organized themselves, striking on railways and in ports across the continent, forming political parties, and setting the stage for the wave of decolonization in the 1960s and 1970s.

Worldwide, communities in post-emancipatory society continued to combat the violent practices developed centuries earlier. The plantation model spread beyond former slave societies in the Americas into rubber plantations in Central Africa, tea plantations in India, and sugar plantations in the Pacific, continuing its legacy of forced labor and ecological devastation. The mistreatment of people based on race continued as well. The threat of racial violence shadowed life for communities across the Atlantic, from the genocide of millions of Congolese people at the hands of King Leopold II of Belgium, to the thousands of lynchings of African Americans. In 1919, a wave of race-based attacks occurred in several cities across the North Atlantic, including Liverpool, England; Glasgow, Scotland; Chicago, Illinois; and Washington, DC, in the United States. The echoes of those outbreaks of white supremacist violence in our world today, from Charleston to Rio de Janeiro to Paris, reveal racism as an enduring structure, one of the most resilient and intractable legacies of slavery and colonialism.

Despite this ongoing violence, the evolving global landscape of the twentieth century was also changed by a symphony of global liberation movements, harmonizing with and resonating through each other. These movements fused spiritual, artistic, and political practice. They ranged from the intellectual debates of the Pan-African Congresses and the Universal Negro Improvement Association to the spiritual resistance embodied by Simon Kimbangu and his growing Kimbanguist movement in defiance of colonialism in Central Africa. They encompassed the vibrant cultural politics of Négritude and embraced unapologetic existential calls to action embedded in the Black Power and Black Consciousness movements. Black

freedom fighters from across the world called for the end of European control in Africa and the racism and segregation faced by Black people in the Americas and Europe, confronting ongoing systems of injustice and imagining freer futures. In 1960, seventeen African nations declared and won their independence, built upon movements that extended back for decades. From Accra to Brazzaville and Kinshasa to Harlem, from Marcus and Amy Ashwood Garvey to Aimé and Suzanne Césaire, Amílcar Cabral to Abdias do Nascimento, Ida B. Wells to Claudia Jones, and Angela Davis to Graça Machel, global Africans redefined politics, identity, and history on their own terms. Periodicals such as *Présence Africaine, Drum magazine,* and the *Black World* and international gatherings from the World Festival of Negro Arts to the Sixth Pan-African Congress (6PAC) joined with direct labor and political actions and active resistance to help this community both imagine and recognize itself in solidarity as a global majority while striving for independence nationally. Together, these movements composed a powerful anthem for freedom and equality, whose echoes resonate in the twenty-first century, inspiring new generations to create a new set of trajectories toward fuller freedom and justice.

Independence demonstration, Saint-Louis, Senegal, ca. 1947. Throughout the colonial era, Africans resisted European rule with armed uprisings, strikes, protests, artistic expression, and political organizing. In this photograph, protestors in the French colonial capital of Saint-Louis, Senegal, gather for an anti-colonial demonstration.

BLACK FREEDOM MAKING BEFORE AND AFTER EMANCIPATION

Minkah Makalani

n October 6, 1969, a twenty-five-year-old Angela Davis entered Royce Hall at the University of California, Los Angeles, to deliver her first lecture as an acting assistant professor of philosophy. That summer, she had been fired for being a member of the Communist Party by the University of California Board of Regents, under the direction of then-governor Ronald Reagan. Ultimately, the California superior court ruled that the Board of Regents could not fire Davis for her political affiliations or ideas, clearing the way for her to teach that fall.

More than 2,000 students, professors, and activists packed the auditorium to hear Davis, who had emerged as a radical intellectual of global importance. Certainly, Davis's training as a philosopher warranted such interest. She had studied at the Institut für Sozialfoschung (Institute for Social Research) at Goethe-Universität Frankfurt in Frankfurt, Germany, and would eventually earn her PhD from the Humboldt University of Berlin, where such figures as G.W.F. Hegel, Karl Marx,

Walter Benjamin, and W.E.B. Du Bois had also studied.

In Royce Hall that day, Davis explained that her course, "Recurring Philosophical Themes in Black Literature," would focus on the concept of freedom, but she did not begin with Greece or examine how various European Enlightenment philosophers understood freedom. She began instead with the premise that Black literature offers "a much more illuminating account of the nature of freedom, its extent and limits," given that "it projects the consciousness of a people who have been denied entrance into the real world of freedom" and who "have exposed, by their very existence, the inadequacies not only of the practice of freedom, but of its very theoretical formulation."

In those first lectures, which are found in the pamphlet *Lectures on Liberation*, Davis encouraged her students to think about freedom as more than a simple state of being in which one's life is free of the control of others. Drawing on the *Narrative of the Life of Frederick*

Previous page
L'Ouverture, Jacob Lawrence, 1986. In 1938, Lawrence completed a series of forty-one paintings on the Haitian revolutionary Toussaint Louverture that presents the life of the iconic leader from his birth on a plantation in the French colony of Saint-Domingue to his time in battle as a general fighting for Haitian independence. This print, based on the original work, was created in 1986 in a collaboration between Lawrence and master printmaker Lou Stovall.

Left
Angela Davis lecturing at the University of California, Los Angeles, 1969. At 25 years old, Davis joined UCLA's philosophy department. Her radical politics and association with the Communist Party made her a target for the university's Board of Regents, who fired her. However, a California Superior Court judge reinstated Davis, and she gave her first lecture to a crowd of more than 2,000 students.

Top
Portrait of Harriet Jacobs, 1894. In her autobiography *Incidents in the Life of a Slave Girl, Written by Herself*, Harriet Jacobs recounted her life under slavery, including the seven years she hid from her enslaver in an attic crawl space. Jacobs's narrative emphasized the depravity of slavery and the importance of the abolitionist cause.

Douglass, Davis called liberation a "dynamic, active struggle for freedom" that involved something much greater than the condition of a single individual. Douglass expressed this sense of liberation when, during an 1864 speech, he described the abolition of slavery as "the comprehensive and logical object of the [American Civil] war, for it includes everything else which the struggle involves." For Douglass, the mission of the Civil War entailed "great moral changes in the fundamental conditions of the people."

The Struggle for Freedom

It is not by accident that Davis found complex articulations of freedom in the Black literary tradition reaching back to slave narratives and wider Black publications of the nineteenth century. Harriet Jacobs, in *Incidents in the Life of a Slave Girl*, similarly reveals an understanding of freedom that goes beyond the matter of individual liberty. Jacobs escaped from slavery, yet she spent seven years in the garret of a house on the plantation where she had been enslaved, intent on freeing her children. She struggled to save her two daughters from bondage, a practice common among enslaved women who found it unbearable to leave children open to the brutality and sexual violence of the plantation. Therefore, whatever degree of individual physical autonomy escaping slavery might provide, Jacobs's freedom would have been incomplete without the freedom of her children. To Douglass and Jacobs, freedom in the 1860s had to mean more than the end of slavery but the inclusion of basic human rights, equality under the law, economic fairness, and full suffrage. A century later, Davis would articulate the same understanding of freedom when she explained, "It is only with the total abolition of the institution of slavery that [Douglass's] misery, his desolation, his alienation will be eliminated." For all three, liberation demanded that a society change its basic understanding of freedom. As Douglass put it, *"No war but an Abolition war; no peace but an Abolition peace; liberty for all, chains for none."*

The radical abolitionism that Douglass had in mind sought the transformation of the larger society through ending slavery. A member of the American Anti-Slavery Society in the United States, he likely drew on ideas that had been circulating within a network of Black abolitionists spanning the Americas and Europe. One of the most radical Black abolitionists, Ottobah Cugoano, an African from present-day Ghana who was kidnapped and sold into slavery as a child, worked alongside Olaudah Equiano (who was similarly kidnapped as a child from present-day Nigeria and sold into slavery) and a handful of others in the London-based organization the Sons of Africa. In 1787, Cugoano penned the first Black abolitionist pamphlet in English, *Thoughts and Sentiments on the Evil and Wicked Traffic of the Slavery and Commerce of the Human Species*. Unlike Douglass, Jacobs, and Equiano, Cugoano eschewed any kind of sentimental appeal to white readers, a common practice of the slave narrative. Instead, he lodged an uncompromising critique of the slave trade, slavery in the British colonies, and the role of slavery in the United Kingdom. In his view, the evil of the slave trade even called into question the sense of freedom that guided European social and political life in an era of self-proclaimed Enlightenment. Regarding the poverty that many suffered in the United Kingdom, which Douglass also witnessed during his time in Europe, Cugoano offered that "liberty and freedom, where people may starve for want, can do them but little good." Despite the dominant view of African barbarism held by most Europeans of his time, he stated that "in many respects, [Africa] may boast of some more essential liberties than any of the civilized nations in Europe enjoy," given that even "the poorest amongst us are never in distress for want, unless some general and universal calamity happens to us." Freedom in this view required not just the end of slavery but also the political and economic equality of the formerly enslaved.

Beyond the printed word, Black abolitionists strove for full freedom through political networks, military resistance, and political manifestations of sovereignty. Black abolitionists in the Francophone world of the late eighteenth and early nineteenth centuries made equally expansive and compelling claims to freedom, some joining the Société des Amis des Noirs (Society of the Friends of the Blacks), established in Paris in 1788. The society's goals of ending slavery in the French Caribbean colonies and France's role in the slave trade gained momentum after the French Revolution began. However, the vaunted Declara-

tion of the Rights of Man and of the Citizen was not immediately applied to freed people or *gens de couleur* (people of African descent who had not been enslaved) in the colonies. One free man of color from Saint-Domingue, Vincent Ogé, had been in Paris at the beginning of the revolution and soon joined the Société des Amis des Noirs after his appeal for greater liberty for *gens de couleur* in the colonies was defeated in revolutionary France's National Assembly. Ultimately, Ogé returned to Saint-Domingue in 1790 and led a revolt of approximately three hundred men in the town of Grande-Rivière. Though unsuccessful, Ogé's revolt brought to the fore the looming questions of racism and the abolition of slavery within the developing French colonies.

Enslaved freedom fighters in Saint-Domingue drew on a separate tradition of Black abolitionism and community-building that had long been nurtured by fugitive slaves in Maroon communities throughout the

Americas and beyond. These were hierarchical, extremely disciplined, and generally patriarchal communities, whose members' social relations and senses of the world were informed by memories of the societies they had left behind. They actively forged vital spaces that were often imperiled and sometimes fraught with the contradictions of creating and carving out imperfect practices of freedom amidst and despite the colonial societies around them. At their most basic, these communities sought to reestablish African modes of life and offer havens from the slave societies that had held them in bondage. At their most ambitious, they were highly organized martial-state formations that threatened the colonial order. In Jamaica, the Maroons were so well organized and militarily adept that they launched campaigns to maintain their independence and destroy the colonial society. Jamaica's First Maroon War (1728–40) prompted the British colonial government to sign peace treaties with

Top
The Maroons in Ambush on the Dromilly Estate in the Parish of Trelawny, Jamaica, F. J. Bourgoin, 1801. This painting depicts a scene from 1795, during the eight-month conflict between self-liberated Africans and colonial British authorities known as the Second Maroon War. Highly organized Maroon communities from Haiti to Brazil engaged in strategic warfare to maintain their sovereignty and dismantle colonial society.

the Leeward Maroons in 1739 and the Windward Maroons in 1740. Similarly, in the Dutch colony of Suriname, the Saramaka Maroons waged a war that lasted from the 1690s until a 1749 peace treaty momentarily halted conflict. They secured their independence in 1769.

In northern Brazil in 1605, escaped slaves established Palmares, perhaps the most famous and one of the largest and longest lasting Maroon settlements in the Americas. Palmares was a constant threat to the local state and repelled Portuguese, Dutch, and Brazilian military incursions. Organized as a federation of smaller communities, or quilombos, Palmares combined several traditional African political and social forms into a quasi-kingdom. An elected king, Ganga Zumba, ruled over lesser chiefs and controlled the distribution of land. While

men such as Zumba and his nephew Zumbi of Palmares loom large as Maroon leaders in the public imagination, women were also important figures in Maroon communities. Paánza in Suriname, who escaped to the Saramaka Maroons, brought with her grains of rice that allowed her new community a degree of self-sufficiency in its decades-long war with the Dutch. In Jamaica, Nanny of the Maroons was renowned for her military brilliance, on display in her campaigns with the Windward Maroons. Through the use of long-range communication (done with the abeng, an animal horn whose name comes from the Akan people in what is now Ghana), camouflage, and guerrilla tactics, Maroon fighters under Nanny's leadership were able to defeat British armies that were much larger and had superior weaponry. A Maroon community was named after her (Nanny Town), and Nanny remains a heralded figure in Jamaica.

Another storied history of Maroons comes from colonial Saint-Domingue— present-day Haiti. François Makandal, who was African-born, lost an arm while working on a sugar plantation and escaped to join a local Maroon community. He was a charismatic figure who had a following as a religious leader among Maroons, the enslaved, and free people—all of whom helped him devise a plot to poison the water supply and kill local whites. Makandal's plot failed, but Maroons proved central to the 1791 rebellion that grew to become the Haitian Revolution. On August 14 of that year, Maroons and slaves gathered at Bois-Caïman for a religious ceremony run by Dutty Boukman, who is believed to have been a leader in Vodou, along with a woman named Cécile Fatiman. Boukman is said to have delivered a speech that implored those gathered to "throw away the image of the god of the whites who thirsts for our tears," directing them instead to "listen to the voice of liberty that speaks in the hearts of all of us." In refusing to accept the colonial order that enslaved them, Boukman avoided drawing on the Enlightenment ideals of the French Revolution. He rejected the dominant world's values because, for him, they were something less than freedom.

Boukman's sensibility conflicted with that of Toussaint Louverture, the revolution's most recognized historical figure. Louverture believed

it imperative to demonstrate that the colony would remain productive under his rule. This led him to enforce a labor regime that conflicted with Boukman's approach. It would be the African-born Jean-Jacques Dessalines who rejected all things French and was able to draw various African groups, or bassoles, under his command. Dessalines had been enslaved but rose to prominence under Louverture's leadership during the revolution, becoming one of his most trusted generals and a feared combatant. In declaring Haiti's independence, Dessalines stated, "It is not enough to have expelled the barbarians who have bloodied our land for two centuries." More than being free of France, Dessalines implored the new nation to "vow to ourselves, to posterity, to the entire universe, to forever renounce France, and to die rather than live under its domination." Following like Boukman, Dessalines believed Haiti would win a lasting freedom by refusing to accept the colonial terms under which it was narrowly conceived and practiced.

The Haitian Revolution enjoys the distinction of being the only successful slave revolt to establish a modern nation-state. It is a telling example of the promise and limits of the freedom that Boukman initially expressed and Dessalines brought into existence. In an age of empire, plantation slavery, and the pervasiveness of the white supremacist belief in the biological inferiority of Black people, the first Haitian Constitution, in 1805, provides a new view of political society. Article 14, which followed a provision naturalizing some white women and the Polish who had fought for Haiti, declared the end of color distinctions and described all Haitians as Black. Translated from French, it offers a powerful sense of Blackness as a foundation for humanity: "All distinctions of color among the children of one and the same family, where the Head of State is the father, will by necessity disappear; Haitians shall henceforth be known by the generic denomination of blacks." Dessalines was guided by what Haitian intellectual Jean Casimir calls the idea of "tout moun se moun," a Krèyol expression meaning "every person is a person." Haiti's founding documents offered a sense of Black people's humanity as the basis for understanding

Général Jean-Jacques Dessalines (1758–1806). Héros de l'Indépendance d'Haïti (1804–1806), artist unknown, 1957. Jean-Jacques Dessalines was a leader of the Haitian Revolution and the first ruler of the independent republic. Under Dessalines's leadership, Haiti became the first nation in the Americas to abolish slavey.

all humanity. Indeed, this impulse also informed the drafting of Article 44 of Haiti's 1816 Constitution, which declared that Black and Indigenous peoples "born in the colonies or in foreign countries, who come to reside in the Republic, will be recognized as Haitians."

Haiti's coupling of Blackness and freedom as one of its founding ideals at the beginning of the nineteenth century ran into conflicting class interests and color differences that shaped struggles over political power. Dessalines perhaps sought to avoid this by appointing himself emperor for life. Over the next century, Haiti's elite guarded its class interests and perpetuated a color hierarchy that privileged property owners, free Blacks, and free people of color, who held in contempt the largely African masses who made up the agricultural and urban workforce.

Despite its challenges in realizing a freedom rooted in Blackness, Haiti nonetheless appealed to many as a bastion of freedom throughout the nineteenth and twentieth centuries. Enslaved people throughout the Caribbean knew of Haiti's Article 44. In 1817, seven enslaved sailors—Dublin, Kinston, Archy, Quashie, Robert, James, and Jem—stole their owner's schooner, named the *Deep Nine*, and set sail from Jamaica for Haiti. When they arrived in South Haiti, then under the rule of President Alexandre Pétion, they found the political haven of which they had heard. As Pétion explained to James McKowen, the Jamaican slaver who sued for the return of his human property, "They were recognized to be Haitians by the 44th Article of the Constitution of the Republic from the moment they set foot on its territory" and thus free. This spirit persisted well after Pétion's death in 1818. Jean-Pierre Boyer, who succeeded him as president, unified the country's north and south in 1820, and in 1822 annexed the Spanish colony of Santo Domingo, abolishing slavery there. In 1824, he offered to pay the passage of any Black person in the United States who wished to settle on Hispaniola, Haiti's island, a proposal that attracted some six thousand free Blacks, mainly from Philadelphia. The program ultimately failed and most of the settlers returned to the United States, but a vibrant community of descendants from that initial group remains in Samaná Bay in the Dominican Republic. Reverbera-

tions of revolution from Haiti extended across the Atlantic. After learning about the Haitian Revolution from visiting sailors, an enslaved Mauritian man named Louis led about 340 slaves in revolt in Cape Town. Reportedly wearing attire similar to Haitian revolutionary Toussaint Louverture, Louis led other enslaved rebels in attacks on grain farms over a period of thirty-six hours. And from the "birthplace" of democracy, Greek revolutionaries wrote a letter to Haitian President Jean-Pierre Boyer in 1822 asking for support in their revolution against the Ottoman Empire. Boyer wrote back acknowledging the Greek people's right to self-rule, and Haiti became the first country to recognize Greece's independence.

Black Movement as Freedom Making

If freedom can be understood as a practice, as something that one engages in with others, one of the more intriguing examples is the willingness to move to escape the grip of white supremacy. Throughout the nineteenth and into the twentieth century, Black people mounted small- and large-scale physical movements. Du Bois, in *Black Reconstruction,* describes how enslaved men and women during the American Civil War left plantations to head for Union lines. By the thousands, slaves engaged in what he called "a general strike against slavery by the same methods that [they] had used during the period of the fugitive slave. [They] ran away to the first place of safety and offered [their] services to the Federal Army." Through their movement, the enslaved freed themselves and brought about a Union victory. In liberating themselves, Du Bois continued, Black people raised the possibility of abolition-democracy in America. Like Douglass's abolition-peace, abolition-democracy would mean control over their own lives, unfettered pursuit of their own desires, regard for others, and political standing and equality.

US generals on the front lines of the war recognized this mass strike for freedom by the enslaved. "Imagine, if you will ... an army of slaves and fugitives, pushing its way irresistibly toward an army of fighting men," remarked the Union general John Eaton. "The[ir] arrival among us ... was like the oncoming of cities." Yet government officials, judges, and industrialists throughout the Americas and Europe in the late nineteenth and early twentieth centuries passed laws, decided court cases, and structured local economies to ensure Black political subordination and financial subserviency. Private citizens and public officials unleashed waves of racial violence at the slightest hint of Black equality in the aftermath of emancipation. As the dominion of legal slavery became increasingly imperiled throughout the Atlantic World, Europe's imperial powers met at the Berlin Conference in 1884–85 to carve up Africa into colonial possessions for each, plunging the continent into its worst period in the modern era and brutally reasserting global white supremacy. In response, Black freedom making in this new era assumed forms that varied but all featured the valuing of Black life.

Spiritual Movements

In the realm of culture—music, visual arts, literature, and spiritual practices—Black freedom making rejected the racist assessments of historians, philosophers, politicians, and mainstream religious leaders. Often, Black people articulated visions of freedom through culture and political activities, not separating the two in their minds. One area where this was readily apparent was the Black spirituality that drew on various African cosmologies. Obeah, Myal, traditional Yorùbá religion, Santería, Candomblé, Islam,

Christian revivalism, Kimbanguism, and Rastafarianism all involved a valuation of Black people that prized African cultural practices and emphasized redemption.

Within the Black Christian tradition, "Ethiopianism" represents one such movement with a diasporic scope. Ethiopia has long held pride of place in Black political life and culture. Part of its allure lies in the biblical reference in Psalms 68:31, "Princes shall come out of Egypt; Ethiopia shall soon stretch forth her hands unto God," which was often read as a prophecy of God's impending redemption of Black people. Ethiopia's standing as one of the oldest Christian nations and its mythological claim to the biblical union of King Solomon and the Queen of Sheba add to its appeal. Ethiopia also held the distinction of being one of the oldest monarchies in the world and the only nation on the African continent never to have been colonized. One of the earliest instances of Black people referring to Ethiopia in church names occurred in the 1780s, when George Lisle, a formerly enslaved Baptist minister born in Virginia, established an "Ethiopian" church in Savannah, Georgia.

When Ethiopia beat back Italian forces at Adwa in 1896, many believed that the biblical prophecy would be fulfilled. This helps explain why, in southern Africa in the late 1800s, Black clergy and parishioners began naming their houses of worship after Ethiopia. In 1892, for example, Mangena

Left
Participants at the Berlin Conference, 1884. The major European powers negotiated the partition of Africa and formalized their claims to its territories at the Berlin Conference of 1884–85. Over the next twenty years, the Europeans—aided by technologies and the weaponry of the Industrial Revolution—increased their control of the continent from 10 percent to 90 percent.

Top
Battle of Adwa, 1896. Ethiopia is important in many Black spiritual traditions. This painting depicts Ethiopian forces defeating Italian colonial invaders in the Battle of Adwa. Many viewed this victory as the fulfillment of a biblical prophecy and a sign of God's coming redemption of Black people.

Maake Mokone, a minister in the Anglican Church in Pretoria, had grown dissatisfied with segregated services and established the Ethiopian Church, which soon drew in other small congregations. Mokone ministered to future political activists, including Sefako Mapogo Makgatho, who would become the president of the African National Congress.

With the help of Charlotte Mannya Maxeke, a singer who was born in 1871 in Ga-Ramokgopa, South Africa, the Ethiopian Church became part of the African Methodist Episcopal Church of the United States. She organized a meeting between the Ethiopian Church leadership and AME bishop Henry McNeal Turner, who was interested in missionary work in southern Africa.

As independent churches continued to flourish throughout the African continent into the early twentieth century, they became spaces in which ministers and

worshipers could criticize the colonial order and express other political views that would not be tolerated in civic forums. Colonial authorities in Africa were aware of this history of the deep connections between political organizing and spiritual spaces and how it was rooted in the work of Black communities during and following enslavement. They would have certainly known about the influence and worked to suppress any inspiration that would be drawn from rebellious spiritual movements such as the 1865 Morant Bay rebellion in Jamaica, when the Baptist preacher Paul Bogle had led poor Black peasants—with an oath to "cleave to the Black"—in a violent confrontation with the police that resulted in more than a dozen deaths and the burning of government buildings.

Pan-African Organizing

Around the time that Ethiopianism assumed institutional form, Pan-Africanism was beginning to take shape as an ideology that challenged racial oppression and colonialism. One of the earliest known formations, the 1893 Chicago Congress on Africa, focused on the feasibility of Black emigration from the Americas to Africa and of lobbying imperial governments for improved conditions in the colonies. In 1900, the Trinidadian lawyer Henry Sylvester Williams organized the First Pan-African Conference. Convened in London's Westminster Town Hall and drawing over thirty delegates from Africa, the Caribbean, Europe, Canada, and the United States, this conference also focused on securing civil and political rights, education, and fair treatment in the colonies for Black people. Modest as its objectives may have been, its participants included some of the most important radicals of the twentieth century. Anna Julia Cooper, the activist and Sorbonne-trained historian who taught at the famed M Street High School in Washington, DC, was in attendance, along with Du Bois, who famously declared at this conference that "the problem of the twentieth century is the problem of the color line." Du Bois spearheaded the Niagara Movement, founded in 1905, a precursor to the National Association for the Advancement of Colored People (NAACP). Dusé Mohamed Ali, a Sudanese-Egyptian stage actor, worked with Williams in London and went on to publish the *African Times and Orient Review* from 1912 to 1918. He was helped in the latter by J. E. Casely Hayford, a polymath from the Gold Coast colony (present-day Ghana) who supported numerous efforts at building a global Black movement, including playing a key role in founding the National Congress of British West Africa.

Henry Sylvester Williams captured something of the Black political imagination in the early twentieth century, which viewed the task of seeking freedom as necessarily international in scope, encompassing the entire world. Du Bois emerged in this period as one of the most important activist-intellectuals to organize for Pan-African liberation. In addition to his work with the NAACP, including as the editor of its magazine,

The Crisis, he convened the first Pan-African Congress (PAC), which met in Paris in 1919 following World War I. This congress, drawing approximately sixty delegates from throughout the Black world, was concerned with the fate of Germany's former African colonies and the plight of Black people in Europe, the United States, and the Caribbean. It proposed a series of gradual reforms, such as the offering of quality education and economic protections, as well as requesting guarantees from colonial governments to provide Africans the opportunity to demonstrate their capacity for self-government. There were three more PACs in the 1920s—in 1921 in London, Brussels, and Paris; 1923 in Lisbon and London; and 1927 in New York—whose resolutions took increasingly militant tones with each meeting. It was not until the Fifth PAC, organized in Manchester, United Kingdom in 1945 by the Trinidadian radical and ex-communist George Padmore along with Kwame Nkrumah, that Africans were the main participants. Indeed, several of those present went on to lead African liberation struggles. This conference provided a platform for such figures as Kwame Nkrumah in Ghana and Jomo Kenyatta in Kenya to lead movements for political independence.

In contrast with the gradualism of many early Pan-African intellectuals, Marcus Garvey offered a more radical vision of Pan-African liberation, which attracted a broader cross section of Black

Bottom
UNIA Parade in Harlem, 1920. Marcus Garvey's Universal Negro Improvement Association offered a radical vision of Pan-African liberation and self-determination that appealed to a diverse, international Black populace. The UNIA became the largest Black political organization in history, with branches throughout the world.

people. Garvey had been politically active in nationalist organizations in his native Jamaica, but his travels would have an even deeper impact on his political outlook. He first went to Panama, where he witnessed the poor treatment of Caribbean migrant workers, with the racism of the United Kingdom and United States on full display. He later made his way to London, where he worked on Ali's *African Times and Orient Review* and gained insight into the importance of publishing a newspaper. Reading Ali's publication also broadened Garvey's understanding of the nature of British colonialism in Africa, the Middle East, and India. He returned to Jamaica and with his first wife, Amy Ashwood Garvey, established the Universal Negro Improvement Association (UNIA), which was headquartered in Kingston, in 1914. In 1916, Garvey began a speaking tour of the United States to raise funds for the organization. His tour coincided with the carnage of the East Saint Louis Race Riot of 1917. In response, and inspired by Black protest activities against the massacre across the United States, Garvey relocated the UNIA's headquarters to Harlem, New York. It was a shrewd

decision; there, he would build the UNIA into the largest Black political organization in history, with branches throughout the Black world.

Among Garvey's strongest qualities were his charisma and wit that drew in Black people from all walks of life, and his vision of a global Black movement that could redeem Africa from European domination. His political platform of "Africa for the Africans, those at home and abroad" presented the continent as a homeland for Black people, where they could build an empire to beat back European colonialism and challenge white supremacy. But possibly more important than Garvey the charismatic leader were the Garvey movement and the constellation of ideals and visions of a liberated Black future to which it gave voice. Among the numerous features of Garveyism, none was more significant than the UNIA's decentralized structure. Where other organizations of the era sought to tightly control the activities of their members, the UNIA allowed its local branches to address concerns that local activists could then situate within a global project of Black freedom. The UNIA newspaper, *The Negro World*,

founded by Amy Ashwood Garvey, was one of the most popular Black periodicals during its run from 1918 through 1932. At its peak, it had a circulation of more than two hundred thousand, carried news from throughout the African Diaspora, and included Spanish and French sections to ensure that it reached more of the Black world than just English speakers. Indeed, its calls for African independence and its criticism of European colonialism led colonial governments throughout Africa and the Caribbean to ban *The Negro World*. Marcus Garvey was ultimately undone by a conviction on federal charges for mail fraud. Though the UNIA would splinter, its display of Black stateliness and the promise of an African empire that would unite and defend Black people around the world still appealed to many.

Arts, Internationalism, and Global Black Freedom

A Black sharecropper in Alabama or a manual laborer in Dakar experienced a different order of racial oppression than an autoworker in Detroit or a dock worker in Marseille. Black migration in the twentieth century was largely driven by the prospect of better jobs or greater social and political liberties, though the achievement of something that approached freedom always proved elusive. But many believed that the goal of freedom had to address both racial oppression and the global structures of European empire. Langston Hughes captured this sense of the need to envision Black freedom on a global scale in his poem "White Shadows":

> I'm looking for a house
> In the world
> Where white shadows
> Will not fall.
>
> *There is no such house,*
> *Dark brothers,*
> *No such house*
> *At all.*

Composed following his 1931 visit to Haiti, Hughes's poem captured the global reach of white supremacy. He had no illusions about the sixteen-year US occupation of Haiti, yet, as his other writings about Haiti reveal, he was also concerned about the country's Black

and mulatto aristocracy, which had grown proud, snobbish, and European in culture and outlook. This class set itself apart from the Black masses, whom it exploited. In his article "White Shadows in a Black Land," published in *The Crisis*, Hughes noted that "the white shadows began to fall across the land as the dark aristocracy became cultured, and careless, conceited, and quite 'high hat.'" These shadows fell well before the US military occupation of Haiti, which protected US business interests from 1915 until 1934.

During his trip to Haiti, Hughes met Jacques Roumain, a Haitian intellectual and poet who was involved in nationalist groups opposed to the US occupation. After Hughes put him in contact with Black Communists in the United States, Roumain established the Parti Communiste Haïtien (Haitian Communist Party) in 1934.

After Haiti, Hughes traveled to Cuba, where he spent time with the poet and future radical Nicolás Guillén. Indeed, Hughes, Roumain, and Guillén reflect a tendency in global Black freedom movements at the time to connect radical politics to artistic production. Influenced by the Harlem Renaissance, Aimé Césaire, Léopold Sédar Senghor, Jeanne "Jane" Nardal, and others inaugurated the Négritude movement in Paris in the 1930s. It would prove equally influential, helping to develop the sense

Top
Smash Jim Crow, Joe Schwartz, 1948. From the factories of Detroit to the railways of Dakar, Black workers experienced racial discrimination and exploitative labor practices in the twentieth century. Workers banded together, forming unions to protect themselves from these abuses. In the United States, Black labor unionism became part of a broader campaign for civil rights.

of a global Black struggle and culture. As Césaire put it, the central questions before Négritude were "Who am I? Who are we? What are we in this white world?" Négritude, like Ethiopianism, Pan-Africanism, and Garveyism, reflected a collective ideal that any practice of Black freedom had to be global in scale.

With the word *Négritude*, Césaire and the other architects of the movement asserted the importance of Africa and African cultures and a break with the French distinction between *noirs* (respectable) and *nègres* (dirty, uneducated) that was generally used to classify Africans. Nardal and Senghor both considered Africa a central focus, with Senghor suggesting that *Négritude* captured "the sum total of the values of civilization of the Black World." Césaire expressed it a bit more poetically, writing that "a voice was rising up . . . a violent and staccato voice, and it said for the first time: 'I, Nègre.'"

A remarkable feature of virtually every wave of the Black freedom movement has been an outpouring of literary, visual, musical, and dramatic artistic works that have been central to how each generation has come to understand freedom. Art may well help achieve a political goal, like securing the right to vote, improving social services, or attaining national independence. When the Cabo Verdean anti-colonial revolutionary Amílcar Cabral, at the height of revolutionary struggle, declared that "national liberation is necessarily an act of culture," part of what he had in mind was the capacity of social movements to draw on those relationships and experiences that can provide a broader conception of freedom than is practiced in the context of empire. The Martinican radical Suzanne Césaire similarly asserted that art offers an emancipatory vision of freedom. She described music and poetry as providing humanity its only "access road toward this other enticing world."

When the Paris-based journal *Présence Africaine* convened its first International Congress of Black Writers and Artists, in 1956, it brought together figures from Africa, Europe, the Caribbean, and the United States to contemplate culture as a political question. In the published proceedings from the second congress, which met in Rome in 1959, *Présence Africaine* suggested that culture constitutes more than an "assemblage of works and norms." Rather, it "lies in the will of the peoples who give its values reality in everyday life," in how they live and relate to one another. Frantz Fanon delivered a version of what would become the chapter "On National Culture" in his *The Wretched of the Earth*. He noted that just as anti-colonial struggles produce formal innovations and new art forms, a successful struggle would bring about "not only the demise of colonialism, but also the demise of the colonized." Cabral echoed Fanon years later when he posited that national liberation "goes beyond the achievement of political independence to the superior level of complete liberation."

The focus on culture and the arts within anti-colonial movements in Africa and the Caribbean was guided by a belief that complete liberation would mean more than merely an end to formal colonial domination. Art was an arena of contestation and struggle. Through the act of liberation, new practices, new social relationships, and new political arrangements might take form that could sweep away what the Guyanese historian

Elsa Goveia describes as "[a] most profound incompatibility [that] necessarily results from the uneasy union which joins democracy with the accumulated remains of enslavement." For Cabral, this insistence on the centrality of culture to manifesting identity and a politics of freedom demanded that national liberation "reduce to ash all aspects of the colonial state . . . in order to make everything possible for our people." For him, complete liberation meant new forms of governance and a new cultural mood.

Postcolonial Black Freedom Making

Global lines of influence form an important part of the history of Black freedom movements. At the 1958 All-African People's Conference in Accra, Ghana organized by Padmore and Nkrumah, Frantz Fanon met with Angolan anti-colonial radicals and invited them to send a small group to train in guerrilla warfare with Algeria's Front de Libération Nationale (National Liberation Front). Such offers of material support made Algeria a hub of radical internationalism. Algeria helped train Lusophone African revolutionaries from Angola and Mozambique, as well as Cabral's Partido Africano da Independência de Guiné e Cabo Verde (African Party for the Independence of Guinea and Cabo Verde). Further, Fanon's *The Wretched of the Earth*, published a few years later, influenced scores of radicals with its demand for an expansive anti-colonial project: "For Europe, for ourselves and for humanity, comrades, we must make a new start, develop a new way of thinking, and endeavor to create a new man." Certainly, Cabral's notion of "complete liberation" echoed Fanon's ideas. Many radicals took up this call "to create a new man," often with all the masculinist implications the phrase suggests.

The example of anti-colonial revolutions and the emergence of independent Black nations in Africa and the Caribbean prompted a new generation of Black activists in the United States to question the goals of the Civil Rights Movement. In his famous 1964 speech "The Ballot or the Bullet," the Muslim minister and intellectual Malcolm X argued for a more expansive, global view that underscored the limits of civil rights: "As long as you fight . . . on the level of civil rights, you're under Uncle Sam's jurisdiction. You're going to his court expecting him to correct the problem. He created the problem." Malcolm X was influenced by William L. Patterson, who, as the head of the Civil Rights Congress, presented the petition "We Charge Genocide" to the United Nations General Assembly, which asked that body to "find and declare by resolution that the government of the United States is guilty of the crime of genocide against the Negro people of the United States." Drawing on this model, Malcolm X sought to have African and Asian nations present charges of human rights violations against the United States in the United Nations as a demonstration of liberation and a rejection of neocolonialism. This was the pressing question that the Cuban Revolution posed about US empire, and it was a question that the West Indies Federation took up as well. Many began to see the wisdom espoused through Malcolm's critique. When all of these were considered alongside the scores of other African, Asian, and Caribbean independence struggles; Portugal's wars in its African colonies; South Africa's apartheid regime; and the United States' involvement in the Vietnam War, its role in the assassination of Patrice Lumumba in Congo, and its attacks on Black political figures in the US.

Black Power emerged as a campaign that broke with the Civil Rights

Movement's focus on citizenship rights and integration. Many Black Power activists sought to build ties to international political movements, arguing that when Black people in the United States were considered in light of colonialism in Africa, the Caribbean, and Latin America, they were clearly a domestic or internal colony, concentrated in urban ghettos. The Black Arts Movement, which emerged alongside Black Power, challenged how Blackness was viewed among Black people and within the larger society. In *Black Power: The Politics of Liberation in America*, Kwame Ture (Stokely Carmichael) and Charles Hamilton drew on Fanon to argue that Black Power should replace the dominant value system, which was rooted in anti-Black racism, and search "for new and different forms of political structure[s] to solve political and economic problems."

Black Consciousness in South Africa similarly focused on bringing about a new social reality through Black struggle. Again, following Fanon, the goal was not to mirror European values or be incorporated into white South African society. Black Consciousness's most well-known thinker,

Steve Biko, argued instead that a society where "the majority of people are African … must inevitably exhibit African values and be truly African in style." In this way, Biko and other Black Consciousness thinkers were after something more than simply the end of apartheid. The goal, according to Biko, was to "reach some kind of balance—a true humanity."

If Black Power and Black Consciousness sought to transform societies, their leadership—overwhelmingly male—often displayed a lack of political imagination on issues of gender. Around the time that Angela Davis delivered her first lectures at UCLA, some male proponents of Black Power criticized her and other Black women for taking leadership roles and thereby allegedly weakening the position of Black men. Frances "Fran" Beal, a member of the Student Nonviolent Coordinating Committee (SNCC) in the late 1960s, recalled that activists would be "talking about liberation and freedom half the night on the racial side, and then all of a sudden men are going to turn around and start talking about putting you [women] in your place." Other Black

Top
Anti-police protest one decade after the Toxteth Riots, 1991. In the summer of 1981, police and residents in the Toxteth neighborhood of Liverpool clashed in a wave of unrest by sparked by long-standing issues of racial tension, police brutality, and economic inequality.

women, like Toni Cade Bambara, have recounted that Black men wanted to assert their power over the groups they joined and over Black women. In many instances, they opposed birth control. But if the male-dominated organizations of this era tended to reduce the role of Black women, it would be Black women's groups, publications, and intellectual work that would elaborate an even more sustained contemplation of what it would mean to create a new society built on more egalitarian principles.

It is not coincidental, then, that the US prison abolition movement—which emerged in the late 1990s as a political critique of the carceral state and seeks to reorient society away from policing and toward social welfare and an ethics of care—grew out of a history of Black feminism extending back to at least the 1960s. In 1968, Beal led the formation within SNCC of the Black Women's Liberation Committee, which became the Third World Women's Alliance two years later. In 1973, Black women radicals from various groups and movements launched the National Black Feminist Organization, and a year later the Combahee River Collective was founded. This group of

Black queer women wanted more attention to be paid to poor Black people and to issues of sexuality. A common theme of all these groups was their awareness of how multiple forms of oppression—colonial domination, racism, sexism, homophobia, and class conflict— simultaneously interacted and thus made a comprehensive approach imperative in seeking liberation. As Beal put it powerfully and plainly in 1969, "The new world that we are attempting to create must destroy oppression of any type."

Black Feminist Abolitionism

Through organizations, collectives, political campaigns, and anthologies over the past sixty years, Black feminists have outlined an abolition feminism that began to gain widespread attention in the summer of 2020 after the killing of George Floyd. As Angela Davis, Gina Dent, Erica Meiners, and Beth Richie state in their book, *Abolition. Feminism. Now.*, "Abolition is unthinkable without feminism and our feminism unimaginable without abolition." Abolition feminism is broad enough to focus on ending interpersonal gender violence as well as building a global, politically informed practice that refuses policing as a solution to the most pressing problems in society.

Prison abolition. Abolish the police. Defund the police. These are terms and political positions that entered the popular lexicon during the BLM protests that stretched around the world in the summer of 2020 after a Minneapolis, Minnesota, police officer murdered George Floyd. BLM began as a broad-based response to the killing of Trayvon Martin in Florida by a white vigilante, George Zimmerman, and the subsequent police killings of Michael Brown in Ferguson, Missouri; Freddie Gray in Baltimore, Maryland; and Breonna Taylor in Louisville, Kentucky. Zimmerman's acquittal and its illustration of the precarity of Black life prompted three Black queer women—

Alicia Garza, Patrisse Cullors, and Ayọ (formerly Opal) Tometi—to launch #BlackLivesMatter, which they envisioned as "an ideological and political intervention in a world where Black lives are systematically and intentionally targeted for demise." In December 2014, various BLM organizations joined with such groups as Black Youth Project 100, Million Hoodies Movement for Justice, and Dream Defenders to form the Movement for Black Lives (M4BL), a coalition that seeks to move society toward a world where freedom and justice are the reality. The M4BL's platform reflects a belief that "a complete transformation of the current systems, which place profit over people and make it impossible for many of us to breathe," is necessary for any manner of redress. As Garza noted, one of their goals was to build a movement that affirmed the lives of "Black queer and trans folks, disabled folks, Black-undocumented folks, folks with records, women and all Black lives along the gender spectrum."

The presence of Black women and queer folk, trans men, trans women, and nonconforming people marks a decided break from previous generations of Black political organizing. Certainly, queer and trans people were always involved in Black political struggles, but they were often hidden, not spoken about, or kept in smaller groups at the margins of larger struggles. Learning from earlier Black feminists and women's practices, Black Youth Project 100 in Chicago has adopted an egalitarian organizational and leadership model built to pursue economic, social, political, and educational freedom for all Black people. What this current moment offers, then, is a new approach to the practice of freedom, and this seems to be what made the Floyd protests so powerful—the clarity with which large segments of the world called for the abolition and/or defunding of the police. The impulse behind such protests was already present around the globe. Since 2015 in South Africa, the Rhodes Must Fall campaign has highlighted the persistence of racism in higher education. In London in 2017, the Grenfell Tower fire killed seventy-one people, displaced hundreds, and underscored a general and long-standing tension with the police. In Paris, particularly in the *banlieues*— working-class suburbs with large Black and Arab populations—harassment and killing of local youths by police have been constant problems. In Nigeria, growing

discontent with the Special Anti-Robbery Squad (SARS), which had a long history of harassment, sexual abuse of young women, and killing, led to the 2017 End SARS campaign.

The history of Black freedom making is diverse and has spanned African peoples' entire encounter with the modern world. The earliest Black abolitionists believed that the end of slavery would have to entail a transformation of the colonial plantation societies. Through various political and cultural movements, many came to realize that merely ending their bondage, establishing Black nation-states, and moving into the larger world without more fundamental change would bring about something less than freedom. Black freedom making since the era of emancipation has been marked by pursuit of another world, which requires not simply the individual freedom of any single person, but the transformation of the globe. In the cultural and spiritual realms, including the arts and movements such as Pan-Africanism and Négritude, Black Power, and Black Consciousness, Black people globally have pursued visions of a world free of any form of oppression. What the history of Black freedom making shows us is that rather than there being a single solution, or a particular program that will bring about such a world, it is the range of actions, struggles, cultural production, and ideas that will re-make the world. As Suzanne Césaire suggested, embracing and continually enacting a set of practices "leads us into 'a new time,' into a new world."

As a more recent iteration of this expansive Black freedom-making vision, abolition feminism—like Douglass's abolition war / abolition peace and Du Bois's abolition democracy—is not the solution to a problem but a way to pose the problem and continue thinking through it so that we might seek solutions and new visions of freedom. As Davis, Dent, Meiners, and Richie explained, "Rather than offering the now as the end point—as in 'at last'—we offer it as a critical and joyful starting point." Black freedom making is a practice with the potential to realize a new kind of freedom. Black freedom making does not reveal a single answer or solution. It is a constant struggle.

The Afro-Brazilian activist and politician Marielle Franco leads a march, 2016. A vocal critic of police violence and an advocate for women's and LGBTQIA+ rights, Franco was tragically assassinated in 2018. Her murder sparked protests across Brazil calling for justice, freedom, and equality.

DRAGON OF THE SEA

Keila Grinberg

In 1881, the abolitionist movement was growing throughout Brazil, and in the state of Ceará in the country's northeast, the situation was no different. The previous year, a group of men in that province had founded the Sociedade Cearense Libertadora (Ceará Liberation Society), which disseminated antislavery ideas through its newspapers and events and purchased manumissions. The group included Francisco José do Nascimento, of Indigenous American and African descent. He was a third-generation fisherman and *jangadeiro* in Aracati, Brazil, who also spent part of his childhood working with his father on a rubber plantation in the Amazon. When he returned to Fortaleza, he worked on local ships. By the time he became involved in the abolition movement, he was second in command of the Port Authority, which was responsible for guiding ships to dock. Nascimento lost his job because he was an abolitionist, as did several of his colleagues. However, the movement continued to grow, receiving support from important activists, including the Black journalist José do Patrocínio, who traveled to Ceará specifically to help with the cause. Together, Nascimento and Patrocínio engaged in fundraising to grant free manumissions.

When slave traders attempted to force Brazilian workers in Fortaleza to transport captive Africans to the south of Brazil aboard *jangadas* (small fishing boats), the society devised a plan to disrupt the slave trade. Under the leadership of Francisco José do Nascimento, the *jangadeiros* collectively refused to transport the enslaved captives. Their strike effectively ended the slave trade in the port of Fortaleza, Ceará's capital. When the strike began, Nascimento probably never imagined that he would usher in an era of abolition in his homeland driven by common people or that he would become one of the leading icons of abolitionism in Brazil. The abolitionist movement spread to the province's municipalities to establish slave-free areas, beginning with Fortaleza in 1881, and, on March 25, 1884, slavery was abolished throughout Ceará.

When abolition was declared, Nascimento traveled to Rio de Janeiro in his *Jangada Libertadora* (raft of freedom) and participated in a formal reception. His likeness appeared on medals minted in his honor, such as the one in the collection at the Brazilian Museu Histórico Nacional. He was simply represented as a Black fisherman at first but was ultimately portrayed as a fearless hero named Dragão do Mar (Dragon of the Sea). Commemorative medals were an important part of the abolitionist campaign in Brazil. The Redenção do Ceará (Redemption of Ceará) medal is one of them; it depicts the *Jangada Libertadora* in Vila do Acarape, which had its name changed to *Redenção* (Redemption).

The abolitionist struggle in Brazil was led by enslaved men and women, freedpeople, and people of African descent, but Brazilian society did not recognize the contributions of most Black activists. The official Brazilian story of abolition was the romanticization of Princess Isabel, who signed the so-called Lei Áurea (Golden Law) of May 13, 1888, which granted freedom to the enslaved. She is inaccurately celebrated as "The Redeemer" (sic), as if she were the chief architect of abolition in Brazil.

Today, there is a powerful movement to recognize and reclaim the true heroes of Brazilian abolition. In 2017, Francisco José do Nascimento was included in the *Livro dos Heróis e Heroínas da Pátria* (Book of National Heroes), which honors people who have served the country. At the Mangueira—a traditional samba school in Rio de Janeiro—Nascimento became the subject of a song in 2019, which contained the lyric "*a história que a história não conta*" (the history that history does not tell). The tune paid homage to the Black and Indigenous peoples—the true national heroes—who, over the centuries, fought for freedom and their right to be true citizens in Brazil. The refrain sung by thousands, "Freedom is the dragon of the sea of Aracati," is a great tribute to Nascimento.

The enslaved and their allies used their economic power as laborers to press the issue of abolition across the Atlantic: From the *jangadeiro* strike, to Samuel Sharpe's rebellion in Jamaica, to the flight from plantations of many thousands of enslaved people in the midst of the American Civil War in what the historian W.E.B. Du Bois later labeled a "general strike," these self-liberating measures struck at the heart of racial slavery by targeting enslavers' profits, and would influence later generations of protests across the Black Atlantic. Globally, as the post-emancipation struggle for total freedom continues, a broader public account of this entire history still waits to be told.

Left
1884 medal commemorating Francisco do Nascimento, the *jangadeiros'* strike, and the abolition of slavery in the state of Ceará, Brazil.

Right
Francisco do Nascimento and the *jangadeiros* of Ceará, 1884. In 1881, Brazilian workers collectively refused to transport for sale captive Africans aboard *jangadas* (small fishing boats). Organized by Nascimento, a fisherman of Indigenous American and African descent, the *jangadeiros'* strike effectively ended the slave trade in Ceará, Brazil.

Francisco Nascimento.

Á testa dos jangadeiros cearenses, Nascimento impede o trafico dos escravos da provincia do Ceará vendidos para o Sul.

PAN-AFRICANISM AND BLACK FREEDOM

Kate McMahon

The first Pan-African Conference was held at Westminster Town Hall in London from July 23 to 25, 1900. Henry Sylvester Williams issued the following invitation to prospective attendees:

> This conference is organized by a Committee of the African Association for the Discussion of the "Native Races" Question, and will be attended and addressed by those of African descent from all parts of the British Empire, the United States of America, Abyssinia, Liberia, Hayti [sic], etc.

Born in the late 1860s, Williams was a Black Trinidadian educated in the United States. He moved to London in 1895 to train as a barrister, later relocating and becoming a prominent member of the South African legal community. Williams had already accomplished much as a Pan-Africanist when he issued the invitation to global Black leaders in his early thirties. His experiences organizing smaller Pan-African groups and meetings while in the United States and the Caribbean prepared him to create a broader Pan-African organization that could respond to the unique geopolitical, economic, and social circumstances of the day.

PAN-AFRICAN CONFERENCE.

WESTMINSTER TOWN HALL,

ON THE

23rd, 24th and 25th JULY, 1900.

This Conference is organised by a Committee of the African Association for the Discussion of the "Native Races" Question, and will be attended and addressed by those of African descent from all parts of the British Empire, the United States of America, Abyssinia, Liberia, Hayti, etc.

YOU ARE CORDIALLY AND EARNESTLY INVITED TO ATTEND.

CONFERENCES—Morning, 10.30 and Evening, 8.

H. S. WILLIAMS, *Hon. Sec.*,
139, PALACE CHAMBERS, S.W.

Top
W.E.B. Du Bois's invitation to the first Pan-African Conference, 1900. Thirty-two delegates attended the first Pan-African Conference, organized in London by the Trinidadian barrister Henry Sylvester Williams. It focused on racial discrimination and Black political leadership and included Black intellectuals from Africa, Europe, and the Americas.

Left
Participants gather in Dar es Salaam, Tanzania, for the Sixth Pan-African Congress, 1974. Photograph by Ozier Muhammad. Also known as 6PAC, this was the first PAC to take place in Africa. It called for the end of all forms of colonialism, racism, and neocolonialism and advocated for the unification of all African people.

The first Pan-African Conference's global delegates included notable figures such as W.E.B. Du Bois, Anna Julia Cooper, and Benito Sylvain. They discussed topics such as the ongoing racism faced by Black people in the United States and the United Kingdom, the Boer War in South Africa, and contemporary slavery on the islands of Zanzibar and Pemba in what is now Tanzania. They passed a series of resolutions, including one addressed to the "Nations of the World," which decried the rampant racism impacting Black people globally as well as slavery, racism, and European colonialism in Africa. The delegates resolved to meet every two years, though it would take nineteen years for another conference to be organized.

This first conference set in motion a series of gatherings of the African Diaspora, known as the Pan-African Congresses, that shaped more than 120 years of political and social activism across the globe. These congresses reflected the unique historical moments. The three documents from the meetings in 1900, 1921, and 1945 symbolized the myriad ways that Black people have engaged in collective, global action to resist racial slavery, white supremacy, and colonialism.

The Pan-African Congress (PAC) of February 1919 was held in Paris and was organized by Du Bois, along with Ida Gibbs Hunt, Edmund Fredericks, and Blaise Diagne. It happened during the aftermath of World War I, in which Black soldiers from across the African Diaspora fought in Europe and elsewhere while Africa was suffering the impacts of European colonization. The return of Black soldiers after the end of the war led to racial violence around the world. The PAC's delegates made a plea at the peace conference being held in Paris at the same time, resulting in worldwide attention for the congress. They appealed to the League of Nations to recognize the racism that people of color experienced owing to various forms of colonial rule. They also advocated for self-government for "all men and nations."

By 1921, Du Bois had become a hardline proponent of a decolonized Africa, and the resolutions passed at the PAC that year reflect this ideological shift. The Congressional sessions were held in London, Paris, and Brussels, with 120 delegates from across the African Diaspora in attendance. Subsequent PACs were held in 1923 and 1927, but the Great Depression and World War II disrupted everything, so the next one was not held until October 1945, in Manchester, United Kingdom. It was co-convened by the Trinidadian activist George Padmore, Du Bois, and others in the Pan-African Federation. This was the congress that shifted focus to decolonization in Africa. Kwame Nkrumah and Jomo Kenyatta, along with dozens of other delegates representing countries across Africa and the Diaspora, shared resources, ideas, and plans for a freer Africa and an end to racism globally. Scholars largely consider the Fifth PAC congress to be the most consequential, because of the presence of leaders of decolonization efforts in Africa. It inspired generations of anti-colonial political action by Africans and African diasporic people.

The PACs continued throughout the twentieth century into the twenty-first century, with a focus on Africa and ending global anti-Blackness, colonialism, and neocolonialism. This cooperative action is one way that Africans and people of African descent have pursued freedom by any means possible.

FASHIONING IDENTITY

Johanna Obenda

In 1957, a striking black-and-white textile circulated the nation of Ghana. Designed to celebrate independence from the United Kingdom, the fabric featured the official portrait of Kwame Nkrumah, the new country's first leader. Nkrumah's portrait is joined by a set of images that reflect on the nation's past and present, including a gold mine to represent the region's historical wealth, a king's sword to symbolize traditional authority, and the new nation's motto: Freedom and Justice. These elements are surrounded by a recurring black star, a Pan-African symbol of hope and unity. While Ghana was the first sub-Saharan African nation to gain independence in the twentieth century, it was not the last, as a wave of decolonization spread across the continent in the 1960s and 1970s. Portrait-printed textiles like the one featuring Nkrumah became a popular medium for expressing messages of African independence, resistance, and identity—a significant departure from the textile's point of origin.

Factory-printed cloth—also known as Ankara, Dutch wax, or African wax—was introduced to the African continent by European traders in the nineteenth century. Early fabrics were based on traditional Indonesian *batik*, where artisans applied melted wax to cotton in intricate designs and then dyed the cloth to reveal the patterns formed by the wax. British and Dutch manufacturers experimented with mechanizing the handcrafted technique to mass-produce cheaper prints for sale. European-made imitation *batik* found success in West African markets, in large part due to local African saleswomen who informed European merchants of popular styles and motifs. Manufacturers adapted their designs and colors to meet local demand, and saleswomen created backstories and names for the imported cloth, embedding local messages into these fabrics. Enriched with new cultural meaning, these factory-printed goods were woven into a broader African tradition of using textiles to express wealth, social standing, and identity.

In the twentieth century, with advancements in photographic reproductions, portraits began to appear on cloth. These new factory-printed textiles, known as fancy cloth, featured large blocks of bold colors, geometric designs, and photographic imagery. As the drumbeat of national liberation

Left
Participant at Ghana's independence celebration wearing a textile with a portrait of Kwame Nkrumah, 1957. Portrait cloths like this one were popular in the era of African independence for communicating political identity and commemorating significant events.

Right
Commemorative cloth of Kwame Nkrumah, 1957. This textile was created to celebrate Ghanaian independence from British colonial rule. It features Nkrumah's official presidential portrait, Ghana's flag, the Ghanaian coat of arms, and a banner with the nation's new motto: Freedom and Justice.

echoed across the continent, a renewed
sense of pride in African heritage
and culture permeated all aspects of
society, including fashion. In Ghana,
Prime Minister Kwame Nkrumah saw
the opportunity to localize wax-print
production, moving jobs and resources
from Europe to the continent and
Africanizing the colonial textile. In the
1960s, several African nations and
manufacturers established their own
textile production factories, creating new
designs to commemorate the era
of independence and using photographic
technology to print images of local and
national leaders directly on cloth. The
faces of African leaders like Léopold
Senghor and Patrice Lumumba adorned
the bodies of a populace eager to
celebrate and define post-colonial
societies on their own terms.

These factory-printed political
textiles spread across the continent,
with portraits printed on a wide range of
fabrics, from *kaanga* in the east,
to *shweshwe* in the south. As the fight
for equality and self-determination
continued into the post-colonial era,
portrait textiles took on new meanings. In
South Africa, for example, it was illegal to
publicly display the anti-apartheid leader
Nelson Mandela's image or to wear the
colors of his African National Congress
(ANC). The South African government
so feared the revolutionary's influence
that, for decades, no pictures of Mandela
were allowed to circulate, publicly or
privately. Displaying or possessing his
image could result in punishment and
arrest. In 1991, after serving twenty-seven
years of a lifetime sentence for treason,
Mandela was released from prison. In

celebration, printed cloth with Mandela's portrait and the ANC's black, green, and gold was mass-produced and worn throughout the country as a visceral symbol of pride and resilience and a bold counterstatement to apartheid.

Draped on bodies, wrapped around goods, and displayed in homes, these portrait textiles were unmistakable, embodied statements of political affiliation and ideology across twentieth-century Africa. These materials remain important documents of African history. Even though many textiles are now manufactured abroad, the tradition of political portrait textiles continues. For example, in 2012, a Nigerian manufacturer issued a factory-printed fabric to commemorate the inauguration of the Liberian president Ellen Johnson Sirleaf, celebrating the first elected woman head of state of an African

nation. Contemporary leaders of the continent and the broader Diaspora, from Malawi's Joyce Banda to the United States' Barack Obama, have likewise been immortalized in textiles, their ideologies activated by those who wear the cloth. From independence, through to the end of apartheid, to our present moment, factory-printed portrait textiles have woven together a story of how fashion can unite communities and both affirm and challenge political orders.

Top
Commemoration cloth of Ellen Johnson Sirleaf, 2012. This factory-printed fabric celebrates the inauguration of the Liberian president, who was the first elected woman head of state of an African nation. The cloth features Johnson Sirleaf's portrait, a repeating pattern of the outline of Liberia, the nation's seal, and a banner that reads "First female president of Liberia/Africa."

Right
Top with Nelson Mandela print, ca. 2010. This shirt is made from *shweshwe*, a dyed cotton fabric with a long history in South African culture and fashion. It features the portrait of Mandela, the anti-apartheid revolutionary who served as the first Black president of South Africa, from 1994 to 1999.

ANASTÁCIA FREED

Yhuri Cruz and Aline Montenegro Magalhães

The French artist Jacques Arago arrived in Rio de Janeiro in 1817 with the mission of recording images of the colony as part of a colonial scientific mission. He stayed in Brazil for two months, then returned in 1820 for another five months, producing illustrations that portrayed life and culture in the colony's cities. During these stays, he captured and described in his diary many scenes, including one of an enslaved man in Rio de Janeiro being punished with a neck iron and bit (sometimes called a Flanders mask). The

Anastácia Livre

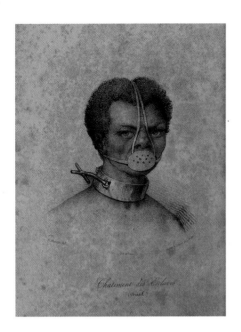

Top
Châtiment des Esclaves (Punishment for Slaves), Jacques Étienne Victor Arago, 1812. Arago, a French artist, drew this image of an enslaved person punished with an iron bit in Rio de Janeiro. The portrait circulated around the Atlantic world and came to be referred to as *Escrava Anastácia* (Enslaved Anastácia).

Left
Monumento à Voz de Anastácia (Monument to the Voice of Anastácia), Yhuri Cruz, 2019. Cruz created a modern monument to Anastácia, reimagining her historic image, and freeing her from the iron device covering her face. In this new portrait, Anastácia is liberated and empowered to use her voice.

latter instrument of torture prevented eating, drinking, and talking. Arago gave no reason for this abuse but called the portrait *Châtiment des Esclaves* (Punishment for Slaves).

When his diaries were published in France in the 1840s, *Châtiment des Esclaves* gained attention in Europe, the Americas, and Africa as a representation of colonial realities. It was one of the most widely circulated images within the Afro-Atlantic world in that era.

In Brazil, the work was renamed *Escrava Anastácia* (Enslaved Anastácia): the perception of the subject underwent a gender transition from a punished man to a punished woman. Not much is known about why this occurred, but a series of myths arose later concerning why Anastácia was punished with an iron bit. Some believed that her rare beauty provoked the jealousy of the slaveholder's wife.

Anastácia's resilience in the face of physical punishment became a core element of her veneration by devotees, who embraced her in ways reminiscent of Catholic martyrs and saints such as Sebastian or Stephen, both of whom were tortured and put to death. Like them, Anastácia is believed to have transcended her suffering because she was miraculously healed. This transcendence of suffering was one key reason why the image and memory of *Enslaved Anastácia* were reclaimed in the 1970s by Brazilians of African descent who found symbolic resonance with her during their own silencing when speaking out against injustice during the years of Brazil's authoritarian regime. She has since become a fundamental part of the pantheon of Afro-Brazilian religions, such as Umbanda, and of the Afro-Catholic church, especially in locations where major shrines of Black fraternal organizations serve the poor, such as Nossa Senhora do Rosário (Our Lady of the Rosary) in Rio de Janeiro and Salvador.

Believers worship her personally as well. Anastácia statues are mass-produced and personally crafted and placed on altars and in public and domestic spaces along with other saints and figures of veneration. Her image is also printed on prayer cards that are carried by devotees.

Instruments of torture, such as those represented in Arago's portrait, are part of museum collections in Brazil and other countries. For example, the Museu Histórico Nacional in Rio de Janeiro preserves an iron bit in its permanent exhibition. For years, the caption did not include the word *punishment*. However, for the museum's recent exhibition *Decolonial Brazil: Other Histories,* which reinterpreted the permanent collection through the lens of reparative justice, the caption was at last changed:

> An iconic image of the pain of enslavement, the iron bit has been associated for centuries with the one worn by Anastácia, a figure of popular devotion. . . . At the same time, it has been given a new meaning, having been transformed into a symbol of the silencing of the Brazilian Black population and of the resistance of Africans and their descendants to the horrors of enslavement.

Anastácia and her memory continue to be reclaimed and redefined. In 2019, the artist Yhuri Cruz created a new work, *Monumento à Voz de Anastácia* (Monument to the Voice of Anastácia). Cruz removed the iron bit and provided a mouth for Anastácia and a golden necklace that adorns her neck, so she no longer wears the suffocating neck iron and bit. Cruz reimagined and subverted the historic image of submissiveness and emphasized the importance of Anastácia's voice. Freed from the iron device, a liberated Anastácia slyly smiles in the face of oppression and assumes a new type of power, one not simply testifying to injustice but asserting dignity. In a reimagined prayer card, Cruz asks for her protection and power to free our thoughts from racism: "Anastácia, you are free, we implore you . . . intercede for us, shield us, enshroud us in your benevolent grace." Anastácia returns from the past, transcending space and time and the forces that silenced her, offering us a chance to use our own voices to speak against injustice.

SONGS OF FREEDOM PLAYLIST

From anticolonial revolution to #BlackLivesMatter, Black artists have composed freedom anthems that echo experiences of frustration and pain, spread messages of hope and joy, and help global listeners imagine freer futures.

Strummed on a *khalam*, chanted at a march, and hummed in a hymn, freedom anthems are the soundtrack to Black life. This playlist, compiled by the international curatorial team of *In Slavery's Wake,* brings together freedom anthems from across the world, beckoning all who support Black liberation to join the dance.

"To Be Young, Gifted and Black"
Nina Simone

"Give Us Our Land (Mabayeke)"
Harry Belafonte

"Ilê Ayê"
Gilberto Gil

"Teacher Don't Teach Me Nonsense"
Fela Kuti

"Nini To Sali Te"
Cité Zaïre

"By Any Means"
Jorja Smith

"Babylon System"
Bob Marley & the Wailers

"Y'En a Marre"
Tiken Jah Fakoly and Yaniss Odua

"Somos los Prietos"
ChocQuibTown

"Brava Gente! O Grito dos Excluídos No Bicentenário da Independência"
GRES Beija-Flor de Nilópolis

"Wet Chen"
Boukman Eksperyans

"Colonial Man"
Hugh Masekela

"Alright"
Kendrick Lamar

"Le Glas a Sonné"
Tabu Ley Rochereau

"Heróis da Liberdade"
Império Serrano

"Birth of Ghana"
Lord Kitchener

"Ata Ndele"
Bankolo Miziki

"Five Nights of Bleeding"
Linton Kwesi Johnson

"Superheroes"
Stormzy

"Freedom"
Beyoncé

"Resistência"
GRES Acadêmicos do Grande Rio

"France à Fric"
Keur Gui

"Indépendance Cha Cha"
Grande Kallé et l'African Jazz

"The Revolution Will Not Be Televised"
Gil Scott-Heron

"Fé Cega, Faca Amolada"
Margareth Menezes

"A Luta Continua"
Miriam Makeba

"We Shall Overcome"
Mahalia Jackson

"Senzeni Na? (What Have We Done?)"
Cape Town Youth Choir feat. Monde Mdingi

"INDÉPENDANCE CHA CHA"

Bambi Ceuppens

"Indépendance Cha Cha," the unofficial anthem of the DRC and the seventeen other African countries that gained independence in 1960, was composed in Brussels, Belgium, on January 31, 1960. A joyous soundtrack to liberation, it was also the first Pan-African hit single: it marked the astonishing and unparalleled spread of Congolese rumba and its later forms, *soukous* and *ndombolo*, throughout the continent and demonstrated the power of music to speak across national boundaries and create societal change.

From January 20 to February 20, 1960, Congolese and Belgian political leaders prepared Congolese independence at a Round Table Conference in Brussels. The Congolese delegation demanded the release of Patrice Lumumba, the founder of the country's first political party Mouvement National Congolais (Congolese National Movement), who was imprisoned in the Congo. When Lumumba arrived at the conference on January 26 the deliberations took a crucial turn and the date for independence was set for June 30.

Before the start of the negotiations, delegation member and journalist Thomas Kanza had suggested forming a band composed of members of African Jazz and OK Jazz, the two most popular Congolese bands at the time. On January 30, bandleader and singer Joseph Kabasele (also known as Le Grand Kallé), maracas player Roger Izeidi, rhythm guitarist Déchaud Mongala (Charles Mwamba), lead guitarist Docteur Nico (Nico Kasanda) and drummer Petit Pierre (Pierre Yantula) of African Jazz arrived in Brussels, joined by bassist Brazzos (Armando Mwango Fwadi-Maya), and vocalist Vicky Longomba (Victor Longomba Besange Lokuli) of African Jazz. The day after their arrival, Kanza asked Kallé to compose a song about the impending independence. On the evening of February 1 at Hotel Le Plaza in Brussels, the musicians played together publicly for the first time under the name African Jazz, at the Independence Ball, which was organized by the journal Congo, owned by Thomas Kanza and his brother Philippe. At 10 p.m., the brothers each gave a speech and Thomas ended his by introducing the band and concluding with an impassioned "Kallé, chauffez Bruxelles!" (Kallé, heat up Brussels!). When they played "Indépendance Cha Cha," it was immediately clear that they had a smash hit on their hands. The ball went on until 5 a.m. In the coming days, African Jazz recorded the song and its flip side "Table Ronde" (Round Table).

In Leopoldville, capital of Belgian Congo, Jean Lema, presenter and supervisor at the Congolese broadcasts of Radio Congo Belge, played "Indépendance Cha Cha" at the beginning of each program. The lyrics serve as a spoken journal, in real time, about the political leaders and parties and the decisions that were made at the round table. In a spirit of national identity, the song is written in two Congolese languages— Lingala and Kikongo—and French.

> *Indépendance cha cha tozui e.*
> *O Kimpwanza cha cha tubakidi.*
> *O Table Ronde cha cha ba gagner o.*
> *O Dipanda cha cha tozui e.*
>
> *O independence cha cha gained.*
> *O Freedom cha cha we conquered*
> *At the Round Table cha cha they won.*
> *Independence cha cha we gained it.*

When the musicians returned home from their European tour, they were paraded through the capital city of Kinshasa in an open-air car while throngs of onlookers shouted, "Indépendance Cha Cha!"

The song spread throughout the colony and served as one of the first markers of a national identity. Its emergence and the craze that followed marked Kinshasa as the birthplace of a whole new type of music that conquered the world. If the political history of the DRC is full of tragedy, its cultural and musical legacy is a source of great pride and national identity. The song's triumphant joy takes on a certain poignancy when one knows how soon the dreams of independence would unravel, but it never fails to lift spirits, and it irresistibly pulls listeners to dance and sing along. It captures the Congolese people's irrepressible desire for and aspiration to the self-determination they have been denied for so long. In 2021, UNESCO added Congolese rumba to its Representative List of the Intangible Cultural Heritage of Humanity.

EXU TRANSFORMS SAMBA!

Vinícius Natal

The feast of São Jorge (St. George)—an important celebration in Brazil's array of popular Black cultural festivals—fell on April 23 in 2022. The acute phase of the COVID-19 pandemic haunted the memories of samba dancers unable to participate in Carnival the previous year. Yet many had experienced a transcendent return just a month prior. It felt like a potential turning point in Brazil, for samba, my city, and the nation. The *orixás*, gods within the pantheon of Candomblé, an Afro-Brazilian religion with deep roots in west and central Africa that was brought across the Kalunga Grande (Middle Passage) by enslaved Africans, spoke powerfully in this crossroads moment.

The most ardent voices of all were Ogum, the prime deity associated with São Jorge's day and of protection against evil in times of danger, and Exu, the god whom my samba school had just celebrated in late February for Carnival. Throughout Rio de Janeiro, rituals for Ogum and Exu, who share energy connected to the streets and sacrifice, were carried out. The city felt poised for protection, for healing, for battle, and for change.

Exu has recently become a major theme in contemporary Brazilian decolonial discourse. Featured in exhibitions, theater performances, books, and countless academic works, the metaphor of Exu has been used to tackle the thorny and unresolved issues of the country's past. In 2022, the Grêmio Recreativo Escola de Samba Acadêmicos do Grande Rio, Grande Rio for short, a samba school in Rio de Janeiro's municipality of Duque de Caxias, honored Exu in the storyline for its theme for the city's internationally renowned Carnival and its parade. Rio's Carnival is considered the biggest in the world, with 2 million people populating the streets daily. "Fala, Majeté! Sete Chaves de Exu!" (Speak Majesty, Seven Keys of Exu!) was the theme of Grande Rio's 2022 Carnival: a call to action, acknowledgment, and prayer. Written by me in partnership with *carnavalescos* (carnival producers) Gabriel Haddad and Leonardo Bora, Seven Keys of Exu presented the *orixá* in a kaleidoscopic way, showing his multiple facets and faces.

Composers Gustavo Clarão, Arlindinho Cruz Jr., Fraga, Cláudio Mattos, Thiago Meiners, and Igor Leal wrote the

Left
Members of the Grande Rio samba school perform during Rio de Janeiro's Carnival, 2022. The group presented the story "Fala, Majeté! Sete Chaves de Exu!" ("Speak, Majesty! Seven Keys of Exu!"), which focused on the Yorùbá and Brazilian deity Exu.

Top
Actor Demerson Dálvaro, representing Exu, stands at the top of the world during Carnival, Vitor Melo, 2022.

music to accompany the theme. The work was a response to the historically virulent intolerance of African-based religions in Brazil and the disparagement of Afro-Brazilian culture and religions since the period of slavery. Claiming that Exu is evil and the embodiment of the devil, neo-Pentecostal religions are making significant inroads in Brazil and are responsible for many attacks on Afro-Brazilian religious sites and *casas de santos* (sacred spaces). This hatred resurged during the pandemic, encouraged by authoritarian politics and its permissiveness toward anti-Black violence. During 2022's Carnival parade, it was said that Grande Rio performers channeled the energy of Exu. The audience, astonished by the electricity of the event, broke out at the end of the

procession with shouts of "They're champions!" In winning its first championship, the Grande Rio samba school made the name of Exu reverberate among the public. Google searches for the *orixá* grew by more than four hundred percent after the parade, and an avalanche of press articles and TV coverage appeared as people sought to learn more about *orixás*. While this enthusiasm for, interest in, and embrace of Exu and the wider pantheon of *orixás* was a surprise for the majority of the population, it was not for the performers within Rio's Black samba schools.

Longtime sites of education that combine culture, politics, and care for primarily poor, Black communities in the city's favelas, samba schools have decisively contributed to the amplification of stories that challenge racist discourse in Brazil. Created by the children and grandchildren of enslaved people after the end of slavery in Brazil as alternative spaces of community, recreation, and empowerment in a country that degraded its Black population, samba schools are cultural organizations that act as powerful vehicles of Black resistance and artistic expression. During the post-abolition period in the early twentieth century, samba dancers armed themselves with powerful strategies to protect and maintain their culture through a series of initiatives deployed for the survival of Black identity and a politics of freedom deeply rooted in embodied movement and cultural expression. Today's clatter and rhythms of tambourines and drums reflect the incongruities of a country still dodging full confrontation with its history of slavery and the reverberations of racism into the present.

This drive for social equity and citizenship through the politics of culture remains palpable and essential. Exu's victory at Rio de Janeiro's 2022 Carnival was heard far and wide. The *orixá* of the crossroads acted as an animating force extolling samba and its ability to address central social themes of memory, history, race, and Black identity that are relevant to Brazilian society as a whole, affirming the role of Black samba practitioners as vital to discussions about Brazil's past, present, and future. Exu and his echoes bridge the Atlantic and help us to face our own inner journey head-on. Let the drums roll. Exu's time has come.

"WE SHALL OVERCOME"

Paul Tichmann

Freedom songs like "We Shall Overcome" transcend geographic, racial, social, and spiritual borders and are testimony to the universal desire for freedom from racism and oppression. This song is regarded as the anthem of the US Civil Rights Movement of the 1950s and 1960s but it was also adopted and adapted during the struggle against apartheid in South Africa from the late 1940s to 1991. For South Africans, this song instilled in us a firm hope, during a time of bitter struggle, that we would eventually triumph over the racism and violence of apartheid, and that "the Black man shall be free someday." This particular lyric was included in the South African version, with the hope that it would come to pass.

In South Africa, "We Shall Overcome" was sung during the Black Conscious-ness Movement in the 1960s and 1970s and through to the United Democratic Front, beginning in 1983. On April 1, 1965, Frederick John Harris, a teacher and member of the African Resistance Movement, who was the only white South African ever executed for treason, sang "We Shall Overcome" as he was led to the gallows. During a visit to South Africa in 1966, Senator Robert F. Kennedy led a crowd in singing "We Shall Overcome." When the veteran anti-apartheid activist Archbishop Desmond Tutu received the Nobel Peace Prize in 1984, he stood with a crowd outside the University of Oslo, singing the song.

Originally composed around 1900 by Charles Albert Tindley with the title and words "I'll Overcome Someday," it was altered in 1945 by Lucille Simmons, who changed the title and words to "We Will Overcome" in 1945. Simmons sang her rendition during a strike by

Black members of the Food, Tobacco, Agricultural, and Allied Workers Union of Charleston, South Carolina. During a workshop in 1947 at the Highlander Folk School in Monteagle, Tennessee, participants further adapted the title and words to "We Shall Overcome."

The song resonates with me as a South African because I often sang it in anti-apartheid protests and gatherings during my student years. On June 16, 1977, as a first-year student at the Howard College campus of the University of Natal (now the University of KwaZulu-Natal), I attended a commemoration of the 1976 Soweto uprising—when police massacred students who were protesting a directive of the Department of Bantu Education that Afrikaans, instead of English, was to be used when teaching mathematics and social science classes in "African" schools. The commemoration was held at the Alan Taylor Residence, a hostel for Black medical students. Soon after the first Black Consciousness Movement speaker took the podium in the packed hall, there was a loud rumbling outside the building, where a semicircle of armored police vehicles was positioned directly across from the entrance to the hall. Unfazed, the speaker urged us to choose whether we wanted to leave or to fight against apartheid to ensure that the students killed in Soweto and elsewhere in the country had not died in vain. As we raised our fists in the air and began to sing "We

Shall Overcome," I drew on the courage of those around me.

My identity book, an aspect of racial classification under apartheid, identified me as "Cape Coloured" (of mixed descent from the Cape Province), although I was born and raised in KwaZulu-Natal. Because of my "race," the institution designated for me was the University of the Western Cape, in Cape Town. I had to obtain special permission to study at the University of Natal, an institution for "whites," where I was part of a Black minority. In the 1980s, we formed a Black Students' Society on the campus, and I was elected to the committee. We organized a boycott of classes in support of equal education. White students, except for a paltry few who joined us in solidarity, continued to attend classes while we occupied the lawns on the campus. "We Shall Overcome" became a theme song for us; the words were easy to remember and the song bound us in unity, in what seemed to be a hopeless pursuit on a majority-white campus. The song not only drew us together, across our political divisions, but also gave us a sense of hope that, in solidarity, we would achieve freedom and justice.

Top
Soweto uprising, 1976. In a series of demonstrations led by South African schoolchildren, protestors rejected the government's plan to make Afrikaans the primary language of instruction in Black schools. More than twenty thousand students bravely participated in these protests in the face of police brutality.

Right
Tobacco workers strike in North Carolina, 1946. In 1945, workers began a strike against American Tobacco in Charleston, South Carolina. The strikers, primarily African American women, sang the song "I Will Overcome" as they picketed for increased pay. One of the strikers, Lucile Simmons, changed the song's lyric from "I" to "We," evoking the sense of solidarity and collective action amongst the group.

UNFINISHED CONVER- SATIONS

A PAST STILL PRESENT

Shana Weinberg

The Unfinished Conversations initiative is an oral history, archival, and curatorial project that documents and shares community memories of how the legacies of slavery and colonialism continue to impact people's lives today. Providing a platform for people to tell their own histories and giving a voice to marginalized communities is the heart of Unfinished Conversations. With contributions from people across four continents, this global collection challenges mainstream narratives that seek to whitewash the history of colonialism, racial slavery, and empire-building, as well as conventions of whose stories should be told and preserved. Led by the Ruth J. Simmons Center for the Study of Slavery and Justice at Brown University, the initiative is jointly organized with Global Curatorial Project (GCP) partners and their communities. Since 2021, these partners have video-recorded communities' stories in Saint-Louis and Fouta, Senegal; Liverpool, United Kingdom; Africatown, Alabama, United States; Rio de Janeiro, Brazil; Cape Town and the Groot Constantia wine estate, South Africa; neighborhoods surrounding Brussels, Belgium; and Kinshasa and the Kimbanguist Church, DRC in Nkamba.

Since its founding, the GCP network has been committed to uplifting lesser-known histories that speak to the lived experiences of enslaved and descendant communities and challenge official state narratives. The stories of regular contemporary people, told in their own voices, have been largely absent from exhibitions on slavery, and the project sought to fill that void. Conversations with communities in Liverpool and Senegal directly shaped the Unfinished Conversations series. People shared family stories of resistance, of searching for belonging, of how their lives today continue to be shaped by racial slavery, and of how they navigate the reverberations of colonialism. The Liverpool community member Ray Quarless shared how his family history reflects the history of the British Empire:

> **My family are a classic example of the British Empire in terms of the geography. It's made up of four component parts: Jamaican, English, Irish, and Bajan [Barbadian]. My great-grandfather arrived in Liverpool in 1868 as a merchant seaman from Jamaica. And he settled in Liverpool, where he met and married my great-grandmother, who was English, from Bilston near Wolverhampton.**

Yet despite the fact that these multicultural communities have lived in Liverpool for hundreds of years, people like Ray do not see their family stories reflected in British histories or school curricula.

Community members across the geographies of the project were clear that they wanted to tell their histories themselves, despite the trauma

Sadio Diallo is interviewed in Senegal, 2023. Unfinished Conversations participants in the Fouta region discussed their families' experiences with slavery, ongoing stigmas tied to local systems of caste and class, and visions for the future.

associated with some of these stories. During a preparatory field visit in 2019, a community member in Senegal stated that documenting these stories requires talking to communities directly, "not to make history in their place." A Senegalese leader of a prominent organization of descendants of slavery advised that the resharing of these histories was important, noting, "History is made up of things that give pleasure and other things that are painful." Community members shared their hopes that presenting these narratives through public-facing projects like the *In Slavery's Wake* exhibition and an accompanying archive at Brown University will help to make them more widely known and begin the process of eroding continually perpetuated false histories.

The first documented Unfinished Conversation interview took place in Senegal, with descendants of the enslaved from former freedom villages in the regions of Saint-Louis, Louga, and Matam, and with members of the international African organiza-

tion Endam Bilali in Orkadiéré in the region of Fouta. Ibrahima Thiaw and Mouhamed A. Ly of the Unité de Recherche en Ingénierie Culturelle et en Anthropologie at Cheikh Anta Diop University led the GCP team in testing a methodology focused on building relationships and trust. Many descendants of the freedom villages' original inhabitants continue to live in the same villages as their parents and grandparents. Their experiences today are deeply shaped by whether their families benefited by working with the colonial powers or whether they were descended from the formerly enslaved. Given the particularly sensitive nature of this history, interviewers opened the conversation by asking people to share their family lineage. Faty Ba, a woman living in the village of Ngano, shared her family's migration story:

> On the paternal side, they say they are from Gabou. . . . They arrived at the village to accompany the Wane families. The Wane family lives in another part of the village. When they arrived, our

Left
Community members in Africatown, Alabama, hold t-shirts from the annual remembrance celebration at Clotilda Landing, the site where the last known slave ship arrived in the United States illegally, 2022. As a part of Unfinished Conversations, members from Africatown and nearby communities in Mobile, Alabama shared their histories.

Bottom
Renzo Carvalho is filmed in the Museu da História e da Cultura Afro-Brasiliera as a part of Unfinished Conversations series in Rio de Janiero, Brazil, 2022. In his interview, Pena spoke about the forgotten histories of Black resistance and importance of preserving memory in the continued fight for freedom.

families moved to this side, and the Wane families moved to the other side. And our grandparents occupied this place.... Our families were dependent on the Wane families. These latter had fields in which our grandparents worked.... We define ourselves as *diéyabés*, or simple slaves.

In her interview, Faty discusses with researchers the cultural norms and social dynamics around the inherited status of different sectors of the community, such as her family's dependence on the Wane family. The particulars of her family's stories help us to better understand how communities continue to live together and navigate these identities today in rural Senegal.

In the United States, interviewees from Africatown, Alabama, also shared how the legacies of racial slavery and forced migration continue to impact the social dynamics between this small community and the larger city of Mobile. Africatown was founded by descendants of the 110 enslaved people who were kidnapped from the African continent and illegally brought to the United States on the slave ship the *Clotilda*, decades after the 1807 Act to Prohibit the Importation of Slaves. The interviewee Emmett Lewis, a descendant

of the *Clotilda* survivor and Africatown founder Cudjo Lewis, shared with researchers at the Smithsonian's National Museum of African American History and Culture how community spaces become vital sites of education and self-empowerment, particularly in the face of historical erasure:

> Knowing that my great-grandfather was Cudjo Lewis, because my dad talked to me about it, because everybody, you know, pushed that history towards me, I feel like, if I didn't know any of that history, when I seen that name in a notebook, I wouldn't have cared. I wouldn't have paid it no attention.... [But] I can go right here to a barbershop and they telling me the complete history of everything. They telling me the names of people.... Ninth or tenth grade, I got a big textbook say "Alabama History." I don't even think there was a page about Africatown history in there.

Community members also spoke of the disproportionate effect of industry on their community, which has had significant environmental and public health impacts. They raised concerns about the lack of opportunities for young people, which leads to high levels of violence in their community. Despite the divisions that go back generations, they also spoke of their work toward community empowerment and finding opportunities for joy.

In Rio de Janeiro, community members also talked about the realities of racism while highlighting practices of empowerment. In Brazil, the last country in the Western Hemisphere to abolish slavery, its legacies continue to deeply shape the lives of people of African descent. The Unfinished Conversations series worked closely with Brazilian partners including the institutions Museu do Samba, Laboratório de História Oral e Imagem (LABHOI), Universidade Federal Fluminense (UFF), Programa Rio: Memória e Ação, and Museu Histórico Nacional, which recorded conversations with community historians, scholars, activists, and musicians, among others. Interviewees discussed how cultural practices of the Diaspora, such as samba and capoeira, serve as powerful acts of knowledge production, community building, spiritual sustenance, and

self-empowerment in a world that is violent toward Black people. Alcino Amaral stated:

> Since the Black body is in the context of slave and colonial logic, it is conditioned to work, to labor; it is conditioned to, finally, be at the mill all the time, to be working, moving, and producing. And since capoeira is another story, it is another narrative, which was made possible here for that body. It's a moment of empowerment of that body; it's a moment of expansion of that body, and it's a process, which I learned in capoeira, that is very personal.

Interviewees shared the historical connection and context for such practices and the ways they provide a spiritual salve for their daily lived experiences shaped by racism.

In the port city of Liverpool, representatives of the Black community spoke to staff at the International Slavery Museum about how their family trees reflected the British slave trade, connecting communities across

Africa, the Caribbean, and the United Kingdom. While their families are part of the oldest Black communities in Europe, their stories are not reflected in official British history. Several of the Liverpool interviews discussed the painful disconnect of learning a whitewashed British history in schools that does not reflect their family experiences. They described their self-education in Black British history and the empowerment found in reclaiming it. Kerry Nugent described feeling like an outsider in their home city despite her family's having called Liverpool home for generations:

> You know, I don't feel accepted as British, but I know that . . . if people tell me to go home, I can only go as far as Parliament Street to my grandmother's home, you know? And I'm under no illusion that if I was to return to Africa that there's going to be an acceptance. I'd be a foreign woman in a strange land.

The staff at the Iziko Museums of South Africa met with workers at the Groot Constantia wine estate, one of the country's leading wine farms, to see if they would be willing to record their stories, particularly given concerns about the possible consequences they might face from their employer. Despite their precarious situation, many went on the record, both individually and in small groups, to speak frankly of their experiences of mistreatment and lack of control over their living conditions. The interviewees made stark connections between enslaved and contemporary laborers on such farms. They discussed the historic *dop* system, which paid workers in wine instead of money, a practice that had devastating impacts on community health, domestic violence, and upward mobility. With so much of their means of support tied up with the wine company, leaving this exploitative work is extremely difficult. Zann Manho said, "I would like to have my own house one day, because when it comes to dying, I am the sole breadwinner. . . . If I have to die, then [the company] are going to kick my children out of the house."

What began as a small set of interviews quickly expanded as people brought family members and neighbors to recording sessions. On the Western

Cape, the Unfinished Conversations project validated the importance of these stories for communities that are not often asked to share their experiences. In her interview, the poet and farmworker Lorna Solomon stated, "We don't have that much freedom of speech. You can't say what you want. . . . You also know who is in charge."

Communities in Belgium and the DRC spoke to the staff of the AfricaMuseum (Belgium), offering an important comparative collection that examines experiences of colonialism on the African continent and within the Afropean Diaspora. Several interviewed individuals currently live in Brussels but were born in colonial Congo, Rwanda, or Burundi. Belgian administrators in colonial Africa sought to control every aspect of people's lives, including the family. Interviewees shared their traumatic experiences as young people growing up as "mixed-race" within a colonial system that claimed the authority to separate them from their families and place them in new homes. Jacqueline Goegebeur shared her memories as the daughter of a Belgian father and a Rwandan mother. Born in Rwanda, she was taken from her mother at the age of three and forced into foster care. As colonial rule was ending in Rwanda, she was sent to Belgium to live with a new family. When asked by interviewers about her work defending the rights of mixed children in Belgium and what work remains to be done, Jacqueline shared the need for governmental recognition of her community's experiences and the importance for these individuals to share their experiences in their own words:

> To start with, acknowledge that there has been abuse. Acknowledge, to start with, that this can be scrutinized and that it can be talked about. Give us this opportunity, and also give us the opportunity to tell our own story ourselves. . . . Indeed I want to do it as well when it comes to colonization and to what we have experienced. Being able to speak ourselves [is] always important.

Experiences like Jacqueline's offer critically important comparative perspectives on life under Belgian colonial regimes across two continents. Such painful stories, marked by both

Mohamed Elmi stands in front of his mosque in Liverpool, England, 2022. In his Unfinished Conversations interview, Mohamed discussed his upbringing in the diverse Black community of Toxteth and emphasized the importance of faith and spirituality in freedom making.

trauma and resilience, reclaim the humanity of this history.

The Unfinished Conversations essays that follow offer brief but, we hope, important windows onto each of the locations where interviews were videotaped. Individuals shared the community histories they felt were the most important. The cadences of storytelling—a pregnant pause, a search for words, a shared knowing laugh between interviewer and interviewee—create an intimacy between speaker and audience that begins to shift the current understanding of racial slavery and colonialism. The interviewees' candor allows the public to begin to understand the human suffering caused by these violent and extractive systems, without scholarly or administrative jargon to mask the experiences.

Words are insufficient to express our immense gratitude to the communities that welcomed GCP members into their homes, neighborhoods, places of worship, and workplaces. In a world that continues to be so deeply shaped by the strata and hierarchies created by colonialism and racial slavery, we do not take lightly the courage it took to share these personal, and often painful, histories. As the title of this initiative suggests, the work remains unfinished. We hope that sharing these stories through this book, the exhibition, the archive, and other platforms will help to further understanding of how the past and present are so closely entwined. We also hope that we have succeeded in making small steps toward acknowledging this history as it really was.

The full archive of recorded stories is available at Brown University in the Global Curatorial Project: Unfinished Conversations oral histories and records collection, Ms.2022.010.

FOUTA & SAINT-LOUIS, SENEGAL

Fatoumata Camara

See page 234 for caption

In the fifteenth century, the destiny of Senegambia was turned upside down. This vast region in West Africa, comprising the Senegal and Gambia river basins, was to be integrated into a new economic system linking the Atlantic world. In addition to producing gold, leather, spices, and ivory, all prized by Western merchants, Senegambia became a hub for the Transatlantic Slave Trade. It was a collection point for slaves, from which those captured in the interior of the continent were exported to the Americas. Its essential role in the expansion of the plantation economy helped foster the emergence of industrial capitalism. On April 27, 1848, slavery was outlawed in the French colonies, including Senegal, sparking keen hopes and initiatives among the formerly enslaved, who believed they were seeing a change in the previously established social order. However, the French colonial conquest, which had begun in Saint-Louis, continued in full force, and the law intended to end this dehumanizing practice did not substantially impact the newly free or their descendants.

In fact, with the abolition of the Transatlantic Slave Trade in the nineteenth century and the subsequent establishment of the colonial system to serve the interests of rapidly expanding Western states and industries, Senegambia became a laboratory for Europe's political control over the continent's interior. Senegambia became a reserve of cheap labor and raw materials for the various colonial powers that settled there, resulting in continued subjugation and exploitation of the region's people and resources. These various processes, along with the forced displacement and voluntary migrations of populations of varied origins and cultural practices, added to socioeconomic and political inequities within Senegambian societies throughout the twentieth century. The consequences of this era are still evident today across the political and geographic landscapes and, above all, in the relationships between various communities that populate the region. This is why descendants of the enslaved continued to fight for better access to resources and against the social hierarchies inherited from the period of slavery. Even now, those legacies keep them at the bottom of the social ladder.

As part of the Unfinished Conversations initiative, the Unité de Recherche en Ingénierie Culturelle et en Anthropologie (URICA) of Université Cheikh Anta Diop collected memories related to the slave trade and its resonance in contemporary societies. A series of interviews was conducted in Fouta, in the northeast near the border of Mauritania, and Saint-Louis, the former French colonial capital, in northern Senegal in 2021 and 2023. During the Transatlantic Slave Trade, enslaved people were sent to or traveled through these areas, and the families of formerly enslaved people live there today.

The Senegal research team focused its efforts on two communities: the *maccudo* and the *bamana*. *Maccudo* means "slave" (plural, *maccube*) and is used today to identify an individual descended from slaves. Bamana communities migrated from French Sudan because of the slave trade or the tumult it caused. It was important for Unfinished Conversations participants from these communities to become familiar with the process and take ownership of it. Identifying the individuals to be interviewed took place through conversations that sometimes lasted late into the night or occurred in the brush away from prying eyes. Recruits were sought following their participation in general meetings or various ceremonies organized by the descendants of the enslaved both in Saint-Louis and in the Senegal River valley.

In Fouta, descendants of the enslaved had established an organization called Endam Bilali, meaning "related to Bilal," a former enslaved person and companion of the Prophet Muhammad. This organization is active across Western Africa, from Mauritania and Senegal to Mali, in the struggle to end the stigmatization and oppression of its members. (See pages 82–83 for more about Endam Bilali.) In Saint-Louis, it was apparent that the *bamanas*, while facing stigmas connected to their past and their origins, had developed strategies to make their mark on the economy, as well as on the physical and cultural landscapes of the city.

More than two dozen people were interviewed across these two regions, telling powerful stories about the trajectories of their ancestors who

Aissata Sy,
2023.

informs her family's former holders each time one of her children marries.

The impact of these continuing practices that organize and police familial lineages through future generations is powerfully encapsulated by Oumar Diallo, a member of the formerly enslaved community in Fouta, who expanded upon the pain that he continues to feel as someone who is still identified as *maccudo*:

> **I have not yet completely cut the cord of slavery, but the way it affects our life has decreased. I live the way I want to; I move around as I like. What still remains in society is the fact of being put down when you say something, and people refer to your slave origins. They hurt you this way. It's like shooting a shotgun at you. The pain is the same. In any group of people, if someone says these words to you, you're no longer considered a human being. They've diminished you.**

In addition to marginalization, stigmas reappear on occasions such as hiring employees or choosing leaders. Insulting terms like "slave bastard" and "*diaamou* Bambara," or Bambara slave, after an ethnic group in the Sudan, are frequently used for descendants of the enslaved. These stigmas are part of the complex relationships in these communities that still revolve around the past.

All interviewees aspired to social and economic equality and shared a willingness to seek secular or religious education to reduce, if not eliminate, their caste station. For example, teaching and learning the Koran is a major element of daily life among Endam Bilali members in the Fouta region, giving them a tool to manage their complex identity and garner more visibility and recognition in the community. Abou Mamadou Ba was not allowed to study the Koran in Mauritania and Mali, but he began to after moving to Orkadiéré, where he still lives. Today, passing down the knowledge he has acquired has become his vocation:

> **When I came back [to Orkadiéré], leading wasn't part of my ambitions, let alone teaching. I wanted to immigrate,**

settled in Senegal. They also shared stories about the measures taken by their forebears and themselves to become free or build a new life. The interviews also dealt with the memories of slavery and colonialism and people's aspirations for a freer, more just life.

In Fouta more than in Saint-Louis—a city in which it is easier to blend into the crowd—the descendants of the enslaved continue to suffer from marginalization akin to a caste system. By design, they are kept at the bottom of the social ladder, to reproduce the relationships that existed among their enslaved ancestors, the former masters of those ancestors, and free people.

According to Sona Sall, who lives in Fouta and is called *ajiyabé*, a term that means "enslaved woman" and is still used today for women descendants of slaves, it is unthinkable that a *maccudo* could marry a member of a noble family. Per traditional customs, some even obtain the consent of their family's former slaveholders to get married. Aissata Sy, a member of Endam Bilali who lives in Orkadiéré, admits that she

to get money like you do, but my Koranic teachers asked me to stay on and teach. . . . I love them, so I decided to accept their wishes. Since then, I've done nothing but teach, I haven't gone anywhere, and I don't think about what they asked me to leave.

Many children and young people come to his home from different regions to acquire Islamic knowledge. "The [Endam Bilali] association has given us what we were looking for in terms of knowledge, has strengthened our bonds. It has also enabled us to practice our religion better; our children are better awake, and so are those of others," Ba observes. Endam Bilali invests in the education of younger generations, including training in the manual trades for those who have not gotten through school. In Diallo's home, all those who cannot succeed in school are guided toward business or woodworking.

In Saint-Louis, the history and legacies of enslavement are lived and expressed much differently than in more rural inland communities like Fouta. As one of the first refuges for the formerly enslaved after the abolition of the slave trade, people whose grandparents experienced slavery in the former colonial capital of Saint-Louis have developed a complex set of strategies to navigate the vestigial effects of slavery in a contemporary urban world. Some distance themselves from that past by claiming royal origins for their grandparents or stating that they came to the former colonial city as part of the colonial project. Others voluntarily "forget" familial histories or resort to creating a heroic past for their ancestors. (See pages 80–81 for more on Saint-Louis.)

Another significant topic in these interviews was the loss of shared memories and history when family members were deported or sold into different regions. Identity development for these communities is difficult. Some members were separated from their biological parents at an early age and remained far from their native land for a long time. These people have difficulty reconstructing their genealogy or even remembering their ethnic group. It is disturbing to see that some individuals have developed an attachment

to the family of their former holder, which remains their only anchor within a society where they remain foreign despite their own family's having lived there for generations. For Kardiata Sall, the long-standing relations with her family's holders ultimately created a kinship relationship between them. Demba Sangaré, who lives in Saint-Louis and identifies as Halpulaar, is much more familiar with the Bambara language and Bambara customs than those of the Pulaar group to which he belongs. He related:

> **My relatives came from Bougouni Circle [in Mali], before immigrating and settling here in Saint-Louis. . . . I can't say exactly when my family came to Saint-Louis, but what I can say is that my mother, the one who gave birth to me, was born in 1905 in Saint-Louis. . . . The reasons that drove them to leave their place of residence in the first place? They were in a bamana kingdom, but specifically in an area that belonged to the Peuls [Fulani] in Mali.**

Descendants also speak to broader patterns of life lived in the wake of slavery and colonialism, regardless of family connections to the experience of being enslaved. From environmental conditions in Saint-Louis, a city that is sinking into the Atlantic Ocean owing to rising sea levels caused by climate

Sona Sall, 2021.

change, to migration forced by poverty, interviewees were just as eager to speak about the present as the past, powerfully articulating the need for deeper independence and justice than currently exist in their lives.

"It's a failure!" claimed Alioune Badara Coulibaly, a writer and member of the bamana community living in Saint-Louis, referring to the recent postcolonial past when asked to speak about justice:

Africa once had its democracy and was developing, and . . . . unfortunately, auxiliaries [Senegalese colonial military forces] helped the French Army occupy our countries, and from there we also lost our freedom. Today even our thinking is Westernized. People don't even know the history of Africa; they don't even know African proverbs. In any case, as [Léopold] Senghor said, when we think for ourselves and by ourselves, we'll move forward. And to do that, we need to know our past: be proud of our past and know how to say no! [They] take resources because we don't have the means. We should have our own means, to be able to dictate to foreigners what we want from our resources. But today

Baila Coulibaly, 2022.

we give our resources, we give them to be able to live. Today we need [to go] beyond the current framework . . . . but today it's the technical and financial powers who dictate their laws to us.

Drawing the lines of experience explicitly back to slavery, Coulibaly asserted, "What still exists from slavery here is more harmful than slavery, where they chained people, because now it's their consciousness that is in chains. Psychological chains make slaves accept their fate and remain passive. . . . A consciousness in chains is almost a lost cause."

Sangaré provided a similar critique of contemporary global politics and tied it to a need for resource independence to deconstruct present inequalities and empower Africans in Senegal and on the wider continent:

Africans, not to speak specifically of Senegalese, need to assume their responsibilities, knowing that today the world has changed. Just as the world has changed, so have they. All those who come here do so because they find something here that they don't find at home. But the intellectuals who have

been given the task of negotiating on our behalf must also understand what's at stake and put the interests of the people first, as long as the people put them in the right conditions, so that our resources can serve the country's development, so that we can take the necessary measures to enable us to live in good conditions. . . . I do think that, as we move forward, Africans, young Africans, understand what's at stake and that they will assume their responsibilities so that the resources that belong to Africans will no longer be used for the development of other countries but will be used for the development of their own people.

Whether speaking about their personal or family identity or about issues of today's global environment or economy, the interviewees in Fouta and Saint-Louis demonstrated a strong desire to connect their lives and experiences to the past. They expressed a common observation that the history of the slave trade also includes the astounding resilience and agency of the enslaved and that these histories must be remembered and taught. From medicinal knowledge and religious practices such as Mariba Yaasa, a ritual showing gratitude after the fulfillment of an urgent prayer to the divinities, to land-management strategies, traditional expertise is honored and sustained among Endam members and in the communities of Khor and Sénofobougou, where the bamanas live in Saint-Louis.

Sangaré evoked the powerful and personal reclamation and practice of rituals and dances, such as *kiring* and *guéré*, performed during traditional festivals. Carrying forward these traditions demonstrates the priceless value of holding onto and passing down culture and freedom making in people's lives today:

> *Kiring* is a kind of languorous dance. In general, it's a dance performed by elderly people going around a circle while being encouraged by the audience. The *guéré* is a much livelier dance. It's performed by young men and women. They form two rows: one row of boys and one row of girls. The drummers are in the middle. The first man who starts

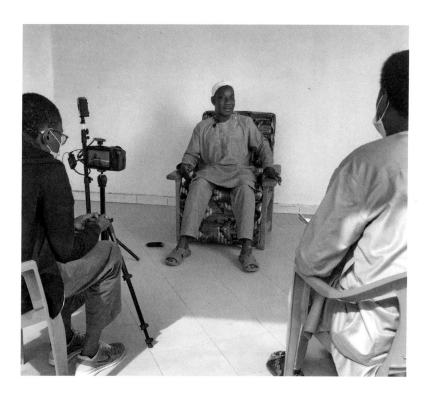

Oumar Diallo, 2021.

> the dance chooses a lady, the one he cherishes in his heart. As he goes, he dedicates the dance to her, but when he returns to his place, the lady joins him, showing her acceptance. This is a dance performed only by the young, not by the elderly. The *kiring*, on the other hand, is performed by notables. Each represents a specific entity. As I am Peulh, when I enter the circle, the dithyrambs fly: "Sangaré Barry" and so on. If a *Diarra* enters too, we do the same to him, and he raises his hands, and so on. That's how it goes. . . . Every year the children organize cultural ceremonies with Bambara dances. I often go at night, just to liven things up, to do a few dance steps . . . to remember my childhood a little, and then go back home. But the young people dance them a lot.

Most crucially, the interviewees in Senegal are aware of a deep and continuing connection with the past that charts their experience of the present and visions for the future.

BELGIUM & DEMOCRATIC REPUBLIC OF CONGO

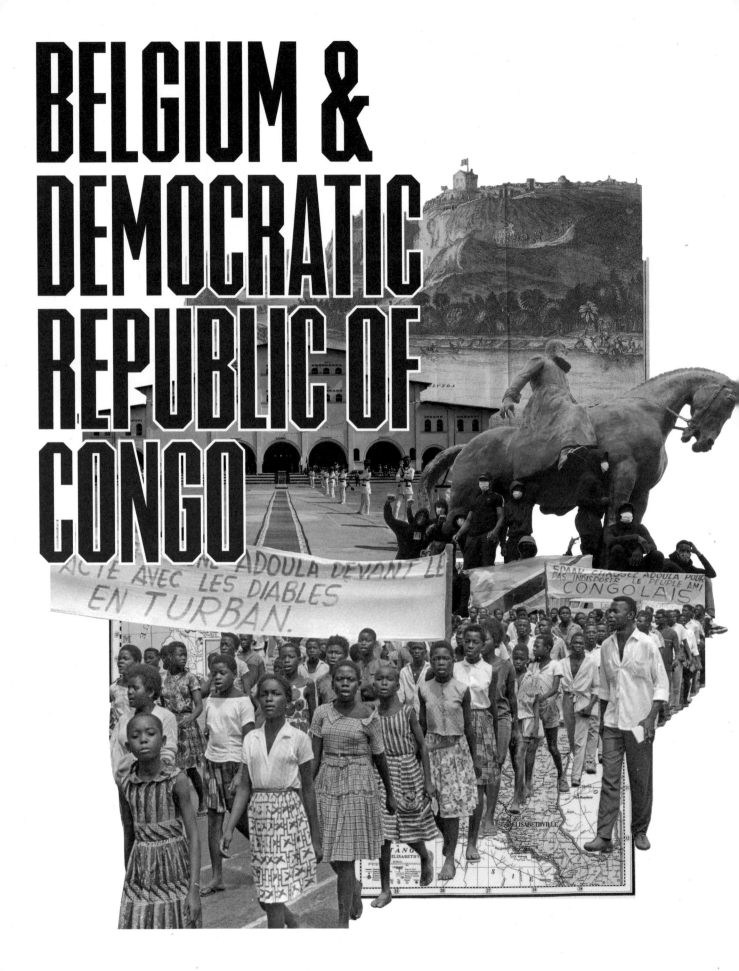

Bambi Ceuppens

See page 234 for caption

The Unfinished Conversations interviews conducted in Belgium and in the Democratic Republic of Congo reveal the ways that people originating from the DRC, Rwanda, and Burundi remember the historical slave trades, colonialism, and racism and experience their continuing impact on their lives, both personally and collectively. Belgium did not exist as a country during the time of the Transatlantic Slave Trade, and not much research has been done on the role it played. While hardly any slave ships departed from or arrived in Belgium's major port of Antwerp, it was the principal importing point for Brazilian sugar and the place where Portuguese traders came to buy goods with which to purchase enslaved people in West Africa.

In 1483, the Portuguese first arrived in the Kongo Kingdom, which covered parts of what are now the DRC, Republic of Congo, Angola, and Gabon. They soon started enslaving its inhabitants and, over time, captured individuals from farther inland as well. Most were shipped from ports in what is now Angola to Brazil and the Caribbean. Hardly any research has been done on the slave port of Boma in the Kongo Central province of the DRC, from which approximately two hundred thousand sub-Saharan Africans were shipped between 1842 and 1867, but in the area, memories of the slave trade linger.

Anna Mawuna Nsiala (ninety-five years old), Thérèse Mantu (ninety-three), Daniel Ndoluvwalu Nadia (eighty-four), and Ernest Léon Vikolo Lelo (seventy-nine), all living in the DRC, had been told about the slave trades organized by whites and Blacks. While Mama Anna told interviewers that people were sold to both Blacks and whites in times of famine, according to Mama Thérèse, only the local slave trade took place in a context of famine: village chief could decide to sell a person who had misbehaved in a local market near the coast, in order to purchase food for villagers with the money earned from the sale. Papa Ernest's reference to one of his great-granduncles shows the difference between the African and European trades: "So, my father. His older sister was married to a slave.... He was free to work, to plant. But he can't return home. He's our merchandise [commodity] that we bought, until he died." Mama Thérèse remembers being told that whites who arrived by sea went from village to village, taking only young men: "They don't buy them with money and go with them to Europe. My grandmother said that one of her uncles disappeared that way, and they never found out where he went."

Papa Daniel described a system of forced labor in Portuguese Angola before Belgium's Leopold II acquired Congo as his private property. People were made to sign contracts they could not read to work as far away as what is now Cabo Verde or even Brazil. Many Angolans who fled that system found salvation across the border in what is now the DRC.

In Belgium, Miezi Bernadette Lusakalalu, who was born after Congolese independence, reflected on a childhood game that girls played in her home village close to the Angolan border. The game helped them to remember and bear witness to the histories of searching for those stolen from their homelands:

> One row would say the name of someone who had gone, and the other row would reply, "Come and fetch me." So it felt like a wave coming and going and always saying, "Come and fetch me." And each time, the group that said, "Come and fetch me," came looking for someone in the group and left.... And before the person could even leave, there was one who fell out of line, and there were two rows who were trying to fight to get the other one back so that they wouldn't leave.

The game stayed with Mama Miezi, and as time went on, she started wondering whether it may have been a reference to the disappearance of villagers because of the Transatlantic Slave Trade.

Inhabitants of the Kongo Kingdom situated the village of the good ancestors "beyond the water." As a result of the Transatlantic Slave Trade, the destination of the transported enslaved people who never returned merged with the afterworld, so physical and social death were considered identical. The lyrics of a song sung by Papa Ernest's Kongo ancestors seem to confirm this:

Thérèse Mantu, 2022.

When a girl was deported, they tell you, "*Mbote* [hello], Mama will come back. Don't worry." And she never came back. . . . Ah, my mother is gone. She'll be back on Tuesday. . . . Will she, will she come back? Ah, father's gone to the forest. I think he'll be back on Friday. No. We mourn the dead. We mourn the dead, who will never come back.

In Belgium, Innocent Muhozi, who was born in Burundi after independence, told interviewers that, contrary to what Burundian history books say, the Arab-Swahili slave trade did reach the country:

A song that was played on the radio—it was a rather sad song about a woman who waits desperately for the return of a loved one and who each time she hears a noise believes that it's the loved one who's coming back. . . . I didn't really understand until one of my brothers told me, in fact, that there's an aunt of ours, so an older sister of our aunt . . . who was taken into slavery. Because I come from a region in Imbo on the shores of Lake Tanganyika where slavers settled at one point . . . who came from Zanzibar . . . and brought a huge number of Burundians into slavery: women, children, men, too. . . . In fact, they didn't manage to cross the [Congo-Nile] ridge, but they occupied the plain[s] region for a few years.

Belgium gained independence from the Netherlands in 1830, and its second king, Leopold II, acquired the Congo Free State as his private property in 1885. In 1908, because of the brutality of his rule, he was forced to hand it over to the Belgian state, which governed |the Belgian Congo until 1960, when |the colony, now known as Democratic Republic of Congo, itself DRC, became independent.

Belgium also administered Ruanda-Urundi, composed of the Kingdoms of Ruanda and Urundi, on behalf of the League of Nations between 1924 and 1946 and then, and afterward, as a trust territory on behalf of the United Nations (UN). Ruanda-Urundi gained independence in 1962 as the separate countries of Rwanda and Burundi. According to Innocent, there were no real differences between Belgian colonization and Belgian tutelage:

Burundi and Rwanda were . . . not colonies as such, even if in the reality of the government of management they were practically colonies. . . . We had this Belgian tutelage . . . which was not different from colonization, in fact, because there was the *chicotte* [a whip made of hippopotamus hide], people paid tribute, you had to donate eggs, you had to give chickens, you had to give milk, etc. People paid constantly, and you had to pay what [was] called . . . the head tax in particular, and people went to work in exile in Uganda . . . to work on these sugar plantations. . . . People went to work to get enough to pay the head tax.

Innocent's father, Barnabé Ntunguka, was a political leader who is considered the first Burundian independence fighter. His struggle for independence started when the colonial administration wanted to expropriate land from his father for the extension of a sugar plantation in Congo and he was eventually jailed:

They did everything they could to chase him away, but [Barnabé Ntunguka] refused. So he took the case to the United Nations, writing petitions and so on. The United Nations ruled in his favor, saying, okay, if it's in the public interest and he's willing to sell and he sells. . . . But if he doesn't want to, there's no way around it, it's his property. And so the administration constantly accelerated the [expropriating] process, with the aim of making him leave in the end. And . . . that's how it started in the beginning. A land dispute that became a downright political claim, in fact, where he wrote a lot of petitions.

The colonial administration was aware of the petitions sent to the UN:

When you were entrusted with trusteeship, you weren't allowed to do just anything—there were rules you had to respect. There were periodic evaluations as well. There were missions from New York to assess the way people were treated, and so on. And so even when he was in prison and writing petitions that went through his Belgian jailers . . . he still forwarded these petitions that denounced to the addressee. And when the addressee sent replies, he received replies in certain cases or for certain cases. . . . There was still a minimum of respect for certain principles of law that were also there.

The treatment of Simon Kimbangu shows how different things were in the Belgian Congo. Born in Nkamba in the Kongo region around 1887, he was a child when men were forced to build a railway on Kongo land. It was a dangerous task, and many lost their lives. Kimbangu was baptized in the Baptist Mission in 1915, and in 1919 he began receiving spiritual visions. He had just recovered from the effects of a sleeping sickness epidemic and was ravaged by the flu. Kimbangu moved to Léopoldville (modern-day Kinshasa), where he worked for Huileries du Congo Belge (Belgian Congo Oil, or HCB), founded in 1911 by the British firm Lever Brothers (one of Unilever's founding companies) which set up the first palm oil plantation in Africa. HCB's headquarters was a hotbed of Marcus Garvey's ideas of self-determination and pride in African heritage.

Kimbangu returned home to Kongo, where he became a messianic religious and political leader. He performed his first miraculous healing in April 1921 and soon drew immense crowds with his prophecies and miracles. The Kimbanguist ministry became

a threat to colonial authorities with its combination of Kongo beliefs, Christianity, and Garveyist ideology, and it wasa powerful liberatory force within the DRC, other parts of Africa, and the world. For Unfinished Conversations, Rémy Muke described Kimbangu's fight for Black liberation:

Simon Kimbangu . . . was born . . . with the mission of fighting slavery. We succeeded in fighting slavery, but then, I would say, the concept changed: we started talking about colonialism. . . . So Simon Kimbangu's struggle—I call it his revolution—was peaceful, because he didn't use a weapon. His weapon was only the word; his weapon was only the Gospel, his weapon was only the Bible; he was going to use his weapon, which was the word of God. . . . He fought colonialism. He wanted freedom for the Black man. He wanted freedom, the legality of [the] Black man. Which is why, later on, his . . . magic phrase—he would say, "The Black man will become white, and the white man will become Black." It's not to change the skin either, [but] for the Black man to regain his freedom. . . . Today we have a president who is . . . African, who is Black, who is himself Congolese by nationality. . . . And when we learned in recent years that there was even an African president in the United States, we said to ourselves: This is the realization of the struggle, of the words of Papa Simon Kimbangu, that the Black man will become white.

If colonial authorities considered Barnabé Ntunguka and Simon Kimbangu threats because of their

Jacqueline Goegebeur, 2022.

actions, they considered mixed-race children a threat merely by virtue of being born. In the strictly racially segregated societies of Belgian Africa, these children were a constant reminder that the racial difference that underpinned the colonial order was inherently unstable.

The few white Belgian men who legally recognized their mixed-race children took them to Belgium, severing all contact with the birth mother. Most mixed-race children, however, grew up with their mother and her family in Africa without any contact with their biological father. Because African women with mixed-race children were said to be prostitutes and thus degenerate mothers, the colonial government regarded their unrecognized children as neglected and believed that they would be better accommodated in mission schools. Cécile Ilunga, the daughter of an African mother and a Belgian father, talked about her experience in the Belgian Congo:

> **All the mixed-race children were rounded up and sent to residential schools at that time. But my family didn't want me to be taken, so they hid me. So they painted my face with soot to hide me whenever a white person passed by. But the whites knew. Someone had informed them, and they came to arrest my two uncles. They were imprisoned for a month and [beaten] for a month with the *chicotte*. And when they got out of prison, they couldn't sit up—they were wounded, and we had to nurse them every night. I remember making hot water to soothe the scars.**

Sixty-seven-year-old Jacqueline Goegebeur was born in Rwanda and taken from mother by the military police as a child. She was put into a boarding school when she was about two-and-a-half years old. In 1959, she and her older sister were sent to Belgium and placed in different foster families. She grew up as the only mixed-race child in her new home:

> **People look at you, people tell all kinds of stories about you. And you know you're being categorized. . . . You're also looked at as someone who's never going to succeed in life. From the start, I was told to behave well. If not, I would . . . definitely end up badly, at best as a prostitute. . . . People find it very hard to accept, for example, that you are the first in the class. And then you get—not from the children, but from the teaching staff and certainly the nuns—then you have to walk on tiptoes, because people do not accept that, as a person of color, you stand out above white children.**

Sibo Kanobana's Congolese father went to Belgium after 1960 to study and met Sibo's white Belgian mother there. Sibo was born in Congo but spent most of his life in Belgium. Having spent a year in Congo as an adolescent, he compared his experiences in both countries:

> **Now, as a person of mixed descent, I am perceived as *muzungu* in Lubumbashi [in the DRC]. Now, *muzungu* means "white" or "white person." I am a white person in that context not just because of my pale skin color but also because I was part of the upper class. And when you call someone *muzungu* in the Congo, it doesn't just have to do with "You're white"—it can also have to do with the language you speak, how you speak French, how well you speak Swahili, how you dress, what school you go to. All those things make you a *muzungu*.**

Rémy Muke, 2022.

... But when I'm in Belgium, I have the experience of being perceived as, yes, brown, Black, immigrant, at least a suspect Belgian. I have to justify myself: Why am I here? Tell me your story. How come you are here? Now, I never experienced that justification in the Congo. In the Congo, I might be a *muzungu* ... but at the same time I am also a "brother." There is no contradiction here between being *muzungu* and at the same time being "a son of the nation.".... Whereas here in Belgium, there is a contradiction. That's the stigma you walk around with in Belgium.

Innocent Muhozi, 2022.

Rachel Kompondo's mixed-race mother grew up in a boarding school in the Belgian Congo without knowing her family. Mama Rachel contrasted the behavior of the white men who abandoned their children with that of the much poorer birth mothers: "The Congo has done much for us with the little means it has: our grandparents and others, they have accepted us, they have fed us *pondu* [a vegetable dish made from cassava], we have food and everything."

According to Ferdinand Lokunda Lokunda Dasilva, who is the president of a nonprofit organization that defends the rights of mixed-race children abandoned by white men, fathers abandon only those whose mothers are Black, now as in the colonial era: "We're looking for a collective solution. Because it's a collective problem. If it were just two or three people of mixed race who were abandoned, we could sometimes overlook the problem. [But] a whole host of people are suffering the same fate, whatever their [father's] origin."

Many Black Congolese are jealous of mixed-race people because they think that, being half-white, they must be rich and privileged, but only a few are. Mama Rachel, who is married to a Belgian, is vice-president of a non-profit that defends the rights of mixed-race persons with a Belgian father born before and after independence. She said that mixed-race people are told, "You are not our children." Despite also belonging to the upper class, she qualifies Sibo's idea that people like them are fully accepted as Congolese: "You can live here; you are born here; you grew up here; people know that you are Congolese. As soon as

you go up a bit, that's when they'll spot you, say, 'No, you're not Congolese.' And that's shocking."

In 2018, the Belgian prime minister officially apologized on behalf of the Belgian government to mixed-race children who were abducted during the colonial era and to their mothers. The Belgian Parliament approved the Mixed-Race Resolution, which opened up access to archives for mixed-race people trying to trace relatives and made it possible for many to finally receive their birth certificates. A group in the State Archives now conducts extensive historical research on mixed-race people in Belgian Africa and tries to establish connections between different colonial archives in order to help individuals find more information on their birth fathers and siblings.

The two Congolese nonprofits in the DRC track these policies but feel that any change in practice is still lacking. They point out that the Belgian embassy in their country refuses to give them information or access to European archives that can help them find their birth parents, and their demands to gain the nationality of their fathers are not taken into consideration. Official visits from Belgian dignitaries, including King Philippe, pass them by, and the Belgian government ignores their communication requests. Unfortunately, it seems that the Belgian authorities have abandoned mixed-race Congolese people with Belgian fathers, in much the same way that those very fathers did themselves.

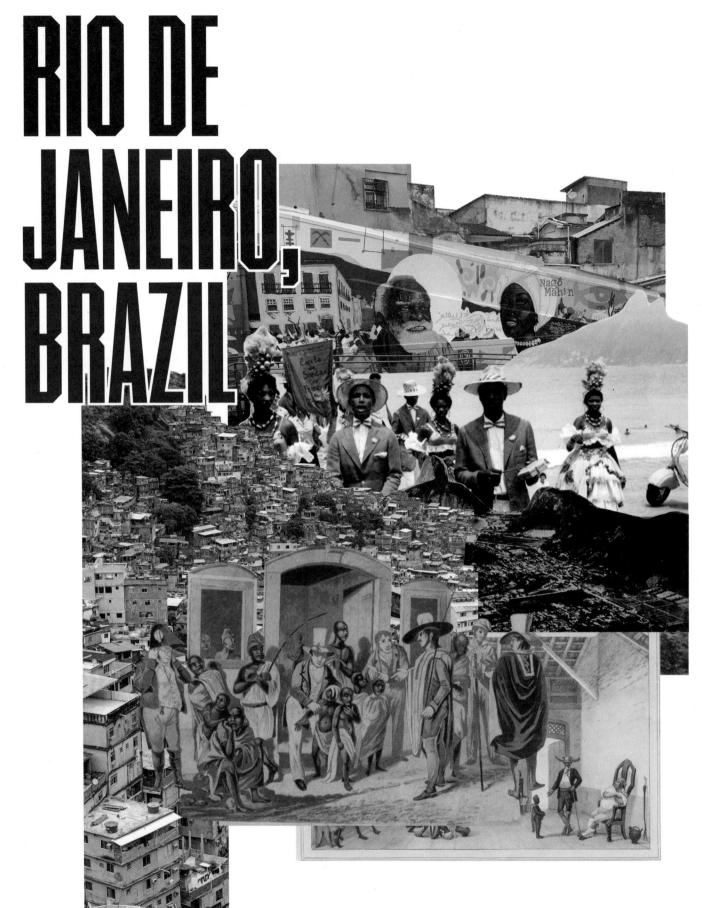

RIO DE JANEIRO, BRAZIL

**Martha Abreu
and Vinícius Natal**

See page 234 for caption

Brazil is a nation profoundly shaped by racial slavery. The largest and most continuous of all the slave societies in the Atlantic world, Brazil was the destination of approximately 40 percent of the more than 12 million enslaved Africans who were forcibly brought to the Americas. For 350 years in Brazil, slavery was a primary tool of colonization and nation-building and was the heart of the economy. It is estimated that at least 2.5 million Africans landed in Brazil in the nineteenth century alone, five times more than all the Africans who were forcibly shipped to the United States. In the city of Rio de Janeiro, the majority of Africans—an estimated nine hundred thousand—arrived at the Valongo Wharf, which has only recently been unearthed and memorialized. (See pages 52–53 for the story of the Valongo reclamation.) Others were taken to secret ports along the coast. Brazil was the last country in the Western world to abolish slavery, in 1888, and has been profoundly shaped by its African presence—culture, religions, expressions—and the long and ongoing Black struggle for freedom and justice.

In late 2022, for the GCP's Unfinished Conversations series, we conducted interviews with twelve Black residents of Rio de Janeiro: Mônica Lima e Souza, Claudio Honorato, Maurício Hora, Ivanir dos Santos, Alcino Amaral, Erick Quirino, Renzo Carvalho, Thayssa Menezes, Nilcemar Nogueira, Nathalia Sarro, Laís Rocha, and Caio Sergio Silva. Confronted by the enormity of the history sketched above, we understood that we needed to make key choices about our intent, scope, and focus in order to create an accurate and personal picture of life lived in the wake of slavery. We focused on this particular intergenerational group of educators, artists, and activists because of what we believed they could teach us about how slavery and resistance have shaped and continue to shape Rio de Janeiro. These interviews provide a small but compelling window into the complexities, danger, beauty, and power of Black life in Brazil, which is often viewed through the lens of samba, the spirituality of Candomblé, or a site of pain and reclamation such as the Valongo Wharf. Some of our interviewees have been researching and teaching Afro-Brazilian religions and the history of slavery since the 1970s or 1980s in Rio de Janeiro. Most actively work in Brazil's *Movimento Negro* (Black Movement). Other interviewees are much younger and represent new ways to confront Brazilian systemic racism in education, history, religion, and Afro-Brazilian arts, such as the dance genres capoeira and samba. The shifts and continuities from generation to generation amid this small group provide a personal, albeit initial, portrait of the legacies of racial oppression that slavery birthed in Brazilian society and continue today.

Importantly, the interviewees also provide a powerful portrait of the resilience and beauty of Black culture in the face of systemic physical, institutional, social, and political violence. This essay represents a small sliver of that picture. Among many moving testimonies, they communicated the central importance of their families and the strength of African ancestry in the continuity of life, in learning Afro-Brazilian culture, and in creating guideposts and markers for Black identity. They felt the continuity of the past in the weight of the legacy of slavery which is inscribed in the memory of family members, and in their social standing, which is marked by the lack of opportunity for upward mobility and formal education. Even though they represent different generations, the main objective of all the interviewees is ending the violence that threatens Black youths on a daily basis.

Laís Rocha, a graduate in history from the Federal University of the State of Rio de Janeiro, said:

> **The legacy of slavery imprisons. It is a burden that we carry of pain and suffering. From it, because of it, perhaps despite it, our ancestors created strategies to maintain themselves in this world. They've invented their culture and reinvented their ways of relating. Because of this courage that they had to reinvent themselves, I can survive today knowing the horror of slavery. ... Being Black in Brazil is dangerous. Above all, it is violent. As a Black woman, this violence is only more specific and horrifying. ... To wake up every day, get out of bed, go to work, come home, kiss your parents, your children, your grandparents—it takes a lot of courage to be Black in our country.**

Erick Quirino, 2022.

Thayssa Menezes, an educator and samba practitioner, described how official culture, through law or medicine, as she explains here, powerfully circumscribes and limits Black lives:

> Before we are born we already know that we are Black. There are studies which show that Black women receive different treatment in their prenatal care. For example, Black women giving birth receive less anesthesia than white women. So before I was born into this world, there was already someone saying, "You are Black." Being Black in Brazil is a place of erasure, but as we become racially literate, we need to escape this structure and think about the power of what it is to be Black. We need to make a movement, especially in education, to enhance the narratives of our people.

Just as important, spaces of Black life and culture provide a wellspring of joy that exists beyond the need for thinking about life simply as resistance. In remembering learning capoeira, an Afro-Brazilian martial art crafted by enslaved Africans and Afro-Brazilians, Laís related the deep sense of embodied freedom and happiness that she felt within the Black spaces of her city, where African-based culture, ritual, and spirituality were practiced:

> My father . . . had been [practicing] capoeira since he was fifteen years old, and when I was, I think, eight years old, I started doing it too. I did it for five, six years, and even though I stopped a long time ago, having moved away—even

a little more than I should from this whole universe—the sound of the *berimbau*, the sound of the *atabaque* [musical instruments central to capoeira] . . . creeps from my pinky finger to my last hair. Being among Black people while they express their culture is sustenance, and not only as a form of resistance but simply because it is part of us and we cannot live without it.

This complexity of embodied cultural forms of expression, of resistance and joy, and of the pain and danger that exist within living memory characterized many interviews.

Among the strategies for social reinvention and the transformation of racism, those interviewed highlighted the power of education and university access, since many were the first in their family to attend an institute of higher education. However, they also valued nonformal education spaces as places to teach and learn, especially regarding combating racism and surviving in a world permeated by it. These spaces, where Black music plays a central role, are also about the protection, connection, and perception of Black people. Black festivals, capoeira and *jongo rodas* (a type of dance circle), religious rituals, and samba schools act not only as temporal links to education and the transmission of knowledge between different generations but also as types of nonformal education and paths for political struggle. For instance, samba schools were formed at the beginning of the twentieth century by the descendants of enslaved people who sought to claim space in a society that suppressed the memories of captivity and of Black resistance. They remain and have grown into powerful institutions.

Erick Quirino, a resident of the west side of Rio de Janeiro and a musician at the samba school Grêmio Recreativo Escola de Samba Mocidade Independente de Padre Miguel, and other artists echoed similar sentiments of tradition, spirit, and creativity that Laís articulated:

> The rhythm was already born in my blood, and I went straight to the drums. And when I got to the drums, that's where we saw that of belonging was that there.

... It's really [about] love. . .and history. Today, my grandfather and my father are no longer alive, so that's where I feel directly connected to them—then we'll get into the idea of sensing something when you're playing near the drums, feeling goose bumps on your body.

Erick not only drew attention to the connection he has with samba, based on his role as a rhythmist in a samba school, but also demonstrated in-depth knowledge and interpretations of African cultural memory, grounded in his main musical instrument, the *cuíca,* which his grandfather and his father also played:

This here is a *cuíca* [*showing drum*]. It's an ancestral instrument, because it's [part of] a sequence of certain African instruments. The *cuíca* belongs to the instrument family of . . . percussion. Its sound comes out only because of the friction of your finger, the friction on the leather that makes the sound, not squeezing or anything—you need to flex the leather for the sound to come out.

During the time of slavery, the sambas and religious meetings of the Brazilian population of Africans and those of African descent were known by the forces of repression throughout the country as *batuques.* Spaces of resistance, identity, and affirmation of African heritage, *batuques* effectively created paths to humanization and limited the effects of the violence and exploitation rife within slavery. Enslaved and freed people fought hard to keep the *batuques,* and the continuity of Afro-Brazilian civilizing values they embodied, as a form of Black freedom in Brazil.

The legal end of slavery in Brazil did little to change the lives of many Afro-Brazilians. A complex web of repression continued to threaten Black lives, cultural expression, and spiritual practices in an era when many hundreds of thousands of formerly enslaved people and their descendants migrated to the urban areas of the state of Rio de Janeiro over the course of a century, transforming the lives of those cities despite the forces of institutional racism that impoverished and degraded their own lives while erasing their enormous contributions. Nonetheless,

Black musicians, their families, and Black cultural and religious associations continued to champion the new challenges of modernity.

At the beginning of the twentieth century *batuques* began to emerge with regional names and styles, such as sambas, *congados, maracatus, bois,* and *jongo.* Samba has become consolidated and recognized as a national Brazilian genre, not just from the perspective of modern, commercial music, but because it always provided an escape from daily struggles and created circles and networks of friendship and solidarity. It has never ceased to embody the dreams of families who see samba as a vision of the world, a political struggle, and the possibility of work, education, and civic training in a country that runs on racism.

Afro-Brazilian descendants today have given new meaning to heritage, memory, and affirmation of Black identities through the lens of social struggle and musical inventiveness. For Nilcemar Nogueira, one of the founders of the Samba Museum and a granddaughter of Cartola and Doña Zica, Black samba leaders from Morro da Mangueira in Rio de Janeiro, samba is not just a musical form:

Samba comes from a social movement, where a group organizes themselves to reoccupy a place from which they were expelled. All the urban reform of our city, it's going to divide the classes—the poor here, the rich there. But this group [samba], whether instinctively or not,

Nilcemar Nogueira, 2022

Alcino Amaral, 2022.

will organize itself to occupy the city. So you see, in the past, for example, religious groups organized themselves to liberate others, like dockworkers and working-class organizations. The samba schools are similar: a Black movement of class organization from the cultural point of view, an expression that is part of everyday life.

Renzo Carvalho, a young law student at the Universidade Federal Fluminense and a practitioner of Candomblé, reiterated the necessity of such strategies of struggle for social affirmation and of culture as politics. In that capacity, he holds the title of *ogã*, an honorary chief or leader of a house of worship:

> **I think that this formulation of oral strategies in the production of communication [such as *capoeira* or *jongo*] that the oppressor can't understand has allowed Black people to endure from generation to generation—not only as a strategy for survival but also for preservation of his culture within the surrounding community.**

Formal education likewise functions as an important mechanism in the search for better living conditions for the Black population. Thayssa Menezes and Alcino Amaral are educators who use their experience as *sambistas* (samba performers) as a tool for transforming the memory of slavery and affirming Black identity in Brazil in general and, more specifically, in Rio de Janeiro.

Thayssa is a teacher with a degree in education from the Universidade Federal Fluminense. She worked as a primary school teacher in the favela of Maré, in the northern part of Rio de Janeiro, and today she is a coordinator for the Management of Ethnic-Racial Relations (GERER) in the Rio de Janeiro Municipal Department of Education. Born into the samba scene, she is the president of the composers' wing of the Grêmio Recreativo Escola de Samba Acadêmicos do Cubango (a samba school) and is the niece of Shanghai, the late *carnavalesco* (carnival producer). Shanghai was one of the few Black artists to break through the predominantly white male and white environment of Rio's samba schools in the 1990s.

Alcino, who lives in the center of Rio de Janeiro, is working toward a master's degree in history at the Universidade Federal Fluminense while also teaching primary- and secondary-level history. He is a capoeira practitioner, serves as a samba event producer performing in circles around the city, and a cultural mediator in downtown Rio de Janeiro's Pequena África, where, together with the musician Thiago Sereno, he produces activities and conducts tours centered on slavery with the project *Rio: Memória e Ação* (Rio: Memory and Action). These tours raise awareness of the genre's African roots and function as a catalyst for memories of Black slavery in Brazil. As residents of Rio de Janeiro, Alcino and Thiago feel the continued absence in schools of debate on ethnic-racial issues. Alcino states:

> **Throughout my education, like in school, I don't remember the very few times I had contact with topics . . . related to Africa or slavery and things like that. And the few times I remember them, I always remember them in a very exact way, very stigmatized. . . . But what surprised me was that I didn't know anything about it—about our history, about slavery. So I**

remember some images, the notebooks, Black people being enslaved, Black people in shackles. But I didn't give any kind of thought to that.

As students, Alcino and Thayssa did not experience the profound transformation that resulted from the implementation of Laws 10639/03 in 2003 and 11645/08 in 2008, which made the teaching of African, Afro-Brazilian, and Indigenous history mandatory in schools across the country. This legislation is considered a landmark in the Black struggle. Alcino and Thayssa graduated as teachers when the possibilities created by these laws would help strengthen the self-esteem of young Black people.

Alcino and Thayssa closely followed the implementation of the quota—or affirmative action—system for Black and poor students at public universities throughout Brazil. These transformations guide their performance as teachers and samba dancers. Alcino related:

One of the things I always say at the beginning of classes [is] that we have to think about the experience of slavery, the experience of Diaspora, the way it was—an experience of tremendous violence, a sensitive experience. But I open a space, which is a necessary space within this class, for us to also think about the legacies of this experience. And the legacies of this experience are directly related to what they [enslaved ancestors] learned and what was brought here by these people, and not only brought, but what was, in short, a tool, what was an instrument to build what we understand to be Brazil.

Thayssa relayed the same sentiment:

So the girl Thayssa always dreamed of being a *carnavalesca*, but my uncle always said that there were two barriers in Carnival: the racial barrier and the gender barrier. And I ended up growing up and life was taking me down other paths, and I now say I'm a teacher education.... I believe that in the classroom, I manage to develop many of the things from the point of view of a samba person, a samba dancer, you know, to develop in education many of the things addressed by the Carnival

performances—through the plots, through the samba themes or stories. So I have always tried to align formal education with samba schools in education, in this curriculum, in activities, in educational proposals.

Black social movements throughout the 1980s and into the 1990s created space for debate and forced changes within the Federal Constitution regarding the recognition of Black communities, history, and people in Brazilian law. A generation of younger samba schools emerged, organized by samba dancers aware of the need to transmit the knowledge that Blackness and Black cultural expression are crucial elements of identity and of freedom making on personal and collective levels. (See pages 162–163 for the story of Exu in the 2022 Carnival.)

What Thayssa, Alcino, and all the other interviewees demonstrate is how much Black cultural forms in Brazil, at different places and times, have played a leading role in the struggle against racism and the affirmation of Black people in society. Samba and education are inextricably intertwined in pushing forward the debate concerning the memory and meaning of slavery in Rio de Janeiro and wider Brazil. Our elders taught us this, and the youngest teach us it as well.

Thayssa Menezes, 2022.

AFRICATOWN, UNITED STATES

WELCOME
To
Africatown
PLATEAU ○ MAGAZINE
HAPPY HILLS ○ KELLY HILLS
LEWIS QUARTERS

Yorktown
MISSIONARY BAPTIST CHURCH

PRAY MORE
WORRY LESS

U.S. COAST SURVEY
Approaches to
MOBILE
ALA.

Gabrielle Chantal Miller
and Johanna Obenda

See page 234 for caption

In 1860, more than fifty years after the legal abolition of the importation of enslaved people to the United States from Africa, the last known slave ship to arrive there docked on the shores of Mobile, Alabama. This schooner, called *Clotilda*, arrived with some 110 Africans on board. The captives, who had been illegally captured in Benin, were smuggled across the Atlantic on a clandestine vessel financed by a politically prominent Alabama family. This family, the Meahers, concealed evidence of their illicit activity by burning the ship and distributing the *Clotilda*'s captives across Meaher-owned plantations and properties throughout the Southern region of the United States. After the US abolition of slavery five years later as a result of the American Civil War and the Thirteenth Amendment, many of those once bound together in the cargo hold of the *Clotilda* came together again with the intent of building new lives. Returning once again to their status as free people, the survivors—alongside the newly emancipated communities of southern Alabama—built a new space of belonging known as Africatown.

Global interest in this historical episode was catalyzed by the discovery of the remains of the *Clotilda* on the banks of the Mobile River in 2021. Numerous documentaries, books, and other publications have brought light to the stories of the survivors and their legacies from the perspectives of their descendants. The predominant narrative surrounding the creation of the Africatown community depicts a vibrant and thriving settlement built by those captives who survived the ship and subsequent years of enslavement. But this provides a limited picture of the broader coalition of free and enslaved people who were establishing Africatown alongside the survivors from the *Clotilda*. Together, this diverse group created a community rich with orchards, businesses, and a support network for navigating their regained freedoms in what would become a new home.

The nuances of these newly built lives were initially documented in the early twentieth century by a local writer who interviewed many Africatown residents but followed the conventions of the time for collecting oral histories: recording respondents' answers but translating their experiences into language more palatable to white society. It wasn't until Black writer and anthropologist Zora Neale Hurston traveled to Africatown that these conversations were revisited. Hurston interviewed many members of the Africatown community, including most notably Cudjo Lewis, born Oluale Kossola. Though she wasn't the first to collect their oral histories, she paved the way for new paradigms by being the first to publish stories from people in their own words and dialects. She also turned her volume of interviews into the book famously known as *Barracoon: The Story of the Last "Black Cargo."* The significance of this work continues to resonate with its modern audience because Hurston's mission to foreground the Black perspective in the historical narrative is still deeply needed in a world where those impacted most by the afterlives of slavery are still rendered invisible.

In Hurston's spirit, Unfinished Conversations highlights the voices of Africatown families who have safeguarded their stories for generations. Descendants continue to make their perspectives known and voices heard. Through their interviews, they collage a picture of a community determined to not just survive but thrive. This community was built by those ferried on the *Clotilda* and by the enslaved and free people in the neighboring areas of Magazine, Plateau, Happy Hills, Prichard, and beyond. This community has always been committed to building freer futures for themselves and for next generations, in the wake of slavery, Jim Crow, urban renewal, industrialization, and systemic injustice. Here, in their own voices, members weave together stories of preserving generational memories and oral traditions, reclaiming access to water, navigating and repairing environmental damage, and, ultimately, defining the meaning of freedom.

Africatown is made of many small towns, and its borders are the waterways that almost entirely surround it: the Mobile River to the east, Hog Bayou to the northeast, and Three Mile Creek to the southwest. As prevalent as the river and its many tributaries are,

Barja Wilson, 2022.

if you were to visit, you would notice industry and transportation infrastructure almost entirely blocking access to these waterways. Barja Wilson, a Mobile native and environmental planner, frequently organizes teams of youths and young adults to clean the historic Old Plateau Cemetery and test the waterways surrounding Africatown for safety and cleanliness. Through her work advocating for better environmental conditions, she has learned a lot about the landscape prior to the encroachment of industry:

> **Before the industry came, I mean, this was vast—this was vast open land. Something you hear the elders talk about is they used to hunt wild boar around here, wild hogs. The trees, the fruit trees, grew plentifully. You didn't really have to go to the grocery store, because everything was here on the land. And then, again, access to the water was very easy. People used to fish and play in the water, boat in the water. Access to Three Mile Creek is pretty much unheard of now because you have industry and industry owners who have purchased parcels all along the river—the Three Mile Creek area—so the citizens don't have a direct access to Three Mile Creek anymore like they used to, except for on Old Perception Road where the Clotilda Landing One is, which the county just recently purchased and, hopefully, that will be put back in use as public space.**

For almost one hundred years, toxic fumes and chemicals from oil, asphalt, logging, petrochemical, paper, coal, and other polluting industries have choked the air, poisoned the waters, spread cancer, and made healthy futures more untenable as time goes by. As these industries have come and gone, Africatown residents have experienced the shrinking of their land, resources, and lifespans. Still, not all natural landmarks have been lost.

At the heart of John Kidd Park, a public site nestled between Africatown's school, community center, and churches, is an almost mystical tree called the Witness Tree. From its robust trunk grows a canopy of branches so large and long that they touch the ground, creating a cocoon. Under its shade, sheltering from the sweltering Alabama sun, we asked Arlean Horton, a great-granddaughter of the park's namesake, If this tree could tell us about all it has witnessed over Africatown's long history, what would it say? Horton stated,

> **My great-grandfather John Kidd was born in 1876. And when he got here, this tree was pretty much the size that you see it now.... It may be as much as three hundred years old....**
>
> **This tree and what it witnessed during its time of being with us.... It has withstood numerous storms. We used to have a barbershop right here under it. We had a grocery store behind me, before it became Kidd Park. We played here under this tree. Swings, wooden-bottomed swings were here before the park was created. We had houses. About four or five houses was here in the park. They were eventually taken down.... This tree used to be a sanctuary.**

As Horton reminisced, a former mortuary owner stepped out of his car to add his memories of how families would bring their recently departed loved ones to this tree to hold services and how in the worst days of industry there were few nights he wasn't busy making preparations for another community member lost. This Witness Tree has been around to see the comings and goings, joys and sorrows, and lives and deaths of many generations.

Like the Witness Tree at the center of John Kidd Park, Lorna Gail Woods holds memories of Africatown past and present. Woods, a descendant of the *Clotilda* survivor Charlie Lewis, preserves the community's photos and objects in a small museum of her own making located in an area known as the Den in the Mobile County Training School (MCTS). Established for African American students in 1880, MCTS was once a high school and now functions as the middle school for Africatown and surrounding areas. Alums include famous athletes such as Tommie Agee, Cleon Jones, and Billy Williams, yet in Woods's museum, any Africatown resident, from survivors of the *Clotilda*, to those who live there today, can be seen and celebrated. Woods also safeguards history and memory through her art of quilt-making, passed down by the women in her family. She finds freedom in these acts of remembrance and described what freedom means to her:

Freedom may not sound like a good word when you're talking about people who know their folk was enslaved and their freedom was cut off, but I feel like freedom is when your mind and body and soul is not restricted. You can think what you wanna think, do what you want to do, but you know the difference of freedom. When those people marched with Martin Luther King, they was tired of being tired. They had worked hard as they could. They had did what the Bible say and they felt like they deserved freedom, but they couldn't have it until people signed a piece of paper. Signing a piece of paper do not make you free....
Look at the Queen [of England Elizabeth II], how they buried her and how people stood on the side of the road and threw flowers and waved at her. We don't get that. We be lucky if a person bought us a flower off the side of the road sometime and give it to us. Not that we got to die to get our flowers, but I think it's freedom when people'll give you flowers while you can still smell them. I love flowers because they're freeing. I love butterflies because they free.

Across town, the local barber Emmett Lewis facilitates a different kind of communal preservation. Lewis, another descendant of Cudjo Lewis, discussed the intimacy of the barbershop as a space where coming together provides a setting for witnessing and safeguarding history. Once they sit in Lewis's chair and are surrounded by the barber's cape, patrons are safe to voice their thoughts, accomplishments, and even hardships. Emmett Lewis, who finds himself sharing and receiving many stories in his barbershop, sees this space as preserving history:

That's why I cut hair—because when you cut hair, you gon' learn more about life than anything.... So many people that just come vent, so many people that talk—and you not understanding that you learning they history. That's why I do it. I do it because I love history. And just hearing what people came from and what ... they stand for now, that was big for me. But being able to understand that, okay, maybe I might be a part of history. Maybe I have something that I stand for.

Joe Womack, an MCTS alum and Africatown environmental activist, sees his role in building a freer future as protecting his community's environment and restoring its relationship with the natural landscape that he experienced in his youth. Swimming in the surrounding waterways, fishing and crabbing, and growing gardens and

Arlean Horton, 2022

orchards were hallmarks of his time growing up in Africatown. Over his life, he has witnessed the ongoing environmental degradation caused by pollution and industrialization. Womack reflected on this degradation and what it would look like to create a future in which residents are healthy and can enjoy the richness of their community's natural environment in perpetuity:

Industry was all around us, but we still found a way to go to the water and try to enjoy as much as we can. What we're doing today is trying to get our kids to recognize that water is right here and to take advantage of it. Now in the meantime, we don't want them to experience pollution like we did. So in order for that to happen, we've got to get the industry[ies] that are here to clean it up. They made it dirty, so we want them to clean it up, and we don't want any more polluting-type industry in the area. And so to do that, what we have to do is get those governmental agencies to do their job, to police the area, to find out what's here, and to clean it up, because this community is something that the people love. We're a resilient community. We fought for it for years, and we really don't want to give it up, because we think that our community is a great spot. . . .

My grandaddy . . . was a storyteller, and he told a lot of different things, and he had a lot of quotes, and one

Lorna Gail Woods, 2022.

that he said that I remember is "Don't let nobody take your watermelon." You know, don't let something that you love be taken away from you 'cause someone else said it ain't good. A lot of times they'll say it's not good because they want it. And if they can get you to run away from it, then they'll get it for little or nothing. So don't let 'em take your watermelon.

At the public pool in the heart of Africatown, we spoke to a swim coach and a lifeguard who have witnessed the impact of the severed relationship between the community and its waterways. Where swimming was once prevalent, now, just a few generations later, drownings of both children and adults have become an epidemic. This interview reunited the lifeguard and pool manager Brandon Hoyt with Coach Derrick Tinsley, his first swim instructor whose mentorship helped Hoyt grow from a near-drowning victim into someone who safeguards life in the water. Coach Tinsley, after his own tragic experience of the drowning death of his wife, left coaching while grieving. Ultimately, though, he came back to swim instruction with a reignited determination to restore the community's relationship with water, one student at a time. In their joint interview, Hoyt and Tinsley discussed their impact on each other's lives and their hope for their community's future.

Hoyt
My earliest memory out of water [is] back when I was maybe five or six at a backyard barbecue. I was playing around the pool and I fell off in the deep end. And I learned the hard way about it by going down in the deep. And somebody had to come save me. And ever since then, I had been determined to learn how to swim.

Tinsley
I'm sixty-three years old, so man, I still go all the way back to a little boy during segregation times. I'm grateful for the community because they taught me how to swim. . . . I have a love for the water. I found my peace at the water, and I share it with the kids in the community because today the kids are more fortunate for the things that was

established as [when] I was a kid, and I had the privilege and the honor of passing it all and allowing them to be part of the overall culture of swimming.

Minister Christopher Williams is the pastor of Yorktown Missionary Baptist Church, one of Africatown's oldest places of worship. Built in 1883 by a group of Christian leaders from the Plateau community, it was originally known as Three Mile Creek Baptist Church. In Africatown, churches are the lifeblood of the community, serving the residents since its inception. Witness to the births, lives, and deaths of Africatown residents, Pastor Williams has unique insight into changes in this community over time:

When I first came here sixteen years ago, the first year I did right at twenty funerals. The pastor down the street, Pastor Brady, he did twenty-one his first year, which was the year before I got here. ... And a lot of those funerals was cancer. A lot of those funerals was breathing problems, and nobody would help. Nobody would help us with it. I contacted the CDC [Centers for Disease Control and Prevention]. I don't know who, I contacted so many people, but they keep telling you it's not a cluster, but you keep having people that died from cancer. ... I believe—this is my opinion, I can't say it's scientifically backed—but I believe that most of the people who have died or is sick is because of the water and because of the poison that came into their lives through no fault of their own.

You go to West Mobile, you see none of this. That is not freedom to me, that's an imprisonment. ... [To] me it is "If we can wipe this community off the face of the map, then nobody'll know about the *Clotilda*, about the people that were kidnapped in Africa and brought here." So freedom in Africatown is totally different than freedom in West Mobile. Freedom in West Mobile means that "Oh yeah, you? You're welcome here," knowing that you're not. ... "We don't want you here, period, because we want to remove you."

... Freedom for some of these people [in Africatown] is being able to wake up without having all the smoke and fog and smog around them, without thinking

Joe Womack, 2022.

and worrying about the dust and the pollution that's coming into their house because of all the heavy traffic and all the stuff. You go to Magazine Point . . . riding down the road at midnight, stirring up the dust and it's blowing into the people's house. They can't turn their air conditioner on. ... Freedom [means] being able to live a comfortable life.

Though this is a small representation of the stories collected for the Unfinished Conversations series, these interviews allow a glimpse into the complexity of the afterlives of enslavement in Africatown. They show that the struggle for dignity, prosperity, health, and freedom doesn't reside only in the past. Recognizing that this struggle is connected to a system that arose with the globalization of slavery and capitalism and continues to impact the descendants of the enslaved today makes it possible to devise strategies that can get to the root of these patterns in history. It is an ongoing and interconnected practice of attention and love, in which imagining and enacting freer futures means caring for the past and the present as well.

CAPE TOWN, SOUTH AFRICA

WOMEN
DO NOT
WANT
PASSES

WITH
PASSES
WE ARE
SLAVES

Shanaaz Galant
and Paul Tichmann

See page 234
for caption

Situated at the southernmost tip of Africa, the Cape Colony was a Dutch and later a British colony. The Cape was a slave society for more than 180 years, until the abolition of slavery in the British colonies in the mid-nineteenth century. In 1652, Jan van Riebeeck, commander for Vereenigde Oostindische Compagnie (VOC), or Dutch East India Company, demanded and enacted the process of slave labor to undertake the arduous tasks of establishing trade and settlements in the colony. The VOC sent the first shipload of enslaved people to the Cape aboard the Dutch ship the *Amersfoort* in 1658, carrying 170 Angolans who had been captured from a Portuguese ship bound for Brazil. In the same year, the Dutch vessel *Hassalt* brought a second shipload of 228 enslaved people from Dahomey (now Benin). As a result of complaints from the Dutch West India Company, which was the VOC's counterpart in the Atlantic and Pacific Oceans and saw the practices of slave trading as direct competition with its burgeoning trade between West Africa and the Americas, the VOC agreed to shift its slave-trading focus to the Indian Ocean. Over the subsequent century, the VOC brought more than sixty thousand enslaved men, women, and children to the Cape, mainly from what are now Mozambique, Madagascar, the east coast of India, and Indonesia.

The VOC was the largest slaveholder on the Cape, and the so-called company slaves were housed in the Slave Lodge in what would grow to be the city of Cape Town. Constructed in 1679, the Slave Lodge epitomized the hybrid and multifaceted systems of exploitation, acculturation, and control that came to define the European colonial project in all parts of the world. Part prison, part fortification, part school, and part hospital, the Slave Lodge was the site where those forcibly brought to the region to work for the VOC were housed. (See pages 114–115 for Jan Smiesing's story and the history of the Slave Lodge.) The building still remains as a stark reminder of the past and now serves as the Iziko Slave Lodge museum, South Africa's social history museum, and a host of the *In Slavery's Wake* exhibition.

Enslaved people were also brought to the Cape to work for the growing settler population, in their households and on their wine, wheat, and stock farms. Capitalizing on the VOC's presence while it advanced trade in the area, including the slave trade, Dutch *vriburgher* (free burghers) and other European settlers began to permanently occupy land at the Cape, displacing the Indigenous populations of the San and the Khoi. Throughout the eighteenth and well into the nineteenth century, enslaved people who had been forcibly migrated to the Cape from across the Indian Ocean labored as domestics, seamen, and, especially farmworkers, constructing, cultivating, and harvesting for the colony alongside Khoi and San people in similarly forced conditions. They were stripped of their names and often assigned replacements from the calendar—Maart (March), September, Februarie (February)—corresponding to the month when their slave ship arrived at the Cape.

Enslaved and Indigenous workers alike were treated as property, had restricted rights, and occupied the lowest rung in Cape society. In 1754, the Cape governor Ryk Tulbagh consolidated various VOC slave regulations into a single *placaaten* (edict), known as the Tulbagh Code. It set down stringent rules for enslaved people, including curfews, limits on the right to gather, and restrictions on movement, and clothing requirements (including a ban on shoes). A slave pass system was instituted wherein a permit or letter was issued to demonstrate that the enslaver had sent the slave and was traveling with their permission.

In the immediate aftermath of emancipation in the British Empire in 1838, a plethora of laws reinscribed the earlier Cape codes into law. The Masters & Servants Ordinance No. 1 of 1841 provided severe punishment for workers who deserted or were disobedient. Laws restricted the rights of Black people to own land. The Khoi and San people, along with former slaves who were now newly "freed," were forced into similar conditions of life and bonded labor as had existed during slavery.

Many wine farms exploited their laborers by using the *dop* (alcoholic drink), or tot, system, paying them in

Carmen Louw, 2022.

daily measures of cheap wine. As a result, the Western Cape still has the highest incidence of fetal alcohol syndrome in the world. Such practices, codes, and laws set the foundations for the racist controls that people of color were subjected to under apartheid, such as pass laws (which strictly regulated their movement), segregation, and widespread political and social violence leading to the authoritarian apartheid regime from 1948 to 1994. (See pages 48–49 for more about passes.)

In 2022, the Unfinished Conversations project in Cape Town gathered a mixed group of people including artists, a poet, educators, a professor, and farmworkers to explore the ruptures and continuities between these seemingly distant pasts and the present. The interviews revealed that despite some gains over the past thirty years, the systems of exploitation forged during the period of enslavement and colonialism continue to impact South Africa.

Touching on identity, personal history, and social and political issues, interviewees provided a collective and diverse portrait of frustration and hope, political action, and the historical knowledge too often ignored in our classrooms, history books, and museums. The interviews frequently reference and link slavery, colonialism, and the apartheid past as a set of continuities, and they articulate a clear sense that freedom is still an ongoing project and an elusive goal.

The poet Diana Ferrus and the artist Roderick Sauls, both descendants of enslaved people, encapsulate similar stories of coming to awareness of the submerged or forgotten past of slavery on the Western Cape. Sauls, who has created a new artwork on display in the Slave Lodge that speaks directly to the history of that place and the pain it inflicted on the people who were enslaved there, reflected on how his research into slavery led him to focus on his own identity in ways that were unexpected:

In my approach I realized I didn't know a lot about enslavement. I then started thinking that if I look at the life of the enslaved it will inform me about it. So as

much as it is about our sorrow and our pain, if we start looking at our own pain and start analyzing, we will discover what that life was all about.

He described how the space of the Slave Lodge created a sense of the lives of the enslaved: "The darkness gave me the sense of how people felt, especially women, children. The fear they had. Especially the fear of the master."

Ferrus voices a similar history of consciousness-building and empowerment through facing the past, stating:

> The awareness for me of slavery didn't come when I was at school, because we weren't really taught about it. . . . I don't know if I must be ashamed about it or what, because people didn't speak about it. It was in later years that my uncle told me that my grandfather was a February. . . . My uncle told me that the Februaries from Worcester were also called *die Masbiekers*, "the Mozambicans,", because they were Mozambican slaves. And as I said before, the awareness of all the other things, of Indigenous people, of slavery, [was hidden]. After 1994 [the end of apartheid], it was as if . . . overtaken by storm, all that information, the consciousness came. Because we were told nothing, nothing, when we were children or even teenagers. So slavery then became something I looked into deeply, because I was worried about what was going on around me. I was looking at my people, and I was thinking, What brought us here? I knew about apartheid. And then when I heard about slaves, I thought, Damn, slavery must have something to do with what is now. And that is when I went to do further research and wrote poetry and [was] even telling stories. Luckily for me, there was always information around. You could go to the archives or African library, even at the university and the Department of History, and so I am very, very glad that that could happen to me. Because now I am sort of at ease, because I know that my people are not like the way they are because of what others said. I could relate that trauma of those years to now. (See pages 56–57 for "My Name is February" by Diana Ferrus.)

While stories of finding and reclaiming a usable past offer a pathway to truth,

reckoning, and repair, our interviews with farmworkers showed us how far we still need to go for justice. Many agricultural laborers in South Africa continue to face poor working conditions that include low wages, long hours, lack of job security, and inadequate housing.

They are also often drawn from marginalized communities, especially for seasonal work. Mercia Andrews, who was born in the Western Cape into a farmworking family and now serves as the director of the Trust for Community Outreach and Education, told us,

> So if you look at farmworkers, how they are today, I think very little has actually changed on some farms. . . . By and large, very little has changed. The master-slave mentality still exists on many of the farms. I see my grandmother, I see myself on the farms. Every day, I see the legacy. The legacy of alcohol and the *dop* system [is] alive on the farms today.

Johannes Warries revealed that his father, a worker on a wine farm in the Malmesbury area, was dismissed after being injured in a tractor accident: "All the years he worked for [the farm owner], and now they won't help him. It is part of slavery. . . . There was slavery and there is still slavery." The continuities between his father's experience and his own have deeply shaped his sense of freedom: "Freedom is when you can talk about how you feel. In South Africa we are not free. There are two things that stop you from speaking, and that is the color of your skin and your class. . . . I am free, but I am also not free."

Mercia Andrews, 2022.

Diana Ferrus, 2022.

He further revealed the sense of dread that one feels as an adult working on a wine farm: "There is heaviness on the farm that comes over you when you enter, and when you leave, it is lifted."

Despite these conditions, "fight" and "struggle" are recurring themes and key words in the interviews. Andrews, who helped lead a large, successful farmworkers' strike in the Cape Winelands District in 2012, painted the portrait of an area called De Doorns as a microcosm of contemporary struggle rooted in systems born under slavery, colonialism, and apartheid:

> I think it's interesting to visit this town De Doorns. De Doorns is a table grape region. In the center, you have these beautiful green vineyards and farmhouses. The white parts and this beautiful landscape that we see on our pictures and so on. And alongside the freeway you see this mass of sprawling squalor and shacks and shacks and shacks. That part is called Stofland. *Stofland* means the "land of dust." So side by side you have beautiful green vineyards and Stofland shacks. It was clear that, for many people coming into the Western Cape as migrant workers, this is the first stop. So they go there into Stofland . . . either as migrant workers or as farmworkers or people coming in undocumented. . . . And then from there [they] would make their way into other farms, into the city, and so on. But in October 2012 one morning, you heard on the radio that the N1 [the road between Cape Town and Johannesburg] was completely barricaded with bricks and stones, and farmworkers were out occupying the street, and it was like the newspaper said. At the time, it was . . . [an historic rebellion, an historic uprising, because farmworkers have never taken to the streets. . . . Thirty-six rural towns were completely organized. Brought the wine and fruit sector, in particular, to a standstill. . . . For me it was unbelievable to see the confidence of the farmworkers, who are normally humble and fearful of these farmers, who come with guns and so on. . . . So there was all this work taking place: organizing, raising consciousness, and so on. And I think also what is important is the seasonality. There were many more seasonal workers, and people were off work, and people had less to lose. There was a new generation of farmworkers—younger, much younger—and there was social media.

Even on farms where conditions are perhaps better, workers still feel frustrated by a range of rules and regulations, as the interview with Zann Manho, Magriet Jacobs, and Lorna Solomon revealed. Among their frustrations are regulations that prevent them from accommodating their children and aged parents in the farmworkers' houses, and the costs of transport for workers not housed on the farms. Similar frustration comes through in the interviews with Adriaan Jordaan, Johannes Warries, and Johan Geduld, who described how they must monitor the volume of the music they play and be careful not to speak too loudly in their residences.

Geduld related stories about his childhood that illuminated the continuing afterlives of slavery and colonialism in the recent past:

> Where I grew up on Ashton [a small town in rural Western Cape] there was still the *dop* system. . . . My parents probably got paid about fifteen rand or ten rand [$.53 or $.80 US] a week. . . . I got to know shoes from my grandmother and grandfather because in Ashton's world the frost is very thick when you go to school. Then we always took "card" boxes, about three card boxes, and made sandals out of them. We fix it, then we go to school.

The example of the De Doorns uprising illustrates the possibility and fragility of freedom making and social justice in the Western Cape and throughout South Africa today. For the Unfinished Conversations interviewees, understanding the past is not merely a memory, but also about making sense of the current space they occupy, shaped by age-old structures of economic, social, and environmental inequity, where the goal of full human rights remains elusive.

Issues of race, class, and inequality continue to dominate three decades after the fall of apartheid, the enshrining of the Constitution of the Republic of South Africa, and the election of Nelson Mandela as president. Carmen Louw, a co-director of the Women on Farms project, evinced the deep sense of disillusionment felt by workers of color in the Western Cape in 2024:

> I thought we had freedom when they could vote in 1994. And with all that euphoria, we thought we were free. But as the years progressed we realized, or I realized, we are not free. We are still slaves to the system that was created by apartheid. Especially the economic inequalities and the land inequalities. Until those things are equalized, we won't be free.

Andrews shares the same sense of disappointment, but also provides a road map to a freer and more just future that offers a fuller sense of freedom beyond the political arena and the right to vote: she includes equal access to land and a better quality of life for all. This is a vision for future generations shared by many of those we interviewed. Andrews noted:

> I have spent my adult life as an activist, and so I have a very big view of what freedom is and should be. I also come from a generation of South Africans that fought for a very different freedom. It wasn't a freedom [only] attached to the ballot box, freedom that [now] is attached to austerity, where there's spatial apartheid and where landholding patterns haven't changed. Where the violence of this country—the structural violence, not only the violence against women and children—[is] so deeply

entrenched in our society. I have a different imagination of a country, of a land, of a world, of an Africa where we can live in peace, where we can have equality, where we can live modestly with nature and with ourselves.... Where the wealth of the world ... its technological wealth as well as its cultural wealth—all of the wealth of the world is shared for the better[ment] of our society and humanity, for our future.

For me, there was a very big moment during COVID when there was an ability to create a vaccine that could be available to everybody in the world and to not have the amount of people that died.... And yet the rulers of the world, through their greed and through the greed of companies, still put a price to the lives of people. Now that, for me, is what we must overcome and destroy, otherwise we will not have freedom. Where simple things like the health of a society and the food—that children go to bed hungry—those are the things that we must challenge and change.

Roderick Sauls, 2022.

LIVERPOOL, UNITED KINGDOM

BLACK LIVES MATTER!

AFRO-CARIBBEAN
DEFENCE COMMITTEE
SELF DEFENCE IS THE
ONLY WAY

LIVERPOOL 8 DEFENCE COMMITTEE

CS GAS
CAN KILL
YOU FAST

Lisa Edison and Alexandra Creighton

See page 234 for caption

By the middle of the eighteenth century, the port city of Liverpool surpassed Bristol and London to become the United Kingdom's slave-trading capital, controlling 80 percent of the British slave trade and 40 percent of the European slave trade. Liverpool became central to the slave trade for several reasons, including its geographic location and its production of commodities, like iron and cotton goods, used for trade in West Africa. Another was the construction of what is now called the Old Dock, the first commercial wet dock in the nation. This enclosed structure meant that merchants could build larger ships and turn them around quickly, because ships could now float in the harbor.

Wealth generated from transatlantic slavery not only created local slave-trading dynasties but also resulted in the city's economic development and contributed to the broader expansion of the United Kingdom's colonial empire. New industries, from banking to shipping, grew exponentially in response to the trade. Ships made in Liverpool alone trafficked more than 1.5 million enslaved Africans across the Atlantic Ocean. This dark history runs through the fabric of Liverpool's built and social environments and can still be felt today.

The Black population in Liverpool also grew because of the city's engagement in the slave trade. In the eighteenth century, Africans begin to appear in the parish records, from Abel, "a Black moor belonging to Mr. Rock," to Samuel Baron, "son of the African king Onramby." A diverse Black community—including enslaved people and domestic servants, the children of African leaders sent to study in the United Kingdom, people escaping enslavement from the United States, and sailors and seamen—contributed to the city's development in the eighteenth and nineteenth centuries. Their presence gave Liverpool the oldest Black community in Europe.

This community continued to grow in the twentieth century when nine million servicemen from across the British Empire provided labor during both World Wars. Many of them arrived in the city in an area called Liverpool 1 (L1) via the Merchant Navy. They raised families with local women in the community called Sailortown, which was begun by earlier sailors who had settled on Pitt Street in L1. These Black residents and their descendants faced discrimination from and displacement by the white population and later migrated five thousand yards from the waterfront to the area known today as Liverpool 8 (L8).

Ray Quarless's great-grandfather was one of the Black sailors who made Liverpool his home. In 1868, he arrived as a merchant seaman from Jamaica, eventually settling and marrying an Englishwoman from Bilston, Ray's great-grandmother. The couple had twelve children and lived on Pitt Street as part of the burgeoning Black community of L1. Ray reflected on the city's long Black history:

> **The first recorded Black person is buried in Saint Nicholas's Church: a man called Abel, and he's buried there on the 1st of October, 1717. So Liverpool's had a Black presence for well over three hundred years. It continues to resist and fight against the grain because that's the way it has been since they settled here as part of Sailortown in Liverpool 1, in the Pitt Street area. And what you have to take into account is that Liverpool 8 as a Black community, as a post–World War II community, its roots are firmly, firmly ingrained within Liverpool 1. It continues to resist and continues to fight.**
>
> **That's where we are today: We continue to struggle, we continue to fight, we continue to campaign in all its formats. And we continue to do that through not necessarily trying to, if you like, shout our way through it or kick our way through the crowd. We do it more strategically now, by working in partnership [with] and alongside the institutions and stakeholders that matter and where we can have an impact. And to a certain extent—not fully, but to a certain extent—that's beginning to come to fruition.**

Kerry Nugent, an activist and advocate for women who have experienced domestic abuse, pointed out the structural inequalities faced by Black people in L8 and connected the "dehumanization of the African people" to white European institutions that used racism as a weapon to justify the enslavement of Africans. She reflected

Ray Quarless, 2022.

on her heritage and the ways that Black children are stereotyped and failed early in Liverpool:

> I am born and bred Liverpool 8. I've been involved in community work for as long as I can remember: always active, working specifically around domestic abuse and women's issues and now looking at health outcomes for our African Caribbean community. My great-grandfather came from Liberia, and he met a Jewish woman, a woman whose surname was Cropper. So they were a family that was involved in the slave trade and had my grandmother Kai. She then met and married a Trinidadian man and then had my mother. And then I came about. So I'm the third generation of Liverpool-born Black women....
>
> Our community, our African brothers and sisters, were treated in a subhuman way that gave rise to [a] kind of white superiority because they had to justify the treatment of slaves by treating them as less than human.... With Liverpool being the capital of the slave trade, that oppression has continued, and we're still struggling today for things like health. We have poorer health outcomes. We don't have the employment opportunities. We're failed in the education system....
>
> I was failed by Liverpool local authority. They failed to provide me with an education. They failed to offer me opportunities on leaving school. They failed to keep me safe, and they failed to do anything about the situation as we stand today. We were often referred to as underachievers in school, and I hate that term. We were failed. Don't put the onus on Black kids to take responsibility for not achieving in school. That was down to the teacher. And that was down to the attitude of white teachers, and that was down to the local authority because they knew what was going on and they still won't stand up and take account for the experience of Black kids in school today. Kids are getting bullied. Kids are experiencing racism from teachers. So nothing's really changed since I left school.

Yinka Yesufu echoed the point that the stereotyping of Black people starts early in Liverpool. He vividly recalled the moment when he first learned of slavery, on a school trip, and how he has had to unpack the discomfort and anger associated with the racism he has experienced:

> If I'm being perfectly honest, I was ignorant of slavery until about the age of nine or ten, and then I was taken to the local main library in the city center, William Brown Street. I still remember,

with my class, going to the top floor, pulling out these drawers, and seeing all these Black Africans in the hull of a cargo ship. And I never realized until later on, me being the only Black guy in my class, how traumatized I was when I saw Black people in the hull of a ship. And then, I don't know, it sparked something in me to investigate my own self-knowledge, etc. And so—yeah, looking at slavery, looking at what's happened to enslaved Africans, I suppose the sadness, the shame of what happened to my fellow man and woman— and so it's impacted me for a lifetime, as far as I can remember. Led me to do a lot of research. . . .

This may appear controversial for a lot of people, but for me, growing up in this city, I consider Liverpool to be the most racist city I know. And I've traveled quite extensively, I'm proud to say. I know just through my name, I know through the color of my skin, I know just being me, how it's impacted me from a young boy to a man to a mature adult growing up, how who I am is seen as a threat to a lot of people. And I suppose

in my younger days I was, without rolling out any tropes, I was the angry young Black man, but I didn't understand why I was angry. And then I started to unpack, uncover the layers to that and realized it was because of the color of my skin that people saw me as a threat. But then over time, I'm comfortable in my own skin.

Like many of the other interviewees, Yinka has spent his life confronting the whitewashing of British history and the exclusion of narratives of Black contributions and triumphs. Yinka believes that through reeducation, people can find stories of Africa and the African Diaspora that are full of heroes and historical icons that will help Black people find a sense of purpose and knowledge of themselves:

It's funny, because you ask a lot of people, "Tell me about the history of Black people." They may start from 1524 with John Hawkins [a British naval commander and pivotal figure in the development of British maritime

Yinka Yesufu, 2022.

dominance, including the slave trade], his first voyage, as it were, to the continent of Africa. But you know what I'll always say. . . . If you want to know a history about Black people in Africa, a starting point—one starting point is Benin bronzes. But if you want to go even further, then check out the literature, check out the research, you know, *Black Athena* [by Martin Bernal], check out the contributions that African people have contributed to the world. And it's been humongous. And we're not just talking about history. We're talking about the sciences. We're talking about mathematics. We're talking about history. We give the world something to be proud of.

History is littered with people who have been forgotten, and the only way to uncover that is to go dig deep in the archives, because the information there—they say that history is written by the victors. To a degree, yes. But you need to dig even deeper to see what the true history is. To see what the authentic history is. To see what my history is. Look at that smile come on. That's freedom. You know, freedom for me is not giving a damn. This is me. Accept me as I am.

Those interviewed noted how the underrepresentation of Black people in the local workforce served as a stark reminder of racism. They feel disenfranchised when stepping out of L88, which they see as a safe place, into the predominantly white areas of Liverpool's city center. Many noted that the lack of access to employment and education makes the possibility of generational wealth a distant dream. Judith Cummings discussed this discrimination:

> [One] of the barriers that face Black people in Liverpool is the opportunity to access further education, the opportunity . . . to gain employment within their chosen field. Again, that's being challenged in many, many years by other movements within the Liverpool 8 area, and I think that sense of belonging is still missing. We're right here in the city of Liverpool, in the center of Liverpool, and yes, if you go to the stores, if you go to the banks, if you go to the law court, how many professional people do you see— Black people—holding certain positions?

That still is a problem, and that still needs to be challenged.

This discrimination colors all aspects of life in Liverpool, including health care. When Judith's family arrived in the city from Trinidad in 1962, her parents faced great difficulty in finding care and support for the learning disability of one of their sons. The Cummings family's story is far too common, and such experiences are as prevalent as ever, as everyday racism and lack of economic opportunity increasingly impact the mental health of the city's Black residents. In honor of her brother, Judith became a mental health advocate and helped to establish the Mary Seacole House, Liverpool's first transcultural psychiatry service, in 1991. She said:

> We have to be quite clear and understand that there is and has been an element of racism throughout the diagnosis of our service users—or even if you're not a service user, anyone who is going through a psychotic episode or who's having challenges within society based on their, you know, their education and their socioeconomic situation. And there always has been this sort of understanding of the terminology "big, bad, and dangerous." . . .
>
> I could share a situation whereby an individual that I was working with was removed from one of the streets, one of the areas within the Liverpool 8 area, Princes Avenue. And because he was acting out in a very bizarre manner, instead of . . . making a phone call to myself or my team, he was detained, he was pushed into a police truck. He was treated really, really appallingly. And instead of . . . speaking to him "What was going on," you know, "How were you feeling?", he was actually detained under the Mental Health Act, which I found totally inappropriate. I do believe, although it's gotten better since 1991, but there is still that biasedness towards treating a Black person one way and treating a white person another way. And again, we need to challenge that over and over again.

While life for Liverpool's Black community is still marred by racism and skewed opportunity, this is not the only

Judith Cummings, 2022.

story people have to tell. Interviewees note the empowerment they feel as people of the African diaspora, asserting their identities proudly and embracing ancestral heritage as a source of knowledge and power. Kerry Nugent discussed her family's Black consciousness:

We were paying close attention to the news coming out of America around the Civil Rights Movement, Martin Luther King. We were listening to Marcus Garvey from Jamaica. We were following Malcolm X's journey. It gave us a sense of pride in our people—you know, we would look to writings, academic writings by Black people around race. My family's very well-read on those issues because it's important that we're conscious. We can't continue the fight without knowing what's going on. So that was all passed down generationally. . . .

Hopefully, them young ones will take this forward, because we can't stop the fight and things aren't okay, you know—we still got police officers murdering our young men and getting away with it.

We're still experiencing harsher sentencing. We in Liverpool, the good thing about us is that we are kind of militant in our approach because we've been here so long—because we've experienced this discrimination, oppression, racism, we have never stood by and let it happen. So we've got a rich history of standing up for ourselves and for our race.

L8's Black population has, against all odds, woven a narrative of unity, strength, and profound cultural significance into the tapestry of Liverpool's history. Many interviewees draw power from the continued struggle against racism, using their resilience as a shield as they navigate white supremacy and anti-Blackness. Despite their diverse backgrounds and experiences, they all touch on a core takeaway: only by understanding the legacies of slavery and colonialism can people address the systemic and contemporary forms of racism and pave the way for a Liverpool that truly champions equity and celebrates its diversity.

ALWAYS MAKING HISTORY: REFRAMING BLACK LIFE

Anthony Bogues

African American essayist and novelist James Baldwin once said, "The great force of history comes from the fact that we carry it within us, are unconsciously controlled by it in many ways, and history is literally present in all that we do." What does it mean to carry history within us? As humans, we create the structures of any society, which are formed and then conditioned by the complex relationships we all engage in. We live within and through these structures. However, we do so recognizing that the past is not detached from the present. Historical narratives allow us to glimpse the past but become more complex as formerly erased histories open up new archives and understandings.

There is never just one view of history. Elites who dominate any society posit their views of history, and when they do, they make assertions and omissions. For example, for a long time, a dominant strain of professional historians argued that racial slavery was not a determining fact of American or Atlantic history and, therefore, its consequences were of little relevance today. In continental Africa there continue to be arguments about what some historians call the "balance sheet of empire," which disputes the way in which the European colonial project supposedly modernized Africa. With this theory, the idea is advanced that, while colonial domination as a form of rule may have been undemocratic, on balance, it benefited Africa by bringing civilization and infrastructural development. Of course, there is abundant evidence contrary to this assertion, as Walter Rodney demonstrated most visibly with a systematic dismantling of the theory in his 1972 book *How Europe Underdeveloped Africa*. This is an argument still in need of broad public recognition. More important, we should note that when myths are debunked, other narratives grounded in evidence must be assembled. Following this assertion, the late African thinker and political personality Amílcar Cabral noted that the European colonial project was not a construction or even interpretation of history, but rather was a process of historical interruption. Only by engaging in anti-colonial national liberation

Ancestral Memorial, Coney Island, Chester Higgins, 1995. In this photograph three women gather in a memorial ritual for enslaved African ancestors. The women are part of The People of the Sun Middle Passage Collective, an organization founded in 1989 to ensure the remembrance of all ancestors who lost their lives in the Transatlantic Slave Trade.

struggles would Africans and other formerly colonized peoples go about the process of a reconstruction or "reclamation" of history.

This act of reclamation is at the core of the GCP network and the *In Slavery's Wake* project, both of which seek to place the voices of those who were enslaved and colonized in the foreground of our view of this history. We do this as part of a long tradition of Black thought and action that has questioned dominant narratives and reframed Black life since the inauguration of racial slavery and the European colonial project. From the very beginning of European colonization and racial slavery, the enslaved and colonized asked themselves: why did this happen? Simultaneously, they also considered methods and acts bent on dismantling these systems of domination. In contending with practices and ideologies of dehumanization and in asking and answering the profound question of what makes us human, they created new ideas about freedom and life while practising and refiguring different forms of history-making. Specifically, by asking the question of why this happened, the enslaved

created stories about exile, exodus, and deliverance. Through speeches, petitions, and especially in published enslaved narratives, like those of the formerly enslaved abolitionist Ottobah Cugoano, a central idea about "the why" was asserted that because of their growing practices of human domination, Europeans were not a chosen or godlike people, as they professed, but were more sinful. In Cugoano's and other narratives, enslaved authors suggested that Africans were a chosen people who one day would rise up against oppression and domination.

Despite alternate views of freedom, which found avenues within the rising world of print culture and commerce, slavery and colonization required and advanced processes that would attempt to strip away the humanity of Africans— and greatly succeeded in doing so in the dominant systems of law, politics, religion, science, and economics. Systems of human classification and hierarchization became embedded practices of racial and colonial domination, employing emerging scientific discourse and entwining it with religious doctrine. One way for the enslaved and the colonized to overturn these classification systems was to create new religious, spiritual, and cultural practices, as well as new political organizations. For these practices to flourish, three elements were crucial: the first was an attempt from within the African Diaspora to answer the question of how to dismantle racial slavery. In North America, so-called *Negro Spirituals* helped to create and advance concepts of exile and exodus—appropriating Biblical narratives of being a people torn from, but destined to return to, a true homeland. In the Caribbean, Afro-Caribbean religions crafted and adapted various stories and gods, sometimes with new cosmologies adapted from African systems, that delivered answers to the why of enslavement and how to destroy it.

The second element was the construction and dissemination of distinctive narratives showing that people of African descent did, indeed, have history. The European colonial project's human classification process constructed a justification for Western stereotypes that pictured Africa as the "dark continent"—in turns ahistorical, exotic, savage, monolithic, timeless, romantic, and primitive. This stereotype was reproduced in some of the most distinguished thought in the Western intellectual tradition, with influential philosophers, like Georg Wilhelm Friedrich Hegel, proclaiming that "Africa had no history" and would ultimately lead to theories and practices of eugenics that developed in later centuries. To correct this act of erasure, people of African descent researched and reclaimed a different story—a recuperative kind of history—that historian and activist Arturo Alfonso Schomburg described in 1925 (implicitly arguing against the eugenicist movement amidst its height of popularity) as a "compendium of exceptional men and women of African stock." This reclaimed history was influenced by the idea that history is about recounting actions of great men and women, of which Europe assumed Africa had none. William Simmons's earlier 1887 book, *Men of Mark: Eminent, Progressive and Rising*, exemplifies this model by telling stories of Black men freed from slavery who shaped American society through public, intellectual, and religious life.

The third element of providing affirmative arguments against the practices justifying slavery and colonialism was the belief in demonstrating progress for people of African descent that provided an alternative genealogy of Black accomplishments, even as they aligned with Western notions of civilization that had been developed during the Enlightenment. Numerous texts from the nineteenth and early twentieth centuries were shaped by the overarching idea of "progress," such as those by Senegalese Muslim scholar Omar ibn Said, who was enslaved and brought to the Americas; works by Black abolitionist Luís Gama from Brazil; or J. J. Thomas in the Caribbean, whose 1889 text, *Froudacity: West Indian Fables by James Anthony Froude*, espoused similar ideologies of progress and civilization on the part of Africans, Afro-Brazilians, or Black West Indians.

But another strain of radical Black abolitionism was developed through the thought and action precipitated by the world-changing events of the Haitian Revolution—which encompassed and successfully coalesced two major struggles during the often-labeled age of revolutions that enveloped the Atlantic world in the late-eighteenth and early-nineteenth centuries. The struggle against both slavery and colonialism in Haiti opened not just ideas of Black sovereignty, but radical collective practices and conceptions of freedom that extended beyond those offered by the American and French revolutions. Unlike in the United States, which had rebelled but preserved slavery, Haitian revolutionaries explicitly tied together the existential fight against slavery with the fight against colonialism on undeiably practical terms. The fear of subsequent revolutions by the enslaved influenced the sale of French American colonies through the Louisiana Purchase and led to the systematic development of a host of codes, laws, and practices across different colonial empires bent on suppressing communication, congregation, and other practices that might lead toward rebellion or revolt. More than just fomenting fear, the influence of this revolution's success in military, social, and cultural spheres for African-descended peoples and others globally cannot be overestimated. As historian Julius Scott has termed it, the "common wind" that developed among enslaved peoples

Creole Republicaine, Edouard Duval-Carrié, 2014. Haitian-born artist Edouard Duval-Carrié engaged with archival materials at Brown University's John Carter Brown Library to create a series of artworks on figures and histories of the Haitian Revolution. In this work, Duval-Carrié features a female revolutionary. Adorned with weapons, she appears to be leaving the scene of a plantation burning in the background.

from Cuba to Colombia to Cape Town as a result of Haitian success sparked hope and provided an object lesson in making a new kind of freedom. The Haitian Revolution formally confronted the dominant conceptions of racial inequality by destroying the so-called hierarchical classifications of humanity. This principle promised a form of philosophical and historical accounting that attacked the underpinnings of Western intellectual tradition. Haitian writer Anténor Firmin's 1885 book *The Equality of the Human Races* was the key example of this kind of account. While Firmin's text was produced in the late nineteenth century, when racial slavery was on the wane, it provided an important argument for a new version of history as told from the Black perspective.

To think with and through the rich examples of African and African Diaspora practices, thought, and history making, from individual publications and petitions to collective acts of revolution, we must reassess what we think we know and grapple with the ways the present is continually shaped by and shaping our understanding of the past. Therefore, we must not relate to the past simply as a bygone time or its social systems as an unchanging juridical or structural matter. When we look at our past as a series of chronological events and benchmarks that divide history into slavery and post-slavery, or apartheid and post-apartheid eras, we often address merely one aspect of the past and ignore continuing social and economic structures. This blindness means not that racial slavery still exists or that formal colonization remains but that the accumulated remnants of catastrophe live on as global sedimented deposits, and have led to conditions in which the lives of ordinary Black people are seen to be disposable. For example, in the United States, Brazil, and the Caribbean, state forces continue to kill young Black men and women with impunity. In many African countries, a colonial presence continues to make daily life almost impossible for ordinary Black people. And in the Caribbean, where both racial slavery and European colonization were the midwives of what would become "modern" society in the late fifteenth century, deep structures of inequality still govern.

Ultimately, when we grapple with and attempt to change conditions born from deeply embedded structures of inequality, we must change our stories of the past—and that process begins with a reframing of our archives of knowledge. Only when we access the historical archive with new perspectives, illuminate new archives, or recognize unacknowledged ones can we begin to change our stories about the past. In this regard, the Unfinished Conversations project being carried out by the GCP is central. For catastrophic histories, memory is a deeply important part of an archive—too often unseen—that exists within descendants of the colonized and the enslaved, deeply buried but ready to surface when activated. If the present is a culmination of the past, then tapping into memory allows space for difficult dialogues and new narratives. Thus, with Unfinished Conversations, memory and oral history become a way for new histories to be told, especially outside of their communities of origin. For example, how does one tell the story of enslavement and colonialism in Senegal and their continued traces in everyday life if one does not listen keenly to the words of those who describe their condition as enslaved people or descendants of slaves? Or how does one understand the contemporary life of women farmworkers in the Western Cape if one does not listen to their words that paint a picture of life still rooted in historical bondage and servitude? Memory allows the past and the present to comingle in ways that bring these human experiences to the forefront.

We need to remind ourselves that the systems of racial slavery and European colonialism were humanmade, and within those structures of bondage, new ideas of freedom, crafted by the enslaved and colonized, were born. From the various petitions for freedom, to acts of refusal, revolts, marronage, and revolutions, practices of freedom by enslaved people emerged that were larger and deeper than Western ideas of liberty. In continental Africa, debates about language, struggles against pacification processes, political petitions, the formation of Ethiopianism, and the emergence of both male and female prophets and spiritual leaders contributed to a similar connected tradition of freedom making. Sometimes these activities remained regionally and locally rooted, but often they were in conversation spanning the

Atlantic world, such as witnessed at the various Pan-African Congresses. In the early twentieth century, movements like Marcus Garvey's Universal Negro Improvement Association demanded Black freedom for the "African at home and Abroad." Beginning in the mid-twentieth century, ideas about Black consciousness and forms of third-world solidarity enveloped what could be called the Black world. Then, in the late twentieth century, the South African Freedom Movement, decolonization, Black Power, and anti-apartheid movements connected Africa and the African Diaspora in a common struggle for a better world. Too often separated from earlier centuries of the Black movement, it is important that we describe the character of these practices of freedom with new eyes and words. If, under enslavement, freedom took the shape of Black abolitionist practices to end racial slavery, then the idea of freedom was organically linked not merely to a conception of individual liberty but to one of collective freedom and equality, based upon and rooted in human dignity, a point frequently made by Frederick Douglass. Likewise, movements in the post-emancipation and "postcolonial" eras drew from these same collective ideas. Anti-colonial freedom, as the psychiatrist and political philosopher Frantz Fanon noted, is rooted in the self-capacity to create the world of the "YOU." Accordingly, freedom does not revolve around the individual but is

Untitled, **Tommy Oliver, 2020. In this photograph Janaya "Future" Khan addresses a large crowd at a Black Lives Matter protest in Hollywood, California, following the death of George Floyd. Floyd's killing sparked protests around the world, where everyday people took to the streets to confront police brutality, decry racism, and demand redress for the ongoing impacts of slavery and colonialism.**

strongly rooted in a deep relationship between community and self. Common to Black abolitionist and anti-colonial freedom projects is the demand for freedom, along with the conviction that humans must not live under any system of human domination.

Human societies have thousands of years of history. We know from many archives that the issue of freedom has always loomed large across many eras. In our modern forms of society, which began to take shape at the same time as European colonialism and racial slavery, freedom and liberty became central philosophies and organizing concepts. But we also know that they became invested with multiple meanings. In this regard, the tendency to conflate liberty and freedom increased over time. Liberty has come to mean a form of freedom: a life unhindered by constraint. As the intellectual historian David Hackett Fischer asserted, "Liberty meant separation. Freedom implied connection." In the Atlantic world, liberty morphed into political liberty. Thus, for example, many of the founding fathers of the American republic proclaimed liberty for themselves yet they simultaneously enslaved Africans. The African American abolitionist Prince Hall petitioned the Massachusetts Assembly in 1777, noting that the revolution was about liberty but that the enslaved did not have freedom. His contrasting of the two words, liberty and freedom, was instructive. By the nineteenth century, when the abolition of racial slavery created liberty for the enslaved, the word liberty was transformed to mean emancipation. But the word emancipation itself had a specific set of meanings, including release from dependency (as if slavery were primarily about the slave's dependency on their enslaver). For the enslaved, articulations of freedom and liberty had far wider definitions than simply emancipation, but they contained and sought to expand a more fulsome sense of equality and democracy in order to manifest freedom. Think of the ways in which those previously enslaved in the United States attempted to tie freedom to education and land ownership in the American South following the Civil War by creating public school systems and advocating for collective land rights—forty acres and a mule. W.E.B. Du Bois called this conception of freedom "abolition democracy," making it clear that the end

of enslavement did not equal freedom. In the anti-colonial movement in the twentieth century, many anti-colonial thinkers argued for a freedom narrowly defined as political freedom: the creation of new, independent state formations through processes of decolonization. However, we need to understand that this definition of anti-colonial freedom was distinct from national liberation, an idea and practice in which decolonization meant not only the creation of a new nation-state but also the transformation of the former colony's economic, social, and cultural relations.

In this wider practice of decolonization as national liberation, freedom became a form of liberation. All these conceptions and practices of freedom that have emerged from Black struggles hold in common an understanding that freedom, equality, and democracy are deeply linked and mutually dependent. In this linkage, one does not mean a limited form of electoral democracy but rather a form of democracy in which there are mechanisms for regular participation in the things that affect everyday life. In numerous stories from the Haitian Revolution, formerly enslaved people complain that they had freedom but no equality. In many politically independent African countries today, this perspective persists, as expressed in the question, "When will independence end?" that was posed to our partners in Senegal while conducting Unfinished Conversations interviews.

Our contemporary world has created versions of liberty that rest upon not only political liberty but also consumer choice. This concept of liberty has become pervasive and shapes much mainstream discourse on liberty. Because we have ignored the ways in which the European colonial project and social system of racial slavery have shaped the making of the modern world, little attention has been paid to the freedom practices and ideas of the enslaved and the colonized. In a world wracked by gross inequalities, where anti-Black racism is on the rise and the norm, do we not need to draw from a different archive of conceptions of freedom? Has the time not come for us to confront the history that has shaped our world? In this regard, Black freedom struggles will now become a rich resource as we attempt to carve out freedom futures and rupture the history that made us all.

SLAVERY, COLONIALISM, AND THE PRESENT: A REFLECTION

Mongane Wally Serote

Rise People Rise, Cliff Joseph, 1970. This painting's three horizontal bands of color resemble the pan-African flag. According to the artist Cliff Joseph, "The red sky symbolizes the conflict; the black center, the people; and the green base, the nurturing life of hope."

The sky formed a concave circle and dovetailed into the horizon to meet the sea. The masters thought they were in total control as they chained and cuffed their human cargo on board ships. The masters must have felt triumphant as they moved farther and farther away from the abode of the slaves, even as some of them still resisted being captured. But seeing the inhuman cruelty of the masters to their resistance, they chose death and drowned themselves or had to be drowned. That was to set the record straight for themselves, and for any survivors and for the masters, that their sacrifice was the price of freedom for all!

In this spirit, the revolutionary movement fights for justice, peace, and freedom for all, or it fights for nothing. There is no middle road. This principle is an important lesson of history and culture. The shared responsibility for carrying out the possibility of freedom, peace, and justice for all was on the shoulders of the oppressed. The slaves and their descendants carried and continue to carry the most gigantic responsibility, because there will be no peace unless they defend it forever. The responsibility of the slave is not to be interested in the guilt of the master.

It is absolute folly and a dangerous assumption for anyone in the world to think that slavery has been abolished. The master must be taught to be free, by all means necessary, because they are blinded by greed, or are fighting, by all means necessary, to maintain their knee on the slave's neck. The slave master, the colonizer, and the neocolonialist act from an uncontrollable desperation, so they make history from the culture of being desperate.

Daniel
saw the stone
that was
hewed out the mountain
Daniel
saw the stone
that was
rolled into Babylon
Daniel
saw the stone
that was
hewed out the mountain
tearing down
the kingdom of this world!

So the slaves sang and are singing now. And so there is no one in the world at this hour who can say that they did not hear the song, because it is too late to say one does not understand it.

Once, not so long ago, the world did split into two. We knew as humanity already that that there is "no more water, the fire next time." What, then, is this humane culture that must be nurtured, that must be entrenched and become the mainstream of all quality of all forms of life? That movement is and must be a global engagement in scope. It must be a cultural engagement through schools and university programs, but also through government policy and structures, and organs of civil society. The nation must encourage cross-pollination of diverse elements through policy and legislation. In other words, humane and progressive culture must be institutionalized, vertically and horizontally, across nations. This, it seems to me, is where the revolutionary forces and movements of the different countries must come together, to undermine the forces of oppression, exploitation, reaction, and counterrevolution.

When in one sunrise moment, it so happened that all of us, in our being so many, are so much more than even the stars: We said, we are one person; the same person; in simple language, brother and sister.

Would we sigh! Would we simply say:

oh at last, and cry and laugh and for
a long while remain in disbelief?
Would we know us?
To be
Brothers and sisters,
under the sun?
In the world, being by ourselves, alone
and agree and say we must start from
the beginning, again
Say so
Without fear
would we?

Would we on that sunrise day say as Thabo Mbeki said that:

I am an African.
I owe my being to the hills and the
valleys, the mountains and the glades,
the rivers, the deserts, the trees, the
flowers, the seas and the ever-chang-
ing seasons that define the face of our
native land.... Whatever the setbacks
of the moment, nothing can stop us
now! Whatever the difficulties, Africa
shall be at peace!

And so
The world, I ask?
Would we
Speak sing whisk or whisper our innate being
And wishes and will
To this the brittle earth of miraculous seasons
Which come and go, go and come
Whether we wish them or not
They come
to earth under the sky
bidding and obeying their protocols
These seasons, through their diversity,
They bring a variety of gifts
to us human beings and to the flora and fauna of the
    land the earth
our land, year after year without fail
        Let us appreciate
        those four diverse seasons
        as they interact in long and elongated
            well wishes
        as they interact and together
        and with us
        of brittle skin and feel and sight and taste
            and thin eardrum
        they come diverse as weather
        how they become they create creativity
        They produce in each province
        Their providence
        not only different,
        but also unique
        not only unique
        but purposeful as the weather
        and therefore, also diverse as reptiles as
            a variety of animal species
        to be
        different types of little lives including
            ants and different species of plants
                This, as the sun comes and goes,
                as the moon together with the stars
                    comes and goes
                These diverse seasons
                do so as summer comes and goes,
                as autumn comes and goes
                change changes and changes change
                oh human race
                change
                as winter comes and goes
                and as spring every September bes
                without fail
                and bestow us new beginnings of life and
                    living

This day this week this month
Comes and goes
Without fail loyal like a dog
time, dapples and splashes and displays nature's
    creative power,
which forever is forever
is us
brittle as heritage
Tangible and intangible as it is
this heritage nudges us, whispers and whistles to us
do not, no never, forget the creative gift
and the power you we have in our spirit, being, and
    breadth
in or minds and in our hearts
in our reality like our eye
which has forever guided us
seeing
and has defined our history and therefore also our
    culture
        It is out of these our social activities together with
            nature's actions and our social development
        So the truth that we shape
        That shapes who we are and must be
        Embrace us
        These us human beings
        developments and realities of powers and being
        as with the seasons,
        have their moods, strengths, and prowess for
            reasons of life
        and creativity
        Look at the renaissance of nature in the land
        as it winks, ululates, rumbles, and dances
        becoming reality
        with its life in the land, in the sky, in the air,

in the being of this our beautiful land and earth
which flaunts its diverse acts and interactions
The mountains in their eternity
In their echo their pasts and presents
quietly quietly affirming that it is in action that
    history is shaped
as it shapes things
as they were shaped by action of thought spirit and
    being,
and so they define the present through the past
and the present day
and minute
life and being

the mathematics of reality
If history speaks to us in the present
and whispers its past now
would we hear
or fear
or freeze like a stillborn baby and not be
see and feel and learn
out of its past, can we, shall we speak to the present
or
be just evidence that has not been
in and about the future
through the truth of our being
and through the being of our truth
and the reality of being our being
We are one with the seasons and nature
remember
We are their diversity as they are our diversity
Inherent in us,
is history, which can also express culture
which finds and speaks to history
which also can determine and decide our being
our history

What we must remember and never forget is that we make
    history
And so culture claims us
And so,
as the seasons come and go
and nature relates through her social rules systems and beings
    hidden in her silences
which we must learn and know,
so must we create and shape
and never say we did not know
that this is the spirit of being
through the song, the dance, the spirit the being of our being
and belonging
and the art of being
and form of being
and so
in the heart of this time
we are here the evidence of being or not being
the spirit and form
and expression are of our spirit, heart, and mind
are we
better than the leopard
the lion
the hyena
the wild dog
better than the eagle and its beak that chicken fears

and the snake fears
that the rat fears
the rat with eloquence waits when the ship sinks
for all to leave first
the rat does
it remains
oh human race
race and rescue the universe the cosmos
the being of things
the little things
like being
lessons
which our hearts hold as a mother would a child
or a father holds a child
when the rain rains and storms the earth
and when the storm like a rock rolls
down
down the slope of the mountain
with a roar
unstoppable and ready to do what it intends to do
is that where we are
oh human race

       where
       where are we are where in this noise
       which we seek to see and find but cannot
       but we hear
       and we know how its peculiar power is
       can be
       Come oh countrymen and countrywomen
       remind me
       and I will remind you too
       for we told time here
       in the longest of time
       to hear us
       when every time
       we remind time
       that we nurtured freedom here
       in the four seasons of this African land
       and the land

              where we walk and work
              come
              come and see us tend it
              come and see us feel and feed it
              this seed
              it sings in the blue sky
              in the myriad colors of many flags
              flailing
              feel its rhythmic calm
              within the diversity of the national anthems of the
                  human race
              we know us and so you too know us now
              come
              and be with us in all the seasons
              which are
              as we forever live and hold hands here
              come
              to till and tend our lives
              and
              one day

When the red or yellow ball
Sails through the gentle mauve yellow red quiet to
    blue space
Soon
When it sails between and across the earth and
    heaven's urge
One day when this everyday beautiful eyeball of
    time
Sails through a whisper and whispers
With a peep
When the concave horizon
Made of earth and sky
Gently gently touch
And whisper
The new day is here
Will we remember
That men and women are bosom friends
And make people
Will we
With love in our hearts as if our hearts
Are our hands
Will we
Remember Palestine
That it is on earth with people
Children men and women
Not slaves of terror

Who
Who will come with me so we hope together
Come oh men and women of the world we live in
come
remind me
and I will remind you too
for we told time here
in the longest of time
to hear us
when every time
we remind time
that we nurtured freedom here
in the four seasons of this African land and world

come and see us tend it
come and see us feel and feed it
this seed
it sings in the blue sky
in the many colors of our flags of the human race
of the world
feel the rhythmic calmness of their cloth and colors
within the diversity of the national anthems
we know us and so you too know us now
come
come let's be and come let's do together and be
    with us in all the seasons
as we forever live and hold hands here
to till and tend our lives
our hearts
will we
as we move and walk and talk as we forever do
remember Palestine being the world
my friend will we
when
you and i
as one will we
walk
talk to teach us
then in the world when there is nothing

ACKNOWLEDGMENTS

This publication—along with the wider project of which it is a part—is a work of remembrance honoring human resistance, resilience, and creativity in the face of a continuing history of exploitation and catastrophe. Realizing a task of such significance depended on assembling an exceptional array of people from around the world. We are indebted first to the contributors to this volume, and also to the founding members of the Global Curatorial Project network, some of whom are represented in these pages and in the exhibition, but all of whom were essential to the broader mission: Geri Augusto, Richard Benjamin, Nancy Bercaw, Anna-Karina Caudevilla, Bambi Ceuppens, Shanaaz Galant, Krystel Gualdé, Bertrand Guillet, Catherine Hall, Wayne Modest, Ibrahima Thiaw, Paul Tichmann, and Tsione Wolde-Michael.

We also owe a significant debt of gratitude to Lonnie G. Bunch III, Christina Paxson, Ruth Simmons, Kevin Young, and the leadership and staff of all collaborating institutions for their vision and recognition of the power of this kind of global collaboration despite its many challenges. We are thankful to the staff of Smithsonian Books, led by Carolyn Gleason and Jaime Schwender, and the expert group of editors and designers they assembled to bring this book to beautiful realization.

We are indebted to multiple artists who were willing to work with us to fill the silences in the archive with their visions, voices, and creativity, including Mongane Wally Serote, Diana Ferrus, Yhuri Cruz, J. Cunha, Angelica Balanta, Lucie Kamuswekera, Will Johnson, Nyugen E. Smith, Tiffany McNeil, Gary Tyler, Pola Maneli, and Juana Ruíz Hernández and the weavers of Mampuján, Colombia. We are especially grateful to Daniel Minter for his artistry and spirit in conceiving *The Universe of Freedom Making* for the exhibition; his designs were translated beautifully into the pages of this volume along with elegant design from Eddie Opara, Jun Jung, and the team at Pentagram.

This project would not have been possible without the generosity of Abrams Foundation and Ford Foundation.

Ultimately, hundreds of collaborators have touched this project, breathing possibility into the wake—only some of whom we are able to list here. Our deepest gratitude goes to the people who shared their lives, stories, courage, and pain with us as participants in the Unfinished Conversations project. Their invaluable contributions and generosity are part of a long lineage of Black freedom making that we, as global citizens, need to continue to recover, remember, preserve, and share to build better futures. We hope that in this project we have honored the pledge we made one night in Senegal when we were charged by a community to "tell their stories."

—Paul Gardullo, Johanna Obenda, and Anthony Bogues

In Slavery's Wake and Unfinished Conversations interns, researchers, and advisers
Ariela Algaze, Kareal Amenumey, Zuri Arman, Antonio Austin, Jordan Barnes, Mariah Bender, Sherri Cummings, Bridget DeLaney-Hall, Karen Eberhart, Yannick Etoundi, Daniel Everton, Marcelo Ferraro, Nélari Figueroa Torres, Julia Gettle, Spencer Gomez, Gustav Lloyd Hall, Arlean Horton, Brandon Hoyt, Kennedy Jones, Marcus Kyles, Yolanda Lamboy, Elizabeth Mathews, Joseph Meisel, Cherise Morris, Stephen Newbold, Lauren O'Brien, Katherine Osby, Anni Pullagura, Marlin Ramos, Marcus Rediker, Channelle Russell, Sean Smith, Dillon Christophe Stone, Amanda Strauss, Laura Tamayo, Malcolm Thompson, Susana Turbay, Hilary Wang, and Emma Yau.

At Brown University and Smithsonian's National Museum of African American History and Culture
Leigh Armstrong, March Baker, Connie Beninghove, Dorothy Berry, Michael Biddle, Dorey Butter, Pascale Boucicaut, Olivia Cadaval, Michelle Commander, Kinshasha Holman Conwill, Deirdre Cross, Colleen Davis, Eric Dixon, Fatima Elgarch, Mary Elliott, Candra Flanagan, Jeannine Fraser, Sabina Griffin, Naiomy Guerrero, Kalyn Hall, Eric Hammesfahr, Tequila Harris, Joanne Hyppolite, Trudy Hutcherson, Steven Lewis, Laura Manaker, Adam Martin, J. Kiku Langford McDonald, Kate McMahon, Gabrielle Chantal Miller, Laura Mina, Sarah Mirekua, Tionna Moore, Kareen Morrison, Kelly Elaine Navies, Dawn Neuendorffer, Antje Neumann, Ivie Orobaton, Candace Oubre, Bianca Pallo, Fleur Paysour, Nick Pedemonti, Elizabeth Purdum, Douglas Remley, Patrick Rey, Maiyah Rivers, Jill Roberts, Sharon Shahid, Africa Smith, Taima Smith, Pamela Steele, Drew Talley, Allison Tolman, Ruthann Uithol, Leslie Walker, Tiffanie Warner, Shana Weinberg, and Melissa Wood.

In Africatown, United States
Emmett Lewis, Nina Major, Patrick Munnerlyn, Jennifer Prince, Corey Richardson, Destineé Rogers, Derrick Tinsley, Samuel Waller, Chris Williams, Barja Wilson, Joe Womack, and Lorna Gail Woods.

In Liverpool, United Kingdom
Ayo Akinrele, Claire Benjamin, Nikki Blaze, Stef Bradley, Darren Brady, Julia Bryan, Stephen Carl-Lokko, Michelle Charters, Alexandra Creighton, Judith Cummings, James Diboe, Janet Dugdale, Lisa Edison, Mohamed Elmi, Ian Freeman, Howard Gayle, Jacqui Graham-Jones, Miles Greenwood, Sandi Hughes, Ranmalie Jayawardana, Adiva Lawrence, Jean-François Manicom, Rita Martelli, Paul McMullan, Kerry Nugent, Michelle Peterkin-Walker, Ray Quarless, Maria O'Reilly, Paul Reid, Anna Ruchalska-Pineda, Alexander Scott, Claire Stringer, Laurence Westgaph, and Olayinka Yesufu.

In Rio de Janeiro, Brazil
Martha Abreu, Alcino Amaral, Marcelo Amaro, Renzo Carvalho, Valéria Farias, Keila Grinberg, Pedro Colares da Silva Heringer, Claudio Honorato, Maurício Hora, Ademir Junior, Elisa Larkin Nascimento, Mônica Lima e Souza, Ana Flávia Magalhães Pinto, Thayssa Menezes, Aline Montenegro, Caio Sérgio de Moraes, Vinícius Natal, Nilcemar Nogueira, Erick Quirino, Laís Rocha, Natália Pires Rodrigues, Ivanir dos Santos, Nathalia Sarro, Thiago Sereno, Matheus Sinder, and Diogo Tubbs.

In Cape Town, South Africa
Mercia Andrews, Jaco Boshoff, Amanda Botha, Loyiso Centane, Najumoeniesa Damon, Shirley Davids, Wayne Florence, Riefqah Franks, Melany Fuma, Esther Esmyol, Johan Geduld, Jake Harding, Miekte Hendriks, Magdelene Jacobs, Magrieta Jacobs, Adriaan Jordaan, Carlyle Lodewyk, Carmen Louw, Nozuko Madokwe, Zann Manho, Ron Martin, Monde Matyumza, Nangamso Memani, Joy Meyer, Aviwe Gift Ndalana, Bongani Ndlovu, Dingi Ntuli, Thulani Nxumalo, Ngoni Nyembe, Maganthrie Pillay, Benjamin du Plessis, Katherine Poggenpoel, Roderick Sauls, Lorna Solomon, Abdul Azeez Stemmet, Dean Tiedt, Johannes Warries, Cobus Wilson, Noleen Wilson, Sky Zulu, Masala Film Works, and Native Creative Productions.

In Dakar, Saint-Louis, and Fouta, Senegal
Abou Mamadou Ba, Amadou Bâ, Faty Ba, Lamine Badji, Mouhamadou Bah, Mame Baledjo, Cyrille Bassène, Fatoumata Camara, Alioune Badara Coulibaly, Baila Coulibaly, Mame Boye Coulibaly, Dounamba Coulibaly, Moussa Diakité Bah, Oumar Diallo, Sadio Diallo, Cheikh Amadou Diarra, Nassou Adama Diarra, Djeumb gui Diaw, Malamine Diaw, Tahirou Diop, El Hadji Abdoulaye Faye, René Ndiana Faye, Modou Gaye, Marius Gouané, Samba Gueye, Mamoudou Dembel Guissé, Aïcha Kamite, Mouhamed Lamine Kane, Oulèye Koné, Mouhamed Abdallah Ly, Youssou Mballo, Ousmane Mbodj, Pasteur Philippe J. B. Mendy, Abdoulaye Ndiaye, Arfang Moussa Ndong, Abdoulaye Niang, Jean Ouattara, Sona Sall, Demba Sangaré, Amar Seck, Badara Seck, Ousmane Sène, Yvette Koussangué Senghor, Khadidiatou Siwaré, Aboubakry Sow, Ibrahima Sow, Aissata Sy, Ibrahima Sy, Amadou Thiam, Ndeye Binta Thioye, Thieman Touré, Yaye Faty Touré, Youssou Touré, Marième Traoré, Anna Karima Wane, and Mariane Yade.

In Brussels, Belgium, and Democratic Republic of Congo
Dominique Ankoné, Bukas Basumbandek, Armand Bayala, Chance Boas, Sofie Bouillon, Christine Bluard, Maurice Carney, Ferdinand Lokunda Lokunda Dasilva, Paul Dilungame Dia Mawonga, Jacqueline Goegebeur, Guido Gryseels, Gaspard Habumuremyi, Cécile Ilunga, Bosefe Iyaku Baluka, Marie-Reine Iyumva, François Kadiebwe Wa Kasangu, Landry Kalla Mballe, Sibo Rugwiza Kanobana, Rachel Kapombo Ilodi, Dieudonné Lakama, Miezi Bernadette Lusakalalu, Betty Mafueni, Thérèse Mantu, Prisca Manyala, Suzanne Matondo, Anna Mawuna Nsiala, Pierre Giscard Mayona Ntangu Zavionso, Déo Mpatu, Innocent Muhozi, Jonas Mukamba Kadiata Nzeba, Rémy Muke, Yvonne Muleka, Daniel Ndoluvwalu Nadia, Ken Ndiaye, Pierre Ngombe Zinga, Léon Nguapitshi Kayongo, Deborah Nsomwe, Daniel Ntumba Wa Tshilumba, Amour Otou-Etoundi, Bart Ouvry, Diana Salakheddin, Paul Shemisi, Annick Swinnen, Jean François Tamba Mabiaca, Géraldine Tobe, Sophie de Ville, Ernest Léon Viokolo Lelo, Jeanine Amusubi Yogolelo, and Salomé Ysebaert.

CONTRIBUTORS

Martha Abreu is co-lead for Unfinished Conversations: Brazil, a professor at the History Institute of the Universidade Federal Fluminense, and a visiting researcher at the Faculty of Teacher Training at the Universidade do Estado do Rio de Janeiro.

Geri Augusto is an exhibition adviser for *In Slavery's Wake*, a senior fellow of International and Public Affairs at Brown University, and a faculty associate at the Ruth J. Simmons Center for Study of Slavery and Justice, as well as in the departments of Africana Studies, Native American and Indigenous Studies, and Portuguese and Brazilian Studies at Brown.

Anthony Bogues, co-director and a collaborating curator for *In Slavery's Wake*, is the director of the Ruth J. Simmons Center for the Study of Slavery and Justice, a professor of Africana studies, and the current Asa Messer Professor of Humanities and Critical Theory at Brown University.

Lonnie G. Bunch III is secretary of the Smithsonian Institution and was founding director of the Smithsonian's National Museum of African American History and Culture.

Fatoumata Camara is a collaborating curator for *In Slavery's Wake* and a research fellow in the Cultural Engineering and Anthropology Research Unit at the University of Dakar.

Bambi Ceuppens is a collaborating curator for *In Slavery's Wake* and a resident anthropologist and senior curator at the AfricaMuseum.

Michelle D. Commander is deputy director of the National Museum of African American History and Culture.

Alexandra Creighton is the curatorial and project administrator at National Museums Liverpool, where she has been involved with the International Slavery Museum and the Waterfront Transformation Project.

Yhuri Cruz is a Brazilian visual artist, writer, and playwright whose practice intertwines literature and action through performance, installation, and collective works.

Sherri V. Cummings is an assistant professor in the history department and the Africana Studies program at Rhode Island College.

Lisa Edison is the community engagement manager for the Maritime Museum at National Museums Liverpool.

Diana Ferrus is a participant in Unfinished Conversations: South Africa and a poet based in Cape Town, South Africa.

Candra Flanagan is a collaborating educator for *In Slavery's Wake* and is the director of the Teaching and Learning unit of the Education Department at the National Museum of African American History and Culture.

Shanaaz Galant is a collaborating curator for *In Slavery's Wake* and co-lead of Unfinished Conversations: South Africa and curator of enslavement at the Iziko Slave Lodge museum, focusing mainly on oral history, community histories, and intangible heritage.

Paul Gardullo is co-director and a collaborating curator for *In Slavery's Wake* and is assistant director of history at the National Museum of African American History and Culture, where he also heads the Center for the Study of Global Slavery.

Miles Greenwood is a collaborating curator for *In Slavery's Wake* and lead curator of transatlantic slavery and legacies at the National Museums Liverpool.

Keila Grinberg is a collaborating curator for *In Slavery's Wake* and director of the Center for Latin American Studies at the University of Pittsburgh, and a professor of history there.

Aline Montenegro Magalhães is a collaborating curator for *In Slavery's Wake* and a professor at the Museu Paulista of the Universidade de São Paulo. Previously, she spent more than twenty years as a historian and curator at the Museu Histórico Nacional in Rio de Janeiro.

Minkah Makalani is the director of the Center for Africana Studies and an associate professor of history at Johns Hopkins University.

Kate McMahon is a historian of global slavery at the National Museum of African American History and Culture.

Gabrielle Chantal Miller is the lead for Unfinished Conversations: Africatown and is a program specialist and archaeologist at the Center for the Study of Global Slavery at the National Museum of African American History and Culture.

Daniel Minter is the creator of the installation a universe of freedom making for *In Slavery's Wake*. He is a painter, illustrator, and educator whose body of work deals with themes of displacement and diaspora, spirituality, and the (re)creation of meanings of home.

Jennifer L. Morgan is a professor of history in the Department of Social and Cultural Analysis at New York University.

Vinícius Natal is co-lead of Unfinished Conversations: Brazil and is a researcher for Vila Isabel samba school.

Johanna Obenda is lead exhibition developer for *In Slavery's Wake* and is a curatorial specialist at the Center for the Study of Global Slavery at the National Museum of African American History and Culture.

Ivie Orobaton is a research specialist at the Center for the Study of Global Slavery at the National Museum of African American History and Culture.

Christina H. Paxson is president of Brown University and professor of public economics and public policy.

Marcus Rediker is an exhibition adviser for *In Slavery's Wake* and is Distinguished Professor of Atlantic History at the University of Pittsburgh.

Alexander Scott is contributing researcher for *In Slavery's Wake* and a project assistant curator at the International Slavery Museum in Liverpool.

Mongane Wally Serote is a poet and author. He was inaugurated as the South African National Poet Laureate in 2018 and has received numerous awards for his many publications.

Mônica Lima e Souza is a participant in Unfinished Conversations: Brazil and the coordinator of international projects at the National Archives in Brazil. She is a professor of African history and coordinator of the African Studies Laboratory at the Universidade Federal do Rio de Janeiro.

Amadou Thiam is part of the Unfinished Conversations: Senegal team and is a doctoral student in archaeology working as a researcher in the ETHOS doctoral school's Unité de Recherche en Ingénierie Culturelle et en Anthropologie.

Ibrahima Thiaw is a collaborating curator for *In Slavery's Wake* and lead in Unfinished Conversations: Senegal. He is a professor of archaeology at the Institut Fondamental d'Afrique Noire at the Université Cheikh Anta Diop in Dakar, Senegal, where he directs the archaeology laboratory and the Unité de Recherche en Ingénierie Culturelle et en Anthropologie.

Paul Tichmann is co-lead for Unfinished Conversations: South Africa. He recently retired as the director of the Collections and Digitisation Department of the Iziko Museums of South Africa and was formerly the curator of the Iziko Slave Lodge museum in Cape Town.

Shana Weinberg is the project manager of Unfinished Conversations and associate director of public humanities programs at the Ruth J. Simmons Center for the Study of Slavery and Justice at Brown University.

Kevin Young is a poet and Andrew W. Mellon Director for the National Museum of African American History and Culture.

REFERENCES

Foreword / Lonnie G. Bunch III
Holmes, Cornelius. Interviewed by W. W. Dixon. *Federal Writers' Project: Slave Narrative Project*, vol. 14, South Carolina part 2 (1941): 294–97. https://www.loc.gov/resource/mesn.142/?sp=301&st=text.

Introduction / Paul Gardullo and Johanna Obenda
Boshoff, Jaco Jacqes, Lonnie G. Bunch II, Paul Gardullo, and Stephen C. Lubkemann. *From No Return: The 221-Year Journey of the Slave Ship São José*. Washington, DC: Smithsonian Books, 2017.
Cooper, Ann Julia. *A Voice From the South*. Oxford: Oxford University Press, 1988. https://search.worldcat.org/title/voice-from-the-south/oclc/123108942.
Ghosh, Amitav. "The Nutmeg's Curse." Chicago: University of Chicago Press, 2021.
Gumbs, Alexis Pauline. "Undrowned: Black Feminist Lessons from Marine Mammals." Chico, CA: AK Press, 2020. https://search.worldcat.org/title/1198713625.
Hall, Stuart. "Cultural Identity and Diaspora." In *Colonial Discourse and Post-Colonial Theory: A Reader*. Edited by Patrick Williams and Laura Chrisman. London: Harvester Wheatsheaf, 1994.
Sharpe, Christina. *In the Wake: On Blackness and Being*. Durham: Duke University Press, 2016.
Walcott, Derek. "The Sea Is History." In *Selected Poems*. New York: Farrar, Straus and Giroux, 2007.
Williams, Eric. *Capitalism and Slavery*. 3rd ed. University of North Carolina Press, March 2021. https://uncpress.org/book/9781469663685/capitalism-and-slavery-third-edition/

The Many Impacts of the Transatlantic Slave Trade / Jennifer L. Morgan
The Black Abolitionist Papers. Vol. 1, *The British Isles, 1830–1865*. Edited by C. Peter Ripley. Chapel Hill: University of North Carolina Press, 1985.
Cadamosto, Alouise Da. *The Voyages of Cadamosto and Other Documents on Western Africa in the Second Half of the Fifteenth Century*. Edited by G. R. Crone. New York: Routledge, 2010.
Ignatiev, Noel. *How the Irish Became White*. New York: Routledge, 1995.
Inikori, Joseph. "Slave-Based Commodity Production and the Growth of Atlantic Commerce." In *Africans and the Industrial Revolution in England: A Study in International Trade and Economic Development*. Cambridge University Press, 2002.
Jefferson, Thomas, to John Wayles Eppes, June 30, 1820. Founders Online, National Archives. Last modified April 12, 2018. http://founders.archives.gov/documents/Jefferson/98-01-02-1352.
Jefferson, Thomas. *Notes on the State of Virginia*. 1785.

Jeffries, Hasan Kwame. "Legacies of Belief." In *Make Good the Promises: Reclaiming Reconstruction and Its Legacies*. New York: HarperCollins, 2021.
Johnson, Walter. "To Remake the World: Slavery, Racial Capitalism, and Justice." *Boston Review* (October 19, 2016). https://bostonreview.net/race/walter-johnson-slavery-human-rights-.
Kaplan, Paul. "Isabelle d'Este and Black African Women." In *Black Africans in Renaissance Europe*, edited by K. J. P. and T. F. Earle. Cambridge: Cambridge University Press, 2005.
Morgan, Edmund Sears. *American Slavery, American Freedom: The Ordeal of Colonial Virginia*. New York: Norton, 1975.
Moszynski, Peter. "5.4 Million People Have Died in Democratic Republic of Congo since 1998 Because of Conflict, Report Says." *British Medical Journal* 336, no. 7638 (February 2, 2008): 235. https://doi.org/10.1136/bmj.39475.524282.DB.
Nunn, Nathan. "The Long-Term Effects of Africa's Slave Trades." *Quarterly Journal of Economics* 123, no. 1 (February 1, 2008): 139–76.
Phillips, Ulrich Bonnell. *American Negro Slavery: A Survey of the Supply, Employment and Control of Negro Labor as Determined by the Plantation Regime (1918)*. Baton Rouge: Louisiana State University Press, 1994.
Robinson, Cedric J. *Black Marxism: The Making of the Black Radical Tradition*. 2nd ed. Chapel Hill: University of North Carolina Press, 2000.
Thornton, John K. "African Dimensions of the Stono Rbellion." *American Historical Review* 96, no. 4 (1991): 1101.
Trouillot, Michel-Ralph. *Silencing the Past*. New York: Beacon Press, 1992.
Wood, Peter H. *Black Majority: Negroes in Colonial South Carolina from 1670 through the Stono Rebellion*. New York: Knopf, 1975.
Zurara, Gomes Eanes de. "The Chronicle of the Discovery and Conquest of Guinea." In *The Chronicle of the Discovery and Conquest of Guinea*, edited by C. R. Beazley and E. Prestage. Cambridge Library Collection, Hakluyt First Series. Cambridge: Cambridge University Press, 2010.

Surveillance and Segregation / Ivie Orobaton
Anderson, David M. "Master and Servant in Colonial Kenya, 1895–1939." *Journal of African History* 41, no. 3 (September 2000): 459–85. Cambridge: Cambridge University Press, 2000. https://www.cambridge.org/core/.
Gershon, Livia. "This Rare Copper Badge Tells a Story of Slavery in Nineteenth-Century Charleston." *Smithsonian Magazine*, June 24, 2021. https://www.smithsonianmag.com/smart-news/slave-badge-found-charleston-180978055/.
Greene, Harlan, Harry S. Hutchins, Jr., and Brian E. Hitchins. *Slave Badges and the Slave-Hire System in Charleston, South Carolina,*

1783–1865. Jefferson, NC: McFarland, 2008.
South African History Online. "Pass Laws and Sharpeville Massacre" Cape Town: June 13, 2011; last updated July 23, 2019. https://www.sahistory.org.za/article/pass-laws-and-sharpeville-massacre.
South African History Online. "Pass Laws in 1800–1994." Cape Town: March 21, 2011; last updated August 27, 2019. https://www.sahistory.org.za/article/pass-laws-south-africa-1800-1994.
Tabaro, Jean De La Croix. "The Passport to Death: Story of Rwanda's Notorious ID." KT Press, July 13, 2015. https://www.ktpress.rw/2015/07/the-passport-to-death-story-of-rwandas-notorious-id/.

Fighting Back / Alexander Scott
Benjamin Golden, Kathryn. "'Armed in the Great Swamp': Fear, Maroon Insurrection, and the Insurgent Ecology of the Great Dismal Swamp." *Journal of African American History* (2021): 1548–1867.
Casteras, Susan P. "'Too Abhorrent to Englishmen to Render a Representation of it . . . Acceptable': Slavery as Seen by British Artists Traveling in America." In *Nineteenth-Century British Travelers in the New World*, edited by Christine Devine, 221–50. Farnham, UK: Ashgate, 2013.
Cutter, Martha J. *The Many Resurrections of Henry Box Brown*. Philadelphia: University of Pennsylvania Press, 2022.
Douglass, Frederick. *Diary, 1886–1894; Tour of Europe and Africa, 1886–1894*. Library of Congress. https://www.loc.gov/item/mss1187900001.
Foster, Thomas A. *Rethinking Rufus: Sexual Violations of Enslaved Men*. Athens: University of Georgia Press, 2019.
"A Fugitive Slave in Liverpool." *Liverpool Albion*, February 22, 1858, 15.
Greenspan, Ezra. *William Wells Brown: An African American Life*. New York: Norton, 2014.
Lamb, John. Personal correspondence with author regarding Frederick Douglass. October 28, 2023.
Longfellow, Henry. "The Slave in the Dismal Swamp." Maine Historical Society, 1842. https://hwlongfellow.org/poems_poem.php?pid=99.
McInnis, Maurie D. *Slaves Waiting for Sale: Abolitionist Art and the American Slave Trade*. Chicago: University of Chicago Press, 2011.
Moody, Jessica. *The Persistence of Memory: Remembering Slavery in Liverpool, "Slaving Capital of the World."* Liverpool: Liverpool University Press, 2020.
Morris, J. Brent. *Dismal Freedom: A History of the Maroons of the Great Dismal Swamp*. Chapel Hill: University of North Carolina Press, 2022.
Murray, Hannah-Rose. *Advocates of Freedom: African American Transatlantic Abolitionism in the British Isles*. Cambridge: Cambridge University Press, 2020.

Olusoga, David. *Black and British: A Forgotten History*. London: MacMillan, 2016.

Parry, Tyler D., and Charlton W. Yingling. "Slave Hounds and Abolition in the Americas." *Past & Present* 241, no. 1 (2020): 69–108.

Todd, Arthur. *The Life of Richard Ansdel*. Manchester, UK: Sherratt & Hughes, 1919.

Wood, Marcus. *Blind Memory: Visual Representations of Slavery in England and America, 1780–1865*. Manchester: Manchester University Press, 2000.

Reverberations

Cugoano, Quobna Ottobah. *Thoughts and Sentiments on the Evil of Slavery*. London: Penguin Books, 1999.

Atlantic Slavery, Colonization, and Shattered Modern Sovereignties / Ibrahima Thiaw

Acemoglu, Daron, Simon Johnson, and James Robinson. "The Rise of Europe: Atlantic Trade, Institutional Change, and Economic Growth." *American Economic Review* 95, no. 3 (2005): 546–79.

Anderson, B. *Imagined Communities: Reflections on the Origin and Spread of Nationalism*. London: Verso, 1983.

Appadurai, Arjun. *Modernity at Large: Cultural Dimensions of Globalization*. Minneapolis: University of Minnesota Press, 1996.

Borrel, Thomas, Boukari-Yabara Amzat, Collombat Benoît, and Deltombe Thomas. *L'empire qui ne veut pas mourir: une histoire de la FranceAfrique, Seuil*. 2021.

Araujo, Ana L. *Shadows of the Slave Past: Memory, Heritage, and Slavery*. Abingdon: Routledge, 2014.

Austen, Ralph. *Trans-Saharan Africa in World History*. Oxford: Oxford University Press, 2010.

Beckert, Sven. *Empire of Cotton: A Global History*. Vintage: New York, 2014.

Beckles, Hilary. *White Servitude and Black Slavery in Barbados, 1627–1715*. Knoxville: University of Tennessee Press, 1989.

Bell, Emma, and David Scott. "Reimagining Citizenship: Justice, Responsibility and Non-penal Real Utopias." *Justice, Power and Resistance Foundation* Vol. (September 2016): 53–72.

Bernier, Celeste-Marie. *Characters of Blood: Black Heroism in the Transatlantic Imagination*. Charlottesville: University of Virginia Press, 2013.

Blackburn, Robin. *The American Crucible: Slavery, Emancipation and Human Rights*. London and New York: Verso Books, 2011.

Blakey, Michael. "Archaeology under the Blinding Light of Race." *Current Anthropology* 61, supplement 22 (2020).

Blaut, James M. *Eight Eurocentric Historians*. New York: Guilford Press, 2000.

–––, ed. *1492: The Debate on Colonialism, Eurocentrism, and History*. Trenton: Africa World Press, 1992.

Bogues, Anthony 2003. *Black Heretics, Black Prophets: Radical Political Intellectuals*. New York: Routledge, 2003.

Boodry, Kathryn S. 2013. *The Common Thread: Slavery, Cotton and Atlantic Finance from the Louisiana Purchase to Reconstruction*. PhD diss., Department of History, Cambridge MA: Harvard University, 2013.

Borrel, Thomas, Boukari-Yabara Amzat, Collombat Benoît, and Deltombe Thomas. *L'empire qui ne veut pas mourir: une histoire de la FranceAfrique, Seuil*. 2021.

Brooks, George E. *Landlords and Strangers: Ecology, Society and Trade in Western Africa, 1000–1630*. Boulder: Westview Press, 1993.

Bruner, Edward M. "Tourism in Ghana: The Representation of Slavery and the Return of the Black Diaspora." *American Anthropologist* 98 no. 2 (1996): 290–304.

Carney, Judith 2001. *Black Rice: The African Origins of Rice Cultivation in the Americas*. Cambridge: Harvard University Press, 2001.

Chakrabarty, Dipesh. *Provincializing Europe: Postcolonial Thought and Historical Difference*. New Jersey: Princeton University Press, 2000.

Cooper, Frederick. *Colonialism in Question: Theory, Knowledge History*. Berkeley: University of California Press, 2005.

–––. *Citizenship, Inequality, and Difference: Historical Perspectives*. Princeton: Princeton University Press, 2018.

Crosby, Alfred W. *The Columbian Exchange: Biological and Cultural Consequences of 1492*. Westport: Praeger Publishers, 2003.

Curtin, Philip D. *The Atlantic Slave Trade: A Census*. Madison: University of Wisconsin Press, 1969.

Curran, Andrew S. *The Anatomy of Blackness: The Science of Slavery in the Age of Enlightenment*. Baltimore: Johns Hopkins University Press, 2011.

Diamond, Jared. *Guns, Germs, and Steel. A Short History of Everybody for the Last 13,000 Years*. London: Jonathan Cape, 1997.

Diouf, Mame Birame. "Les sociétés médiévales, villes et campagnes, face à la question de la soudure alimentaire et au manque en général, dans les derniers siècles du Moyen Age occidental et au début de l'époque moderne." PhD diss., University of Clermont Auvergne, 2021.

Ebron, Paula A. "Tourists as Pilgrims: Commercial Fashioning of Transatlantic Politics." *American Ethnologist*, 26, no. 4 (1999) : 910–32.

Fall, Y. K. *L'Afrique à la Naissance de la Cartographie Moderne, XIVe/XVe siècles: les cartes majorquines*. Paris: Edition Karthala 1982a.

Forte, Jung R. 2007. "'Ways of Remembering': Transatlantic Connections and African Diaspora's Homecoming in the Republic of Benin." *Social Dynamics* 33, no. (2007): 123–43.

Ferdinand, Malcom. *Une écologie décoloniale: penser l'écologie depuis le monde caribéen*. Paris: Editions Seuil: 2019.

Ferguson, J. 2005. "Seeing Like an Oil Company: Space, Security, and Global Capital in Neoliberal Africa." *American Anthropologist* 107, no. 3 (2005): 377–82.

Galloway, J. H. "Sugar." In *Cambridge World History of Food*, edited by K. F. Kiple and K. C. Ornelas, 437–49. Cambridge: Cambridge University Press, 2000.

Gellner, E. *Nations and Nationalism*. Oxford : Basil Blackwell, 1983.

Gilroy, Paul. *The Black Atlantic: Modernity and Double Consciousness*. Cambridge: Harvard University Press, 1993.

Gonzalez, Johnhenry. 2019. *Maroon Nation: A History of Revolutionary Haiti*. New Haven: Yale University Press, 2019.

Hartman, Saidiya. *Lose Your Mother: A Journey along the Atlantic Slave Route*. New York: Farrar, Straus and Giroux, 2007.

Harrison, Faye V. 2012. "Building Black Diaspora Networks and Meshworks for Knowledge, Justice, Peace and Human Rights." In *Afro-Descendants, Identity, and the Struggle for Development in the Americas,* edited by B. Reiter and K. E. Simmons, 3–17. Ruth Simms Hamilton, African Diaspora Series. East Lansing: Michigan State University Press, 2012.

Hobhouse, Henry. *Seeds of Wealth: Four Plants that Made Men Rich*. Oxford: MacMillan, 2003.

Hudson, P. J. *Bankers and Empire: How Wall Street Colonized the Caribbean*. Chicago: University of Chicago Press, 2017.

Holsey, Bayo. *Routes of Remembrance: Refashioning the Slave in Ghana*. Chicago: University of Chicago Press, 2008.

Jones, Eric L. *The European Miracle: Environments, Economies and Geopolitics in the History of Europe and Asia*. Cambridge: Cambridge University Press, 1981.

Jones, Hilary. "Fugitive Slaves and Christian Evangelism in French West Africa: A Protestant Mission in Late Nineteenth-century Senegal." *Slavery & Abolition 38, no. 1 (2016)*.

Joyner, Brian D. 2003. *African Reflections on the American Landscape, Identifying and Interpreting Africanisms*. Washington, DC: National Park Service and National Center for Cultural Resources, 2003.

Klein, Martin. "Studying the History of Those Who Would Rather Forget: Oral History and the Experience of Slavery." *History in Africa. Vol. 16 (1989): 209–17.*

–––. *Slavery and Colonial Rule in French West Africa*. Cambridge: Cambridge University Press, 1998.

–––. "The Slave Trade and Decentralized Societies." Journal of African History 42, no. 1 (2001): 49–65.

Lamko, Koulsy, Amy Niang, Samba Sylla Ndongo, and Lionel Zevouno. "De Brazzaville à Montpellier, regards critiques sur le néocolonialisme français." Collectif pour le Renouveau africain (CORA), 2021.

Leiris, Michel. *L'Afrique fantôme*. Gallimard: electronic edition, 2014.

Lovejoy, Paul E. "The Context of Enslavement in West Africa: Ahmad Baba and the Ethics of Slavery. In *Slaves, Subjects and Subversives: Blacks in Colonial Latin America*. Edited by Jane G. Landers and Barry M. Robinson, 9–38. Albuquerque: University of New Mexico, 2006.

Lovejoy, Paul E. *Transformations in Slavery: A History of Slavery in Africa*. New York: Cambridge University Press, 2000.

Ly, M. A., and I. Thiaw. "'A Quand la Fin de l'Indépendance?' Notice sur les Arènes Mémorielles Sénégalaises." In *La Quête du Sens. Mélanges offerts à Paulin Hountondji à l'occasion de xes 80 ans*. Edited by P. C. Kiti, D. Medegnon, and A-R. Ndiaye. Star Editions, 2021.

MacEachern Scott. "Seeing Like an Oil Company's CHM Programme: Exxon and Archaeology on the Chad Export Project." *Journal of Social Archaeology* 10 (2010): 347. DOI: 10.1177/1469605310378801.

Manning, Patrick. *Slavery and African Life*. Cambridge: Cambridge University Press, 1990.

Merry, Sally Engle. "Transnational Human Rights and Local Activism: Mapping the Middle." *American Anthropologist* 108, no. 1 (2006): 38–51.

Mintz, Sydney W. *Sweetness and Power: The Place of Sugar in Modern History*. New York: Viking, 1985.

Monga, Célestin. *Anthropologie de la Colère. Société civile et démocratie en Afrique Noire*. L'Harmattan: 1994.

Morgan, H. Lewis. *Ancient Society or Researches in the Lines of Human Progress from Savagery through Barbarism to Civilization (1877)*. London: MacMillan, 1877.

Mudimbe, Valentin Y. *The Invention of Africa: Gnosis, Philosophy and the Order of Knowledge*. Bloomington: Indiana University Press, 1988.

Murphy, S. *Financing Southern Expansion in the Antebellum United States*. Chicago: University of Chicago Press, 2023.

Nuun, Nathan, and Nancy Qian. "The Columbian Exchanges: A History of Disease, Food and Ideas." *Journal of Economic Perspectives* 24, no. 2 (2010): 163–88.

Ogundiran, Akinwumi, and Toyin Falola. *Archaeology of Atlantic Africa and the African Diaspora*. Bloomington: Indiana University Press, 2007.

Pratt, Mary L. *Imperial Eyes: Travel Writing and Transculturation*. London and New York: Routledge, 1992.

Pierre, Jemima. *The Predicament of Blackness. Postcolonial Ghana and the Politics of Race*. Chicago and London: University of Chicago Press, 2013.

Restrepo, Eduardo and Arturo Escobar. 2005. "Other Anthropologies and Anthropology Otherwise: Step to a World Anthropologies Framework." *Critique of Anthropology* 25 no. 2 (2005): 99–129.

Richard, G. François. *Reluctant Landscapes. Historical Anthropologies of political Experience in Siïn, Sénégal*. Chicago: University of Chicago Press, 2018.

Roberts, Richard, and Martin Klein. "The Banamba Slave Exodus of 1905 and the Decline of Slavery in the Western Sudan." *Journal of African History* 21 (1980): 375–94.

Rodet, Marie. "Listening to the History of Those Who Don't Forget." *History in Africa* 40 (2013): 27–29.

———. "Escaping Slavery and Building Diaspora Communities in French Soudan and Senegal, ca. 1880-1940." *International Journal of African Historical Studies* 48, no. 2 (2015): 363–86.

Rodney, Walter. *How Europe Underdeveloped Africa*. Washington, DC: Howard University Press, 1982.

Sansone, Livio, Elisée Soumonni, and Boubacar Barry, eds. *Africa, Brazil, and the Construction of Trans-Atlantic Black Identities*. Trenton and Asmara: Africa World Press, 2008.

Santos, Boaventura S. *The End of the Cognitive Empire: The Coming of Age of Epistemologies of the South*. Durham and London: Duke University Press, 2018.

Shaw, Rosalind. *Memories of the Slave Trade: Ritual and the Historical Imagination in Sierra Leone*. Chicago: University of Chicago Press, 2002.

Seyram, Apoh, Wazi, James Anquandah, and Amenyo-Xa. "Shit, Blood, Artifacts, and Tears: Interrogating Visitor Perceptions and Archaeological Residues at Ghana's Cape Coast Castle Slave Dungeon." *Journal of African Diaspora Archaeology and Heritage* 7, no. 2 (2018), 105–30.

Shilliam, Robbie. *The Black Pacific: Anti-Colonial Struggles and Oceanic Connections*. London: Bloomsbury, 2015.

Stahl, Ann. B. "Political economic mosaics: archaeology of the last two millennia in tropical-Sub-Saharan Africa." *Annual Review of Anthropology* 33 (2004): 145–72.

———. "Circulations through Worlds Apart: Georgian & Victorian England in an African Mirror." In *Materializing Colonial Encounters,Archaeologies of African Experience*, edited by F. G. Richard, 71–94. New York: Springer, 2015.

Swingen, Abigail. *Competing Visions of Empire : Labor, Slavery, and the Origins of the British Atlantic Empire*. New Haven: Yale University Press, 2015.

Thésée, Gina, and Paul R. Carr. "The International Year of People for African Descent (IYPAD): The Paradox of Colonized Invisibility within the Promise of Mainstream Visibility." *Decolonization: Indigeneity, Education and Society* 1, no. 1 (2012): 158–80.

Thiaw, Ibrahima. "Anthropology and the End of Independence: What's Next?" In *Pathways to Anthropological Futures*. Edited by C. L. Ribeiro and D. Rutherford, 2022. Wenner-Gren FORUM: https://wennergren.org/forum/pathways-to.anthropological-futures/.

———. "Archaeology of Two Pandemics and Teranga Aesthetic." *African Archaeological Review*, 2020. https://doi.org/10.1007/s10437-020-09403-9.

———. 2008. "Every house has a story." In *Africa, Brazil and the Construction of TransAtlantic Black Identities*. Edited by L. Sansone, É. Soumonni, and B. Barry. Trenton: Africa World Press, 45–62.

———. "Slaves without Shackles: An Archaeology of Everyday Life on Gorée Island." In *Slavery in Africa: Archaeology and Memory*. Edited by P. Lane and K. MacDonald, Proceedings of the British Academy 168: 147–65. London: British Academy, 2011.

———, guest editor, and D. Mack. "Atlantic Slavery and the Making of the Modern World: Experiences, Representations, and Legacies, an Introduction to Supplement 22." *Current Anthropology* 61, supplement 22 (October 2020).

Thornton, John. *Africa and Africans in the Making of the Atlantic World, 1400-1680*. Cambridge: Cambridge University Press, 1992.

Trouillot, Michel-Ralph. *Silencing the Past: Power and the Production of History*. Boston: Beacon Press, 1995.

———. *Global Transformations: Anthropology of the Modern World*. New York: Palgrave Macmillan, 2003.

Valognes, Stephane. "Slave Trade Memory Politics in Nantes and Bordeaux: Urban Fabric between Screen and Critical Landscape." *Journal of African Diaspora Archaeology and Heritage* 2, no. 2 (2013): 151–71.

Webber-Heffernan, Shalon. "Performing Monument: Future Warnings." *Performance Matters* 4, no. 3 (2018): 76–90.

Whitten Jr., Norman E., and Arlene Torres. *Blackness in Latin America and the Caribbean: Social Dynamics and Cultural Transformations: Central America and Northern and Western South America*. Vols. 1 and 2. Bloomington: Indiana University Press, 1998.

Williams, Eric. *Capitalism and Slavery*. Chapel Hill: University of North Carolina Press, 1944.

Wolf, Eric. *Europe and the Peoples without History*. Berkeley: University of California Press, 1982.

Wright, Gavin. *Slavery and American Economic Development*. Baton Rouge: Louisiana State University Press, 2006.

Wynter, Sylvia. "After Man, Towards the Human: The Thought of Sylvia Wynter." Keynote response at conference in honor of Sylvia Wynter. Centre for Caribbean Thought, University of West Indies, Mona Campus, June 14-15, 2002.

———. "Unsettling the Coloniality of Being?Power/Truth/Freedom: Towards the Human, After Man, Its Overrepresentation—An Argument." *New Centennial Review* 3, no. 3 (2003): 257–337.

Youngquist, Paul. 2005. "The Afro Futurism of DJ Vassa." *European Romantic Review* 16 (2005): 181–92.

Ironwork and Speculative World Making / Michelle D. Commander

Equiano, Olaudah. *The Interesting Narrative of the Life of Olaudah Equiano, or Gustavus Vassa, the African. Written by Himself*. London: Penguin Books, 2004.

Tahro: Shaping Spiritual Vessels / Johanna Obenda

Arzeno Mooney, Claudia, April L. Hynes, and Mark M. Newell. *African-American Face Vessels: History and Ritual in 19th-century Edgefield*. The Chipstone Foundation. N.d. https://www.chipstone.org/article.php/537/Ceramics-in-America-2013/African-American-Face-Vessels:-History-and-Ritual-in-19th-Century-Edgefield.

Gartman, T. *Facing History: Lessons from the Potter's Wheel. Smithsonian Center for Folklife and Cultural Heritage. February 1, 2021.* https://folklife.si.edu/magazine/facing-history-jim-mcdowell-black-potter.

McCurnin, M. *From the Old to the New World: The Transformation of Kongo Minkisi in African American Art. VCU Scholars Compass. N.d.* https://scholarscompass.vcu.edu/etd/78/

Montgomery, C. J. "Survivors from the Cargo of the Negro Slave Yacht Wanderer." *American Anthropologist* 10, no. 4 (1908): 611–23. https://doi.org/10.1525/aa.1908.10.4.02a00110

Spinozzi, A. *Hear Me Now: The Black Potters of Old Edgefield, South Carolina*. Metropolitan Museum of Art, 2022.

Industry and Extraction / Ivie Orobaton

Bakewell, Peter. "Mining in Colonial Spanish America." In vol. 4 of *The Cambridge History of Latin America, edited by Leslie Bethell, 105–52. Cambridge: Cambridge University Press, 1984.* https://www.cambridge.org/core/

Birchard, Ralph E. "Copper in Katanga Region." *Economic Geography* 16, no. 4 (October 1940): 429–36. https://doi.org/10.2307/140952.

Brown, Kendall W. *A History of Mining in Latin America: From the Colonial Era to the Present. Albuquerque: University of New Mexico Press, 2012.*

Green, James N., and Thomas E. Skidmore. *Brazil: Five Centuries of Change*. 3rd ed. Chap. 2: "A New Colonial Order, 1695–1821," sec. 2.1: "Gold Discovered." New York: Oxford University Press, 2021. https://library.brown.edu/create/fivecenturiesofchange/.

Kara, Siddarth. *Cobalt Red: How the Blood of the Congo Powers Our Lives*. New York: St. Martin's Press, 2023.

Mawe, John. *Travels in the Interior of Brazil.* London: Longman, Hurst, Rees, Orme, and Brown, 1812. Adopted by Michael Hardy and Tzun Hardy, July 17, 2023. Joseph F. Cullman 3rd Library of Natural History. https://library.si.edu/.

McQuade, Joseph. "Earth Day: Colonialism's Role in the Overexploitation of Natural Resources." *The Conversation, April 18, 2019.* https://theconversation.com/earth-day-colonialisms-role-in-the-overexploitation-of-natural-resources-113995.

Schwartz, Gabriel L., and Jaquelyn L. Jahn. "Black People More than Three Times as Likely as White People to be Killed During a Police Encounter." In *Mapping Fatal Police Violence Across U.S. Metropolitan Areas: Overall Rates and Racial/Ethnic Inequities, 2013–2017*, edited by Jonathan Jackson. *PLOS One* 15 (June 24, 2020). https://doi.org/10.1371/journal. pone.0229686

Sguazzin, Antony. "South Africa Wealth Gap Unchanged Since Apartheid, Says World Inequality Lab." *Time*, August 5, 2021. https://time.com/6087699/south-africa-wealth-gap-unchanged-since-apartheid/.

Varanasi, Anuradha. "How Colonialism Spawned and Continues to Exacerbate the Climate Crisis." In *State of the Planet, Columbia Climate School, September 21, 2022.* https://news.climate.columbia.edu/2022/09/21/how-colonialism-spawned-and-continues-to-exacerbate-the-climate-crisis/.

Whitcomb, Joshua. "Inequality in South Africa Since 1960." University of Bayreuth. March 23, 2022. https://www.eh-exhibition.uni-bayreuth.de/en/cs/South-Africa/index.html.

Winsor, Morgan. "'Apartheid and Jim Crow Are Really No Different': Why George Floyd's Death Reverberated in Africa." ABC News Online, July 12, 2020. https://abcnews.go.com/International/apartheid-jim-crow-george-floyds-death-reverberated-africa/story?id=71556630

Zinkel, Benjamin. "Apartheid and Jim Crow: Drawing Lessons from South Africa's Truth and Reconciliation." *Law Journals at University of Missouri School of Law: Article 16.* University of Missouri School of Law Scholarship Repository, 2019. https://scholarship.law.missouri.edu/cgi/viewcontent.cgi?article=1830&context=jdr.

Weaving History and Healing / Johanna Obenda

Human Trafficking: Sophie Hayes Foundation: England. 2022. https://www.sophiehayesfoundation.org/.

Jewsiewicki, B., and M. Hendriks. "Present Pasts of Colonial Modernity: Embroideries by Lucie Kamuswekera." *African Arts* 56, no. 2 (2023): 30–47. https://doi.org/10.1162/afar_a_00708.

Domestic World Making of the Enslaved / Geri Augusto

Augusto, G. "For Marielle: Mulhere(s) da maré– Danger Seeds and Tides." *Transition* 129 (2020) (20200101): 246–64.

Barickman, B. J. "'A Bit of Land, Which They Call Roça': Slave Provision Grounds in the Bahian Recôncavo, 1780–1860." *The Hispanic American Historical Review* 74, no. 4 (1994): 649–87.

Brito, Luciana. "Enfeitando o Passado: Um olhar para a ancestralidade entre saias, fitas e rendas." In *Escrita de Mulheres Negras em Conta Gotas: sobre futuros*, vol. 2. Analu Souza e Kassandra da Silva Muniz (Org.), 88–97. Sao Paulo: Instituto Langage, 2023.

Carney, Judith Ann, and Richard Nicholas Rosomoff. *In the Shadow of Slavery: Africa's Botanical Legacy in the Atlantic World.* Berkeley: University of California Press, 2011. https://search.worldcat.org/title/759158601.

Chamoiseau, Patrick, et al. *Texaco*. First Vintage International ed. New York: Vintage International (Penguin), 1998.

"Domestic Worldmaking by the Enslaved." Society of Architectural Historians virtual symposium, February 19, 2022. https://www.domesticworldmaking.com/.

Gonzalez, Lélia. "A categoria político-cultural de amefricanidade." *Tempo Brasileiro* (Rio de Janeiro), no. 92/93 (January/June 1988): 69–82.

Hammond, John. "Mística, Meaning and Popular Education." *Interface* 6, no. 1 (May 2014): 372–91.

Ligia, Margarida Gomes de Jesus. *Ganhadeiras e Zungueiras: autonomia e participação em rede em Salvador e Luanda.* Dissertação de Mestrado em Desenvolvimento e Gestão Social. Universidade Federal da Bahia, Salvador, 2014.

Martins, Leda M. *Afrografias Da Memória: O Reinado Do Rosário No Jatobá.* 2nd ed. Mazza Edições/Perspectiva, 2021.

McKittrick, Katherine. *Demonic Grounds: Black Women and the Cartographies of Struggle.* University of Minnesota Press, 2006.

Perry, K.-K. Y. *Black Women against the Land Grab: The Fight for Racial Justice in Brazil.* Minneapolis: University of Minnesota Press, 2013.

Reis, João José, and A. Brakel. *Slave Rebellion in Brazil: The Muslim Uprising of 1835 in Bahia.* Translated by Arthur Brakel. Johns Hopkins University Press, 1993. https://search.worldcat.org/title/slave-rebellion-in-brazil-the-muslim-uprising-of-1835-in-bahia/oclc/434716635.

Santos, Renato. (Org.) *Questões urbanas e racismo.* Petrópolis, RJ: DP et Alii Editora/Associação Brasileira de Pesquisadores Negros (ABPN), 2012.

Wynter, Sylvia. "Novel and history, plot and plantation." *Savacou*, 1971, 95–102.

Paánza: Seeds of Memory / Johanna Obenda

Carney, Judith. "Rice and Memory in the Age of Enslavement: Atlantic Passages to Suriname." *Slavery & Abolition* 26, no. 3 (2005): 325–48. https://doi.org/10.1080/01440390500319562.

–––. "'With Grains in Her Hair': Rice in Colonial Brazil." *Slavery & Abolition* 25, no. 1 (2004): 1–27. https://doi.org/10.1080/0144039042000220900.

Ideal Film. Serious Films. VRIZA. *Stones Have Law.* Netherlands, 2018.

Price, Richard. *First-Time: The Historical Vision of an African American People.* Chicago: University of Chicago Press, 2002.

van Andel, T., H. Maat, and N. Pinas. "Maroon Women in Suriname and French Guiana: Rice, Slavery, Memory." *Slavery & Abolition* (2023): 1–25. https://doi.org/10.1080/0144039X.2023.2228771

"1992 Festival of American Folklife." Smithsonian Folklife Festival. https://festival.si.edu/past-program/1992.

Tòya: Drumbeats of Revolution / Sherri V. Cummings

Bello, Bayyinah. https://www.google.com/books/edition/Jean_Jacques_Dessalines/6G6-zQEACAAJ?hl=en.

Jan: Notes from a Healer / Shanaaz Galant

Dick, Archie L. *The Hidden History of South Africa's Book and Reading Cultures.* Toronto: University of Toronto Press, 2012.

–––. "The Notebook of Johannes Smiesing

(1697–1734), Writing and Reading Master in the Cape Slave Lodge." *Quarterly Bulletin of the National Library of South Africa* 64, no. 4 (2010).

Ross, Robert. *Cape of Torment: Slavery and Resistance in South Africa*. London: Routledge and Kegan Paul, 1983.

Shell, Robert, and C. H. Shell. *Children of Bondage, a Social History of the Slave Society at the Cape of Good Hope, 1652 to 1658*. Johannesburg: Witwatersrand University Press, 1994.

Roosje: A Mother's Testimony / Candra Flanagan

Cowling, Camillia. *Conceiving Freedom: Women of Color, Gender, and the Abolition of Slavery in Havana and Rio de Janeiro*. Chapel Hill: University of North Carolina Press, 2013.

"Decisions of the Court of Criminal Justice, 1819–1823." Fiscals' Reports, part 2. National Archives UK: CO 116/139.

"The Health Divide: Too Many Black Babies Are Dying So Doulas Are Coming to the Rescue." https://centerforhealthjournalism.org/our-work/insights/health-divide-too-many-black-babies-are-dying-so-doulas-are-coming-rescue.

"How Racism and Microaggressions Lead to Worse Health Outcomes." https://centerforhealthjournalism.org/our-work/insights/how-racism-and-microaggressions-lead-worse-health.

"Infant Mortality and African Americans." https://minorityhealth.hhs.gov/infant-mortality-and-african-americans.

"Maternal Mortality." https://www.who.int/news-room/fact-sheets/detail/maternal-mortality#Overview.

Morgan, Jennifer Lyle. *Laboring Women: Reproduction and Gender in New World Slavery*. Philadelphia: University of Pennsylvania Press, 2004.

"Our Black Maternal Health Crisis Is an American Tragedy." https://www.ama-assn.org/about/leadership/our-black-maternal-health-crisis-american-tragedy.

"The Persistent Joy of Black Mothers." https://www.theatlantic.com/culture/archive/2021/08/black-mothers-joy-weapon/619713/.

Turner, Sasha. *Contested Bodies: Pregnancy, Childrearing, and Slavery in Jamaica*. Philadelphia: University of Pennsylvania Press, 2017.

"Unwanted Epidurals, Untreated Pain: Black Women Tell Their Birth Stories." https://www.nytimes.com/2023/05/06/upshot/black-births-maternal-mortality.html.

"What Drives Black Maternal Health Inequities in the U.S." https://www.ama-assn.org/delivering-care/population-care/what-drives-black-maternal-health-inequities-us.

"Working Together to Reduce Black Maternal Mortality." https://www.cdc.gov/healthequity/features/maternal-mortality/index.html.

Rebellion at Sea / Kate McMahon

"Estimates." *SlaveVoyages*. https://slavevoyages.org/assessment/estimates.

"Libel of Thomas R. Gedney, Aug. 29, 1839," *Thomas R. Gedney &c. v. The Schooner Amistad, &c.,* case files. US District Court, District of Connecticut, M1753.

Lithograph. *Art by Isaac or James Sheffield, lithography by Moses Yale Beach*. Boston: Joseph A. Arnold, Prints and Photographs Division, Library of Congress, https://www.visitthecapitol.gov/artifact/lithograph-joseph-cinquez-cinque-sengbe-pieh-c-1839.

Marques, Leonardo. *The United States and the Transatlantic Slave Trade to the Americas, 1776–1867*. New Haven: Yale University Press, 2016, 61–64.

Rediker, Marcus. "The African Origins of the Amistad Rebellion." *International Review of Social History* 58, no. 21 (2013): Mutiny and Maritime Radicalism in the Age of Revolution: A Global Survey, 20–21.

———. "African Origins": 20.

Trans-Atlantic Slave Trade Database. *SlaveVoyages*. https://www.slavevoyages.org/voyages/SoGfTfoN.

United States v. *Amistad* 40 US 518; 10 L. Ed. 826 January 1841.

Black Freedom Making Before and After Emancipation / Minkah Makalani

Abrahams, Peter. "The Congress in Perspective." In *History of the Pan-African Congress: Colonial and Coloured Unity, a Programme of Action*. Edited by George Padmore. London: Hammersmith Bookshop, 1963. https://www.marxists.org/archive/padmore/1947/pan-african-congress/ch05.htm.

Beal, Fran. "Double Jeopardy: To Be Black and Female." In *The Black Woman: An Anthology*. Edited by Toni Cade-Bambara, 1970. Reprint, New York: Washington Square Press, 2005.

Biko, Steve. *I Write What I Like: A Selection of His Writings*. London: Pearson Education, 1987.

Bogues, Anthony. *Black Heretics, Black Prophets: Radical Political Intellectuals*. London: Routledge Press, 2003.

Brown, Vincent. *Tacky's Revolt: The Story of an Atlantic Slave War*. Cambridge: Harvard University Press, 2020.

Cabral, Amílar. *Revolution in Guinea: An African People's Struggles*. New York: Monthly Review Press, 1970.

———. "The Weapon of Theory." In *Unity and Struggle: Speeches and Writings of Amílcar Cabral*. New York: Monthly Review Press, 1979.

———. "National Liberation and Culture." In *Return to the Source: Selected Speeches of Amílcar Cabral*. New York: Monthly Review Press, 1973.

Cade-Bambara, Toni. *The Black Woman: An Anthology*. 1970. Reprint, New York: Washington Square Press, 2005.

Casimir, Jean. *The Haitians: A Decolonial History*. Chapel Hill: University of North Carolina Press, 2022.

Césaire, Aimé. *Discourse on Colonialism*. 1955. Reprint, New York: Monthly Review Press, 2000.

———. "Who am I." *Nègre je suis nègre je resterai. Entretiens avec Françoise Vergès*. Paris: Albin Michel, 2005.

Césaire, Suzanne. *The Great Camouflage: Writings of Dissent (1941–1945)*. Edited by Daniel Maximin. Middletown, CT: Wesleyan University Press, 2021.

Cugoano, Quobna Ottobah. *Thoughts and Sentiments on the Evil of Slavery*. London: Penguin Books, 1999.

Davis, Angela Y. *Angela Davis: An Autobiography*. N.p.: International Publishers, 1988.

———. "Lecture on Liberation." In *Narrative of the Life of Frederick Douglass, an American Slave, Written by Himself*. San Francisco: City Lights Publishers, 2009.

———, Gina Dent, Erica R. Meiners, and Beth E. Richie. *Abolition. Feminism. Now.* Chicago: Haymarket Books, 2022.

Douglass, Frederick. *Narrative of the Life of Frederick Douglass, an American Slave, Written by Himself*. San Francisco: City Lights Publishers, 2009.

———. *My Bondage and My Freedom*. London: Penguin Books, 2003.

———. *The Life and Writings of Frederick Douglass: The Civil War, 1861–1865*. Edited by Phillip Foner. N.p.: International Publishers, 2020.

Du Bois, W. E. B. *Black Reconstruction in America, 1860–1880*. Los Angeles: Free Press, 1998.

DuBois, Laurent. *Avengers of the New World: The Story of the Haitian Revolution*. Cambridge: Cambridge University Press, 2005.

Dupuy, Alex. *Rethinking the Haitian Revolution: Slavery, Independence, and the Struggle for Recognition*. Lanham, MD: Rowman & Littlefield, 2019.

Eddins, Crystal. *Rituals, Runaways, and the Haitian Revolution: Collective Action in the African Diaspora*. Cambridge: Cambridge University Press, 2022.

Edwards, Brent Hayes. *The Practice of Diaspora: Literature, Translation, and the Rise of Black Internationalism*. Cambridge: Harvard University Press, 2003.

Equiano, Olaudah. *The Interesting Narrative of the Life of Olaudah Equiano, or Gustavus Vassa, the African. Written by Himself*. London: Penguin Books, 2004.

Esedebe, P. Olisanwuche. *Pan-Africanism: The Idea and Movement, 1776–1991*. Washington, DC: Howard University Press, 1004.

Fanon, Frantz. *Black Skin, White Mask*. Translated by Richard Philcox. 1952. Reprint, New York: Grove Press, 2008.

Ferrer, Ada. "Haiti, Free Soul, and Antislavery in the Revolutionary Atlantic." *American Historical Review* (February 2012): 40–66.

Garza, Alicia. "A Herstory of the #BlackLivesMatter Movement." *Are All the Women Still White? Rethinking Race, Expanding Feminisms*. Albany: State University of New York Press, 2016.

Getachew, Adom. *Worldmaking after Empire: The Rise and Fall of Self-Determination*. Princeton: Princeton University Press, 2019.

Goveia, Elsa. *Slave Society in the British Leeward Islands at the End of the Eighteenth Century*. Caribbean Series 8. New Haven: Yale University Press, 1965.

Harris, Christopher Paul. *To Build a Black Future: The Radical Politics of Joy, Pain, and Care*. Princeton: Princeton University Press, 2023.

Hughes, Langston. *Good Morning Revolution: Uncollected Writings of Langston Hughes*. Edited by Faith Berry. New York: Citidel Press, 1992.

———. "White Shadows in a Black Land." *The Crisis* (May 1932): 157.

James, C. L. R. *The Black Jacobins: Toussaint L'Ouverture and the San Domingo Revolution*. New York: Vintage Books, 1963.

Jenson, Deborah. "Sources and Interpretations: Jean-Jacques Dessalines and the African Character of the Haitian Revolution." *William and Mary Quarterly* 69, no. 3 (July 2012): 615–38.

Jones, Kellie. *South of Pico: African American Artists in Los Angeles in the 1960s and 1970s*. Durham: Duke University Press, 2017.

Lahouel, Badra. "Ethiopianism and African Nationalism in South Africa before 1937." *Cahiers d'Études Africaines* 26 (1986): 681–88.

Magaziner, Daniel R. *The Law and the Prophets: Black Consciousness in South Africa, 1968–1977*. Columbus, OH: Ohio State University Press, 2010.

Mokhtefi, Elaine. *Algiers, Third World Capital: Freedom Fighters, Revolutionaries, Black Panthers*. London and New York: Verso Press, 2018.

Mwase, George Simeon. *Strike a Blow and Die: A Narrative of Race Relations in Colonial Africa*. Cambridge: Harvard University Press, 1967.

Neal, Larry. *The Black Arts Movement*. New York: New York University Press, 1968.

Nkrumah, Kwame. *Neo-Colonialism: The Last Stage of Imperialism*. N.p.: International Publishers, 1966.

Patterson, William. *We Charge Genocide: The Crime of Government against the Negro People: A Petition to the United Nations*. Civil Rights Congress, 1951.

Presence Africaine 8-9-10 (June–November 1956).

Presence Africaine 24-25 (February–May 1959).

Pretorius, Hennie. "Nehemiah Tile: A Nineteenth-Century Pioneer of the Development of African Christian Theology." *Journal for the Study of Religion* 3, no. 1 (March 1990): 3-15.

Romney, Particia. *We Were There: The Third World Women's Alliance and the Second Wave*. New York: Feminist Press, 2021.

Shepperson, George. "Ethiopianism: Past and Present." In *Christianity in Tropical Africa*. Edited by G. C. Baëta. Accra: University of Ghana, 1965.

–––, and Thomas Price. *Independent African: John Chilembwe and the Origins, Setting and Significance of the Nyasaland Native Rising of 1915*. Edinburgh: University Press of Edinburgh, 1969.

Smethurst, James Edward. *The Black Arts Movement: Literary Nationalism in the 1960s and 1970s*. Chapel Hill: University of North Carolina, 2005.

Taylor, Keeanga-Yamahtta. *How We Get Free: Black Feminism and the Combahee River Collective*. Chicago: Haymarket Books, 2017.

Thébia-Melsan, A., ed. *Aimé Césaire, pour regarder le siècle en face*. Paris: Maisonneuve & Larose, 2000.

Third World Women's Alliance. *Black Woman's Manifesto*.

Thompson, Kristina. *Shine: The Visual Economy of Light in African Diasporic Aesthetic Practice*.

Durham: Duke University Press, 2015.

Tishken, Joel E. "Neither Anglican nor Ethiopian: Schism, Race, and Ecclesiastical Politics in the Nineteenth-Century Liberian Episcopal Church." *Journal of Africana Religions* 2, no. 1 (2014): 67–94.

Tomás, António. *Amílcar Cabral: The Life of a Reluctant Nationalist*. London: Hurst & Company, 2021.

Trouillot, Michel-Rolph. *Haiti: State against Nation*. New York: Monthly Review Press, 1990.

Ture, Kwame and Charles V. Hamilton. *Black Power: The Politics of Liberation in America*. New York: Vintage Books 1992.

Widener, Daniel. *Black Arts West: Culture and Struggle in Postwar Los Angeles*. Durham: Duke University Press, 2010.

Wilder, Gary. *Freedom Time: Negritude, Decolonization, and the Future of the World*. Durham: Duke University Press, 2015.

Woodard, Komozi. *A Nation within a Nation: Amiri Baraka (LeRoi Jones) and Black Power Politics*. Chapel Hill: University of North Carolina Press, 1999.

Woodly, Deva R. *Reckoning: Black Lives Matter and the Democratic Necessity of Social Movements*. Oxford University Press, 2022.

Dragon of the Sea / Keila Grinberg

Alonso, Angela. *The Last Abolition: The Brazilian Antislavery Movement, 1868–1888*. Cambridge: Cambridge University Press, 2022.

Morel, Edmar. *Dragão do Mar, o jangadeiro da abolição*. Edições do Povo, 1949.

Rocha, Saulo Moreno. *Esboços de uma biografia de musealização: o caso da Jangada Libertadora*. Master's thesis. Rio de Janeiro, UNIRIO/Mast, 2018.

Santos, Claudia. *Disputas políticas pela abolição no Brasil*. Petrópolis, Vozes, 2023.

Xavier, Patricia Pereira. *Dragão do Mar: a construção do herói jangadeiro*. Fortaleza, Museu do Ceará, 2011.

Pan-Africanism and Black Freedom / Kate McMahon

"Letter from Pan-African Congress to League of Nations." Pan African Congress. Ca. September 1921, p. 2. Amherst: University of Massachusetts. https://credo.library.umass.edu/view/full/mums312-b017-i345.

The Pan-African Connect: From Slavery to Garvey and Beyond (N.p.: Majority Press, 1984).

Report of the Pan-African Conference Held on the 23rd, 24th, and 25th July, 1900, at Westminster Town Hall, Westminster, S.W. (London: Veale, Chifferiel, 1900), 1. https://credo.library.umass.edu/view/pageturn/mums312-b289-i003/#page/1/mode/1up.

Rabaka, Reiland. "Introduction: On the Intellectual Elasticity and Political Plurality of Pan-Africanism." In *Routledge Handbook of Pan-Africanism*. Edited by Reiland Rabaka (New York: Routledge, 2020), 1–32.

–––. "W. E. B. Du Bois: From Pioneering Pan-Negroism to Revolutionary Pan-Africanism." In *Routledge Handbook of Pan-Africanism*.

Edited by Reiland Rabaka (New York: Routledge, 2020), 197.

Sherwood, Marika. *Origins of Pan-Africanism: Henry Sylvester Williams, Africa, and the African Diaspora* (New York: Routledge, 2011), 1–2.

Fashioning Identity / Johanna Obenda

Bowles, L. R. *Dress Politics and Framing Self in Ghana: The Studio Photographs of Felicia Abban*. Cambridge: MIT Press, December 1, 2016. https://direct.mit.edu/afar/article/49/4/48/54944/Dress-Politics-and-Framing-Self-in-Ghana-The.

Canales, K. *Fabric of the African Diaspora*. V&A Blog. October 12, 2021. https://www.vam.ac.uk/blog/museum-life/fabric-of-the-african-diaspora.

Checinska, C., O. Akerele, A. Bendriouich, G. Casely-Hayford, S. Dolat, B. Greer, M. L. Miller, E. Murray, N. Ngumi, H. Osman, and R. A. Walker. (2022). *Africa Fashion*. V&A Publishing, 2022. https://www.vam.ac.uk/shop/books/all-books/africa-fashion---official-exhibition-book-hardback-163878.html.

Deconstructing the Concept of "African Print" in the Ghanaian Experience. Free Library. (n.d.). https://www.thefreelibrary.com/

Record Factory Printed Cloth. Smithsonian Institution: Collections Search Center, n.d. https://collections.si.edu/

Teaching History with 100 Objects—Cloth Celebrating Ghanaian Independence. London: British Museum, n.d. http://teachinghistory100.org/objects/about_the_object/cloth_celebrating_ghanaian_independence.

UPI Archives. "First Mandela Photo in 24 Years." February 10, 1990. https://www.upi.com/Archives/1990/02/10/First-Mandela-photo-in-24-years/7636634626000/.

Anastácia Freed / Yhuri Cruz and Aline Montenegro Magalhães

Chuva, Marcia, et al. "Brasil decolonial: outras histórias. " In *Sobre sonhos que sonhamos juntos... parte 2*. Exporvisões: miradas afetivas sobre museus patrimônios e afins. May 27, 2022. https://exporvisoes374227711.wpcomstaging.com/2022/05/27/sobre-sonhos-que-sonhamos-juntos-parte-2-brasil-decolonial-outras-historias/.

Conceição, Jessy Kerolayne Gonçalves. "A máscara não pode ser esquecida." *Poiesis, Niterói* 21, no. 35 (January/June 2020): 345–62. https://periodicos.uff.br/poiesis/article/view/36386/23370.

Handler, J. S. and K. E. Hayes. "Slave Anastácia: The Iconographic History of a Brazilian Popular Saint." *African Diaspora* 2 (2009): 25–51. https://www.studocu.com/en-ca/document/university-of-ottawa/introduction-to-spanish-american-culture/10-lecture-handler-escrava-anastacia/24866046.

Hertzman, Marc, and Giovanna Xavier. "Let's Build a Monument to Anastácia." Public seminar. June 30, 2020. https://publicseminar.org/essays/lets-build-a-monument-to-anastacia/.

Johnson, Paul C. "Modes and Moods of 'Slave Anastácia,' Afro-Brazilian Saint." Porto Alegre, *NER Debates* 21, no. 40 (August/December

2021): 261–324. https:journals.openedition.
org/jsa/pdf/15584.

Songs of Freedom (Intro) / Johanna Obenda
Makeba, Miriam. "*A Luta Continua*." Lyric epi-
graph, ca. 1989.

"Indépendance Cha Cha" / Bambi Ceuppens
Brain, Alan. *Les autres chevaliers de la table
ronde*. 2021. https://pan-african-music.com/
table-ronde-independance-cha-cha/.
Raspoet, Eric. "Misschien woont er echt een
zwarte in mijn blanke lijf." *De Morgen* (May
15, 2010). https://www.demorgen.be/nieuws/
misschien-woont-er-echt-een-zwarte-in-mijn-
blanke-lijf~bdeee6a7/.

"We Shall Overcome" / Paul Tichmann
Adams, Noah. "The Inspiring Force of 'We Shall
Overcome.'" August 28, 2013.
https://www.npr.org/2013/08/28/216482943/
the-inspiring-force-of-we-shall-overcome.
Dozier, Eric. "We Shall Overcome: Birth of a World
Anthem." November 17,
2013. http://www.ericdozier.com/blogdash-
board/2014/11/17/we-shall-overcome.
Neal, Brandi Amanda. "We Shall Overcome: From
Black Church Music to Freedom Song." MA
thesis, University of Pittsburgh, 2006.
"Remembering Archbishop Desmond Tutu."
The Elders, 27 December 27, 2021. https://
theelders.org/news/remembering-archbish-
op-desmond-tutu.
"'We Shall Overcome': The Theme Song of Civil
Rights." *Rolling Stone*, January 13, 2012,
https://www.rollingstone.com › culture › cul-
ture-lists.

**Rio de Janeiro, Brazil / Martha Abreu and
Vinícius Natal**
Abreu, Martha, and Hebe Mattos."Jongo,
Recalling History." In *Cangoma Calling: Spirits
and Rhythms of Freedom in Brazilian Jongo
Slavery*, edited by Pedro Meira Monteiro and
Michael Stone. University of Massachusetts
Dartmouth, 2013. http://www.laabst.net/
laabst3/
Butler, Kim, and Petrônio Domingues. *Diásporas
Imaginadas: Atlântico Negro e Histórias
Afro-Brasileiras*. São Paulo: Perspectiva Press,
2020.
Cunha, Carlos Fernando, Nathalia Sarro, and
Vinícius Natal. *A Kizomba da Vila Isabel:
Festa da Negritude e do Samba*. Rio de
Janeiro: EDUERJ (Editora da Universidade do
Estado do Rio de Janeiro), 2023.
Gomes, Nilma Lino. *O Movimento Negro
Educador: Saberes Construídos nas Lutas por
Emancipação*. São Paulo: Editora Vozes, 2017.
Fischer, Brodwyn, and Keila Grinberg. *The
Boundaries of Freedom: Slavery, Abolition,
and the Making of Modern Brazil*. Cambridge:
Cambridge University Press, 2022.
Lopes, Nei. *O Negro no Rio de Janeiro e sua
Tradição Cultural. Partido-Alto, Calango,
Chula e Outras Cantorias*. Rio de Janeiro:
Pallas Editora, 1992.
Reis, Desirree. "I Encontro Internacional Samba,
Patrimônios Negros e Diáspora." *Samba
em Revista* 14, no. 13 (December 2022). Rio
de Janeiro: Museo de Samba. https://www.

museudosamba.org.br/patrim%C3%B-
4nios-negros.
Santo, Spirito. *Do Samba ao Funk do Jordã*. São
Paulo: SESC, 2012.

**Always Making History: Reframing Black Life /
Anthony Bogues**
Baldwin, James. *The Price of a Ticket: Collected
Nonfiction: 1948–1985*. Boston: Beacon Press,
2021.
Bogues, Anthony. *Empire of Liberty*. Chicago:
University of Chicago Press, Dartmouth
College Press, 2010.
Cugoano, Ouobna. *Thoughts and Sentiments on
the Evil of Slavery*. London: Penguin, 1999.
Ferguson, Niall. *Empire: How Britain Made the
Modern World*. London: Allen Lane, 2003.
Fischer, David Hackett. *Liberty and Freedom:
A Visual History of America's Founding Ideas*.
Oxford: Oxford University Press, 2005.
Grossman, James. "James Baldwin on History:
Perspectives on History: AHA." AHA, August
3, 2016. https://www.historians.org/re-
search-and-publications/perspectives-on-his-
tory/summer-2016/james-baldwin-on-history.
Roman, C. V. *American Civilization and the
Negroes; The Afro-American in Relation to
National Progress*. Circa 1920. Reprint,
Forgotten Books, 2018.

**Slavery, Colonialism, and the Present: A Medita-
tion / Mongane Wally Serote**
Baldwin, James. *The Fire Next Time*. New York:
Dial Press, 1963.
Mbeki, Thabo. "I Am an African." Cape Town:
African National Congress, May 8, 1996.

CREDITS

154: Courtesy Saint Louis Art Museum, Johnson Publishing Company Archive. Courtesy J. Paul Getty Trust and Smithsonian National Museum of African American History and Culture. Made possible by the Ford Foundation, J. Paul Getty Trust, John D. and Catherine T. MacArthur Foundation, Andrew W. Mellon Foundation and Smithsonian Institution; **155:** National Museum of African Art, Smithsonian Institution, Gift of Donald A. Theuer and Lilburne Theuer Senn, Photograph by Franko Khoury, 2002-9-32; **156–157:** National Museum of African Art, Smithsonian Institution, Gift of Dr. Johnetta Betsch Cole, Photograph by Brad Simpson, 2015-3-1; **157:** Iziko Museums of South Africa; **158:** Monument to the Voice of Anastácia, Yhuri Cruz, 2019; **159:** Universidad Complutense de Madrid; **160:** Collection of the Smithsonian National Museum of African American History and Culture, 2023.39.7ab, Gift of the Estate of Carroll Parrott Blue, © 2024 Mora-Catlett Family / Licensed by VAGA at Artists Rights Society (ARS), NY; **162:** HP.2005.60.7, collection RMCA Tervuren; photo R. Stalin (Inforcongo), 1960 © RMCA Tervuren/Stalin ; **163:** Vive Le 30 Juin 1960 Zaire Independence Tshibumba Kanda-Matulu, 1947-ca. 1981, Democratic Republic of the Congo, ca. 1974-1976. Paint on canvas H x W x D (image): 45.7 x 64.8 cm (18 x 25 ½ in.) 2020-17-4, gift of Marshall and Ginger Adair, Photograph by Brad Simpson, National Museum of African Art, Smithsonian Institution; **164:** Buda Mendes/Getty Images; **165:** Vitor Melo; **166–167:** UWC-Robben Island, Museum Mayibuye Archives; **167:** Courtesy of Forsyth County Public Library Photograph Collection, Winston-Salem, N.C.; **171:** Unité de Recherche en Ingénierie Culturelle et Anthropologie (URICA)/IFAN-UCAD, Global Curatorial Project (Ms.2022.010) sponsored by Abrams Foundation and Brown University; **172:** Smithsonian National Museum of African American History and Culture, Global Curatorial Project (Ms.2022.010) sponsored by Abrams Foundation and Brown University; **173:** Museu Histórico Nacional; Museu de Samba; LABHOI - Laboratório de Historia Oral e Imagem (UFF) Programa Rio, Memória e Ação, Global Curatorial Project (Ms.2022.010) sponsored by Abrams Foundation and Brown University; **175:** Iziko Museums of South Africa, Global Curatorial Project (Ms.2022.010) sponsored by Abrams Foundation and Brown University; **176, *clockwise from top left*:** Chronicle/Alamy stock photo; Factory printed cloth, F.W. Grafton, Liberia, After 1960–1964, Cotton, dye, H x W: 177.8 × 116.2 cm (70 × 45 3/4 in.), 2013-7-2, Gift of Leon and Nancy Weintraub, Photograph by Brad Simpson, National Museum of African Art, Smithsonian Institution; Unité de Recherche en Ingénierie Culturelle et Anthropologie (URICA)/IFAN-UCAD, Global Curatorial Project (Ms.2022.010) sponsored by Abrams Foundation and Brown University; Archives nationales du Sénégal, sous-série 4Fi, nº 4FI - 0407; Unité de Recherche en Ingénierie Culturelle et Anthropologie (URICA)/IFAN-UCAD, Global Curatorial Project (Ms.2022.010) sponsored by Abrams Foundation and Brown University; *A New and Accurate Map of the European Settlements on the Coast of Africa, from the River Senegal to that of Benin, Comprehending the Gum, Grain, Ivory & Slave Coasts*, Courtesy Dr. Oscar I. Norwich collection of maps of Africa and its islands, David Rumsey Map Center, Stanford Libraries, https://purl.stanford.edu/fk510dj5628; **178–181:** Unité de Recherche en Ingénierie Culturelle et Anthropologie (URICA)/IFAN-UCAD, Global Curatorial Project (Ms.2022.010) sponsored by Abrams Foundation and Brown University; **182, *clockwise from top left*:** Antiqua Print Gallery / Alamy Stock Photo; REUTERS/Yves Herman; INTERFOTO / Alamy Stock Photo; Bruxelles : J. Lebègue & Cie, [1896], World Digital Library; John Wessels/AFP via Getty Images; **184–187:** Musée Royal de l'Afrique Centrale/Musée Royal de l'Afrique Centrale/Koninklijk Museum voor Midden-Afrika, Global Curatorial Project (Ms.2022.010) sponsored by Abrams Foundation and Brown University; **188, *clockwise from top left*:** Courtesy of Paul Gardullo; Michael Serraillier/Gamma-Rapho via Getty Images; Collection of the National Library Foundation – Brazil; Courtesy of the John Carter Brown Library; Jean Carlos/Unsplash; **190–193:** Museu Histórico Nacional; Museu de Samba; LABHOI - Laboratório de Historia Oral e Imagem (UFF) Programa Rio, Memória e Ação, Global Curatorial Project (Ms.2022.010) sponsored by Abrams Foundation and Brown University; **194, *clockwise from top left*:** Library of Congress, Geography and Map Division; Smithsonian National Museum of African American History and Culture, Global Curatorial Project (Ms.2022.010) sponsored by Abrams Foundation and Brown University; William Lovelace/Daily Express/Hulton Archive/Getty Images; Carmen K. Sisson/Cloudybright / Alamy Stock Photo; Associated Press; Smithsonian National Museum of African American History and Culture, Global Curatorial Project (Ms.2022.010) sponsored by Abrams Foundation and Brown University; ·

196–199: Smithsonian National Museum of African American History and Culture, Global Curatorial Project (Ms.2022.010) sponsored by Abrams Foundation and Brown University; **200, *clockwise from top left*:** Iziko Museums of South Africa, Social History Collections; Georges De Keerle/Getty Images; courtesy of the National Library of South Africa, Cape Town; Carte de l'Afrique méridionale au pays entre la ligne Cap de Bonne Espérance et l'Isle de Madagascar, Courtesy Africana Historical Maps Collection, David Rumsey Map Center, Stanford Libraries, https://searchworks.stanford.edu/view/gx299hy1611; photo by Jurgen Schadeberg, the Schadeberg Collection; **202–205:** Iziko Museums of South Africa, Global Curatorial Project (Ms.2022.010) sponsored by Abrams Foundation and Brown University; **206, *clockwise from top left*:** Wikimedia Commons; Photo by Andrew Teebay for the *Liverpool Echo*, © Reach PLC; Wikimedia Commons; © David Sinclair; © Imperial War Museums; **208–211:** International Slavery Museum, National Museums Liverpool, Global Curatorial Project (Ms.2022.010) sponsored by Abrams Foundation and Brown University; **213:** Collection of the Smithsonian National Museum of African American History and Culture, 2022.18.3, © Chester Higgins, All Rights Reserved; **215:** Courtesy of Edouard Duval-Carrié; **216:** Collection of the Smithsonian National Museum of African American History and Culture, 2021.31.65, Gift of Tommy and Codie Oliver, © Tommy Oliver; **218:** Collection of the Smithsonian National Museum of African American History and Culture, 2022.80.3, © Cliff Joseph Estate.

Unfinished Conversations collage captions, listed clockwise from top left

Fouta & Saint-Louis, Senegal: Saint-Louis from the Senegal River, 1865; factory printed cloth featuring Léopold Sédar Senghor, the first president of Senegal, ca. 1960s; protestant church in Saint Louis Senegal, 2023; postcard of Saint-Louis, Senegal, 1900; community gathering in memory of Marème Diarra, 2023; man reflecting in prayer during a ceremony honoring Marème Diarra, 2023; map showing European settlements near Senegal, ca. 1781.

Belgium and Democratic Republic of Congo: *The Bansa, or Residence of the king of Kongo called St. Salvador from Dapper,* G. Child, 1746; demonstrators stand on the statue of Leopold II in a protest organized by Black Lives Matter Belgium, 2020; demonstration against Prime Minister Cyrille Adoula's visit to Democratic Republic of Congo, 1964; map of the Belgian Congo, 1896; Nkamba Temple during Christmas celebrations, 2017.

Rio de Janeiro, Brazil: Mural at the Museum of Afro Brazilian History and Culture (MUHCAB) in the Pequena África neighborhood of Rio de Janeiro, 2023; samba group, 1899; slave market at the Valongo Wharf, 1835; Morro da Providência as seen from the Cidade do Samba, Rio de Janeiro, 2023.

Africatown, United States: Map of Mobile Bay, 1864; Yorktown Missionary Baptist Church in Africatown, Alabama, 2022; Martin Luther King Jr. and his wife, Coretta Scott King, lead a Black voting rights march from Selma, Alabama, to Montgomery, Alabama, 1965; Welcome to Africatown sign, 2021; Major League Baseball (MLB) player and Mobile County Training School alumnus Billy Williams, 1969; photograph of industry near Africatown, Alabama, 2022.

Cape Town, South Africa: Painting of Table Bay South Africa, 1700s; Nelson Mandela during a rally in Soweto, 1990; women protest apartheid passbook laws, 1956; map of southern Africa between the Cape of Good Hope line and the Island of Madagascar, 1730; African National Congress speakers protesting unjust laws as a part of the "Defiance Campaign," 1952.

Liverpool, England: Liverpool Sailors' Home, ca. 1850s; protests of the Liverpool 8 Defense Committee, 1981; Caribbean troops in Britain during World War I, 1917; Black Lives Matter protest on St. George's Hall Plateau, 2020; map of Liverpool, 1765.

INDEX

Note: Illustrations are indicated by
page numbers in italics.

women, 40, *40,* 101, 108-9, *108-9,* 111, 116-17,
    146-48
Woods, Lorna Gail, 197, *198*
Wretched of the Earth, The (Fanon), 143-44

Yantula, Pierre, 163
Yesufu, Yinka, 208-10, *209*
Yorùbá, 138

Zephirin, Frantz, *135*
Zica, Cartola, 191
Zimmerman, George, 147
Zumba, Ganga, 135
"Zungueiras, or Are They Ganhadeiras?" (Gomes
    de Jesus), 106-7
Zurara, Gomes Eanes de, 34

Section introductory essays by Paul Gardullo and Johanna Obenda
Section opener artwork by Daniel Minter
Captions by Johanna Obenda and Ivie Orobaton

Published by Smithsonian Books
Director: Carolyn Gleason
Senior Editor: Jaime Schwender
Editor: Julie Huggins
Editorial Intern: Paige Elliott
Digital Imaging Technician: Bill Whitcher

Developmental Editor: Karen Taylor
Proofreaders: Holly Edgar, Juliana Froggatt, and Joanne Reams
Designed by Eddie Opara, Jun Jung, Inês Ayer, and Wendy Hu, Pentagram New York

National Museum of African American History and Culture
Director: Kevin Young
Deputy Director: Michelle D. Commander
In Slavery's Wake Publication Team: Kate McMahon, Ivie Orobaton, and Douglas Remley

In Slavery's Wake is supported by grants from Abrams Foundation and Ford Foundation.

Hardcover ISBN: 978-1-58834-779-4

Library of Congress Cataloging-in-Publication available upon request.

Printed in Canada, not at government expense
28 27 26 25 24
1 2 3 4 5